How to Gain the Professional Edge
Praise for the Previous Edition

"At last, a book that contains vital and timely information concerning achieving your career goals. This book is a must-read for everyone who wants to attain career success without having to go through the school of hard knocks. Sue Morem equips you with the tools and techniques necessary during this time of radical and drastic change to enhance your visibility and recognition in the organization to rapidly advance your career." —Helena C. Douglas, Management Development Director, Clemson University

"*How to Gain the Professional Edge* does an excellent job presenting information and insights critical to success in the workplace. The real-world examples are right on target, and they powerfully substantiate the general principles underlying the text. I would recommend this book to individuals preparing to enter their careers—it succinctly describes what to do (and not to do) in professional interpersonal situations, but more important, perhaps, it thoughtfully explains why. The book will also be helpful to individuals seeking to revitalize and move ahead in their professional lives. This book will definitely be on the recommended reading list for our business students." —Jerry Rinehart, Director of Undergraduate Studies, Carlson School of Management, University of Minnesota

"Sue's material was well received and the evaluations from her students were excellent. Sue's presentation makes learning a positive and enjoyable experience." —Susan Mortenson, Training Coordinator, Honeywell Corporation

"Susan's keen insights and personal experience are evident all through the book. She identifies all of the 'points of difference' essential for winning presentations." —Richard L. Knowlton, Chairman, The Hormel Foundation

"Nothing is more powerful in service than the instantaneous impression customers get the first time they come in contact with your organization. The most powerful impact comes from your employees, who are, in the customers' minds, the organization. In her book, *How to Gain the Professional Edge,* Sue Morem has captured the essence of that first impression and shares the tools to make that ever-important moment not only dazzling but unforgettable." —Petra A. Marquart, Author, *The Power of Service*

"Extremely helpful and informative. The information is of great interest, and she shares wonderful material." —Jon S. Carlson, Vice President of Income Development, American Cancer Society

"Sue and her powerful message are a driving force behind many successful careers. Must-reading for anyone looking for a formula that magnitudes their dreams." —Kay Lewis, Executive Producer, La Jolla Project Production Company

"Susan's presentation was superb! She demonstrates a great deal of professionalism mixed with a wonderful sense of humor. Her material is up-to-date and appropriate for any audience." —Maurice Chenier, Operations Manager, Ceridian Corporation

"Our associates responded well to Sue's message, which was both informational and entertaining. She has helped us to develop insight and awareness, which was our goal." —Donald R. Melton, Senior Vice President, Resident Manager, Dain Bosworth, Incorporated

"As a result of using the information in Sue's book, our employees are treating each other more respectfully and professionally. Consequently, we are having more fun and our service has improved dramatically. Sue's book offers answers to problems and provides a successful plan to use for anyone looking to succeed." —Randy Stanley, General Manager, Ruth's Chris Steak House

"The enthusiastic manner in which Sue presents her information makes learning fun. It is evident that she believes in the importance of being at your personal best at all times." —Jean Johnson, Office Supervisor, 3M

"The reason I like Sue Morem's work is that she's a good teacher of something in short supply today: people skills." —Letitia Baldrige, Author of *Letitia Baldrige's New Manners for New Times*

"Sue Morem walks her talk. She looks more pulled-together for a casual lunch than most people look at the Oscars! Her warm, witty presentations instruct and inspire, and this great book does too!" —Susan Vas, Author, speaker and comedian

"Image and presence are an integral part of every professional success story. Unfortunately, very little of value is available. With *How to Gain the Professional Edge*, Susan Morem rights this wrong and will help you climb higher on the ladder of success." —Martin Yate, Author of the *Knock 'Em Dead* job-hunting books

How to Gain the Professional -Edge-

Achieve the Personal and Professional Image You Want

SECOND EDITION

SUSAN MOREM

Ferguson
An imprint of ☑ Facts On File

How to Gain the Professional Edge, Second Edition

Copyright © 2005 by Susan E. Morem

Ferguson
An imprint of Facts On File, Inc.
132 West 31st Street
New York NY 10001

Library of Congress Cataloging-in-Publication Data

Morem, Susan.
    How to gain the professional edge / Susan E. Morem.—2nd ed.
       p. cm.
    Includes bibliographical references and index.
    ISBN 0-8160-5674-9 (hc : alk. paper)
    1. Success in business. 2. Business etiquette. 3. Self-presentation. 4. Clothing and dress.
I. Title.
    HF5386.M755 2005
    650.1—dc22   2004011930

Ferguson books are available at special discounts when purchased in bulk quantities for businesses, associations, institutions, or sales promotions. Please call our Special Sales Department in New York at (212) 967-8800 or (800) 322-8755.

You can find Ferguson on the World Wide Web at http://www.fergpubco.com

Text design by Mary Susan Ryan-Flynn

Printed in the United States of America

MP FOF 10 9 8 7 6 5 4 3 2 1

This book is printed on acid-free paper.

CONTENTS

Acknowledgments

I am truly grateful for the support and encouragement given to me by so many people over the years. My thanks goes to my friends, colleagues, clients, and to the hundreds of business people who read and respond to my columns, purchase my books, and attend my seminars. You have given me motivation in my work and have been an inspiration in writing this book.

Thank you Dr. Pamela Cain, Nancy Rains, and Sharron Stockhaussen for sharing your expertise, your honest feedback, and your continued support of everything I do. I mean it when I say that this book wouldn't have been possible without your wisdom and encouragement.

To my friends and family, thank you for your friendship, your interest in my work, and for overlooking my inattentiveness during the months I spent writing this book.

To my editor James Chambers, from the first time we spoke you were receptive and open to my ideas. Thank you for the opportunities you've provided me, your support of my work, your faith in me, and above all, thank you for your flexibility.

To my parents, Rose and Jules Levin, you are the best teachers and role models. I'll never stop learning from you and the standards you have set.

To my incredible three daughters, Stephanie, Stacie, and Samantha, for reminding me that success shows up in many ways—you are my greatest success in life and my pride and joy.

To my husband Steve, you've encouraged me, supported me, tolerated me, and have *always* believed in me. Thank you for being my most loyal fan.

And finally to Drew Carey, although we've never met, you will always be a part of my story and the success of this book. Thank you for your appreciation of and interest in self improvement books and for bringing the first edition of this book on to your television show and into the national spotlight.

INTRODUCTION

Global workforces. Changing demographics. Outsourcing. Downsizing. Streamlining. Restructuring. We're all running as fast as we can to keep up with changes in business and within our fields of expertise. In our quest to keep up with the times and move ahead, it seems something critical is getting lost in the shuffle.

Advances in technology have dramatically changed our lives and the way we do business. We recognize the importance of and rely on the equipment we use, but we are losing sight of the most important factor for success—*our relationships with other people*. Due to the ease and efficiency of electronic communications, more and more of our correspondence is completed this way rather than dealing with people directly. As the workplace becomes increasingly impersonal, many of us are no longer sure how to act toward our bosses, peers, employees, customers, and colleagues.

In addition to the skills or expertise needed to do your job, the "people" skills, enthusiasm, and leadership qualities you possess—and display—are critical to your success. Your ability to work smoothly with others, communicate effectively, maintain a positive attitude, and resolve problems will distinguish you and enable you to *gain the professional edge*.

Maybe you're content with your current position; maybe you're itching to make a change. Perhaps you are young, just starting out, or perhaps you've had a long career and fear you may soon be forced to leave your job. You could be unemployed and looking for ways to improve your job search, or you could have a job and be looking for ways to improve *yourself*. If you manage others, are self-employed, or are a budding entrepreneur; if you're unappreciated, working in unpleasant conditions, or dread the thought of going to work each day, it doesn't have to be that way. This book can help you make the changes you want to make.

It doesn't matter if you are reaching the peak of your career or hitting your lowest point; if you want to increase your chances of success, this book was written for *you*. Don't read it as a novel or hurry your way through; don't assume it doesn't apply to you. If you read it to benefit from it, you will. You will become a better you.

How to Gain the Professional Edge made its debut in February 1997. Just two weeks after its release, I received a call from the producer of *The Drew Carey Show*. I assumed that when I heard from a television producer, it would be someone from a talk show or morning news program. I couldn't imagine why a sitcom would be interested in a self-help book, but the producer told me she wanted permission to use it for an upcoming episode. "Are you sure you have the right book?" I asked. After all, the book had been out for such a short time. "I have the manuscript with me," the producer said, then proceeded to read the cover page, verifying the title of the book and my name. She told me someone had given it to her. At first I was nervous about my book being featured in a sitcom, but then I felt honored that *The Drew Carey Show* wanted to use *my* book. I knew it was a once in a lifetime opportunity.

How to Gain the Professional Edge first appeared on national television on April 27, 1997. Drew and Mimi, the main characters of the show, were competing for a new position. Wanting to gain the edge and outshine the competition, Drew buys *this book* for tips to help him improve his image. He succeeds and manages to impress the members of the board. Mimi, who is wondering what Drew is up to, discovers the book, takes it, and decides to use it to her advantage. When the finalists meet with the board in the company dining room, Mimi and Drew seem to be making a favorable impression, but before long they both slip up.

The entire episode centers on the first edition of this book, which has now been revised and greatly expanded, with twice as many chapters as the previous edition.

Sometime after the episode aired, in an interview with Matt Lauer, Drew Carey talked about his lifelong interest in reading self-help books and the influence they've had on his life. As he held the first edition of this book in his hands, he talked about how some books have inspired ideas for his show.

The plot played out on *The Drew Carey Show* was fictitious and the characters' behavior a bit extreme, but they were not all that far removed from reality. Similar scenes play out in real life every single day. People become complacent, don't know what to do or how to act, and they too slip up.

Don't wait until *you* slip up to realize you're missing something or need to improve. Continuously update and improve both your "softer" and "harder" skills. Knowledge is power; protect yourself and your career by being knowledgeable and staying informed. Be eager and willing to continue to learn, change, and grow, both personally *and* professionally, for the rest of your life. It is the key to your personal happiness and career success.

In seeking to identify the top characteristics employers look for when hiring an employee, Chuck Martin, author of *Managing for the Short Term,* surveyed more than 2,000 senior executives and managers. An overwhelming majority of the respondents—87 percent—said they would look for and hire people who are willing to learn.

Are *you* willing to learn? *Business* is changing. *Technology* is changing. *The workplace* is changing. *People* are changing. Are *you* changing too? If you aren't interested in learning and changing, don't be surprised if employers show little interest in you. Continue to learn about yourself and others. Know what is expected of you. Don't do it because you *have to;* do it because you *want to.*

Whether you purchased this book yourself or received it from someone else, read it with the expectation of *learning something new.* If you do, I guarantee you will find information in this book that was written just for *you.* It's never too late; you can become the successful person you were meant to be.

Go for the edge!
Sue Morem

Chapter 1

It's All About *You*

WHAT DO YOU WANT?

Imagine two people starting out in their careers; both are bright, talented, and likely to succeed. They share similar goals and both work hard to achieve them. However, over the years only one of them excels; the other remains stagnant.

Have you ever wondered why some people are more successful than others? What enables some people to succeed and what limits the success of others? Why will some people reach their dreams while others never come close to reaching theirs?

Does what we *do* determine how successful we will be, or is success a matter of chance or good fortune? If you've ever questioned your chances of success, you are not alone. Success and happiness are hot commodities but remain somewhat elusive.

Are you where you want to be in your career and in your life? Do you have a vision for your future? Do you have a plan to help you reach your goals or the hope that you will? How do you define success for you? How will you know if you are successful?

Not too many years ago, maintaining employment with one company until retirement was the norm. Today, permanent employment with one company has become somewhat of an anomaly, and increasing numbers of seniors are postponing their retirement. Times have changed, and so have the reasons people do the work they do. Money is a driving factor, but not the only one. More and more people seek meaning from their work and look for ways to increase their efficiency.

Do you measure your success by your income or your status? If you are striving to be in a position of authority, earn more money, or acquire material possessions, are you sure you will be satisfied when you do? Success shows up in many ways; what are the indicators of *your* success?

Opportunity is abundant and most anything is possible, but you need to know what your "anything" is. When you know what you want and declare your vision, you have a greater chance of achieving it. As you become clear about your goals, share them with others. Don't keep your dreams and vision a secret. When you talk about your goals, they become more tangible. There are resources and people available to help you reach your dreams, but it's up to you to tap into them. Don't hesitate to ask people for advice; most will be delighted to share the things they've learned. There are mentoring programs, workshops, seminars, tapes, and books all designed to help you gain confidence and skills that lead to success.

IT DOESN'T HAVE TO BE COMPLICATED

Life can be complicated; at times we keep ourselves so busy, we're left with little time to think about the things that really matter. We're busy creating lists of things to do that never get done because we run out of time. We have good intentions, but we deliver poor results when we overcommit or put things off. We strive to be effective managers, business owners, and employees and do our best to be compassionate family members, friends, and lovers. We are expected to be decent citizens, community members, and coworkers and are responsible for our children, pets, homes, and personal belongings.

We've got deadlines to meet, appointments to make, and commitments to honor. When we want something, we want it *now,* and we can't imagine what life was like before there were cell phones, fax machines, computers, and overnight delivery.

As busy as we are, we aren't always productive, and we waste a tremendous amount of time. We spend endless hours waiting; we wait for people, we wait in lines, and we wait for answers. We get caught up in traffic, held up on the computer, and slowed down when we're put on hold or waiting for a response. We put up with constant interruptions—the phone, the computer, the meetings, the customers, the coworkers, the questions, the requests, the children, the dog, the cat, the deliveries, and the unexpected problems.

It is easy to become overwhelmed with all we have to manage, but most of us have more control over our time and our lives than we think. Instead of taking control, too often we say yes when we should say no, and we agree to do more than we should. It's easier to blame someone else than it is to be held responsible, or to give up instead of hanging on. Too often we accept failure instead of pursuing success.

Take control of what you can; don't leave the odds of your success to chance. Take the time to think about what you want, and never allow yourself to become so busy that you fail to create your vision for your future. If you want to reach your goals, you need to know what you want and effectively communicate your needs to others.

How to Gain the Professional Edge will help you take an honest look at yourself and help you succeed, no matter where you are in your life or career. Throughout this book you will have the opportunity to evaluate yourself and identify areas you need to work on. You will gain new skills and knowledge that will help you become the person you want to be. Take the time to read, think, and really work through the suggested exercises to get the most out of this book. Then take what you've learned and put it into practice. Knowledge alone isn't enough; what you *do* with the knowledge you've gained makes all the difference.

EVALUATE YOURSELF

It's important to begin by thinking about what brought you to where you are today. Once you do, it will become easier to lead yourself to your tomorrow. Do you know how others see you? Do you know how you *want* others to see you? How do you see yourself, and what do you reveal about yourself to others? It's not always easy to conduct an honest assessment, but it is important. Complete the following personal evaluation.

1. Describe how you see yourself in three words.
   1. _____
   2. _____
   3. _____

2. What are your three greatest strengths? Capitalize these to remind yourself to capitalize on them. Know what you're good at.
   1. _____
   2. _____
   3. _____

3. List three of your greatest or proudest accomplishments.
   1. _____
   2. _____
   3. _____

4. What three things do you like best about your image?

   1. _____
   2. _____
   3. _____

5. What three aspects of your current job do you like best?

   1. _____
   2. _____
   3. _____

6. Think of the best job you've ever had. What were the three main reasons you liked that job?

   1. _____
   2. _____
   3. _____

7. What makes you great at what you do?

   _____
   _____
   _____

Before you move on, if you didn't fill in all of the spaces, take the time to go over each question again. This can be a challenging exercise if you were taught not to brag about your accomplishments or speak too highly of yourself. While some people have no problem singing their praises, others have a difficult time. They find it easier to focus on what they lack, rather than what they have. It's vital to know your individual strengths and what makes you unique.

Once you've finished responding to the first set of questions, move on to the following questions:

1. Describe how you would like to see yourself in three words.

   1. _____
   2. _____
   3. _____

2. What are three areas you could improve on?

   1. _____
   2. _____
   3. _____

3. List three reasons you are dissatisfied with your image.
    1. _____
    2. _____
    3. _____

4. Identify three mistakes you've made.
    1. _____
    2. _____
    3. _____

5. Identify the three things you complain about most often in your life.
    1. _____
    2. _____
    3. _____

6. Identify the three things you complain about most often in your job.
    1. _____
    2. _____
    3. _____

7. If you could change three things about your current job, what would they be?

    1. _____
    2. _____
    3. _____

If it was easier for you to answer this set of questions, evaluate the reasons why. We all have strengths and weaknesses, and both should be acknowledged. However, if you are used to focusing on what you *aren't,* you're missing out on all that you *are.* When you focus on your weaknesses, you aren't able to focus on developing your strengths. When you portray yourself positively to others, others tend to see you positively. When you belittle yourself in front of others, you are drawing attention to your perceived inadequacies. When you portray yourself negatively, people tend to see you more negatively.

As you review your answers, you'll begin to see that the way you see yourself and the way you describe yourself are an integral part of your sense of self-confidence and self-esteem. Do you find agreement between the way you see yourself and the way you would *like* to see yourself? If not, what changes do you need to make so that the two sets of descriptions match, or in other words, so you *become* who you want to *be?*

The key to professional success is something you've probably heard before: Accentuate the positive. To be successful and to project a positive image, you must know what your strengths are and be proud to name and develop them. If you have trouble coming up with answers to these questions, work on them—know what makes you great!

Write each of the strengths you've listed in bold letters on a 3" × 5" card and tape the card someplace you look frequently; tape it to your mirror, to the sun visor of your car, or in your daily planner. Do whatever it takes to remind yourself of what you have going for you and what you—and only you—have to offer.

Before you can gain the professional edge, you need to believe you can be successful. Don't compare yourself to others; focus on the kind of person *you* want to become. When you believe in yourself and feel deserving of the success you're after, you've taken the most important step toward having it. Success can be achieved by anyone; you can achieve the success you seek.

ARE YOU AN EMPLOYEE OR AN ENTREPRENEUR?

When you think of an employee or an entrepreneur, what comes to mind? If you assume an entrepreneur is someone who is self-employed and too independent to work for anyone else, think again. Many employees of companies have learned to think and act like an entrepreneur as a strategy of their success.

Are you an employee or an entrepreneur? Take a moment to read through the following statements to find out. As you read each one, make a note of the statements you agree with—the ones that reflect your mind-set about yourself and your job.

1. I am responsible for my success, or lack of it.

2. My success, or lack of it, is out of my control.

3. I take care of myself.

4. I expect others to take care of me.

5. I am a self-starter.

6. I need direction.

7. Time flies when I am working; my days pass quickly.

8. I watch the clock when I am working; my days are long.

9. If something doesn't work out, I've got other avenues to pursue.

10. If I lost my job, I don't know what I'd do.

11. I enjoy the challenges that come with change.

12. I resist change.

13. I am open-minded.

14. I am close-minded.

15. I am responsible for what happens to me.

16. I blame others for what happens to me.

17. I learn from my mistakes.

18. I fear making a mistake.

19. I like the work I do.

20. I dislike the work I do.

21. I look forward to going to work each day.

22. I dread going to work each day.

23. I keep in touch with a broad range of people.

24. I've let many of my contacts go.

25. I would keep working even if I didn't need the money.

26. I would quit tomorrow if I didn't need the money.

27. I am a leader.

28. I am a follower.

29. When I have a problem with someone, I resolve it.

30. When I have a problem with someone, I ignore it.

31. If I want something, I ask for it.

32. If I want something, I hope I'll get it.

33. I reach out to people I do not know.

34. I wait for people to seek me out.

35. I seek opportunities for self-improvement.

36. I can't change; this is who I am.

37. I exceed the expectations others have of me.

38. I try to meet the expectations others have of me.

39. I resolve problems.

40. I find problems.

41. I am growing in my career.

42. I am stuck in my career.

43. I am empowered to make a difference.

44. I am powerless to make a difference.

45. I am disciplined.

46. I am controlled.

47. I like people and people like me.

48. People don't pay attention to me.

49. I know what I want.

50. I don't know what I want.

Look over your selections. Did you note more even-numbered or odd-numbered statements? Count the number of even-numbered statements you selected, and then count the number of odd-numbered statements you chose. Then discover in the following paragraphs what your selections say about you.

The odd-numbered statements convey an attitude of personal responsibility, optimism, and self-control. The even-numbered statements suggest feelings of helplessness, resignation, and a dependence on others. If you agreed with the majority of the odd-numbered statements, you possess many of the attributes of an entrepreneur. You may work for yourself or for someone else, but you don't depend on others; you rely on yourself. You realize that you are responsible for what happens to you and that what you do determines your happiness and success. You are willing to take risks, and you look for new ways of doing things.

If you agreed with more of the even-numbered statements, you think more like an employee than an entrepreneur. Chances are, you don't take too many chances, prefer to play it safe, and tend to rely on others. You may feel you work hard, but you rarely do more than what's required. You're not likely to be working in your ideal job, but if you're not sure what else to do, you stay where you are.

If you found you lean toward an employee in some areas and an entrepreneur in others, that's fine. It is possible that you think like an entrepreneur in some ways but resemble an employee in others. Not all entrepreneurs will agree with all of the odd-numbered statements, and not all employees will relate to all of the even-numbered statements.

Think about the pros and cons of your mind-set. For example, if you resist change, is that helping you or hindering you? Do you have any control over the things that change at work? What if you dislike the work you do *and* you resist change; what options will you have? If it is easier for you to stay in a job you dislike than it is to make a change, what are the implications?

If you are a self-starter and a leader, and you work for someone who prefers to direct and control *you,* will your qualities be an advantage or a disadvantage? Are you able to take direction from someone, and if not, what are the potential consequences connected to not taking direction?

Review the 50 statements once again. This time, as you read each one, think about your current position and your future goals. Which statements are an asset, reflecting attitudes and behaviors likely to help you achieve your goals? Which statements are a hindrance and reflect traits that could work against you?

You will be most effective when your style is a good fit with your work environment. If a behavior is hurting your chances of success, you can change it. As you increase your awareness, you increase your ability to identify what's working and what isn't. Don't settle for less than your best, and don't assume your job will be secure forever. No job is permanent, and there are no guarantees that the company you work for today will even be there for you tomorrow.

Most people work many different jobs throughout the span of their careers. The more prepared you are and the more open you are to change, the easier it will be each time you make a move. Never allow yourself to become stagnant. Do whatever you must to stay employable. Keep in touch with former coworkers, bosses, clients, and associates, and do what you can to advance your knowledge and skills. If you've been waiting for a promotion or hoping for a better opportunity, stop wishing and start taking action; if you want something to happen, you need to make it happen.

BE OPEN TO CHANGE

When I started my business many years ago, I knew it would not be easy. I had entered a small and misunderstood industry, and I offered training on topics that were personal and controversial. I prepared myself to expect that for every 20 calls I made, perhaps one person might be interested in hiring me. I had to gather all of my courage to get on the phone to contact companies. I found that once I was able to secure an appointment, a pattern emerged. When I'd meet face-to-face with the president of a company, a manager, or someone in human resources, I found we all shared similar philosophies. The conversation would lead to some of their concerns, and I heard many of the same comments over and over again:

"I've got this talented person who's smart, hardworking. I would love to promote her, but I can't. She doesn't look the part of management," or "He doesn't present himself well," or "She can't communicate effectively."

I've even had people tell me, "He's chauvinistic; she smells like an ashtray; he never stops talking." In fact, it is often so difficult for managers to confront these seemingly small but significant issues that I've made presentations to a group of 30 because only one person really needed to hear the message.

Personal image and habits are a sensitive issue. No one wants to be the bearer of such delicate information; it's difficult to tell someone that he or she smells and embarrassing to admit you see more than you should when someone sits down.

We often are unaware of the things getting in our way of success. We miss the cues others are giving us because we don't want to hear what they have to say. Yet it's often the little things that stall a career—things that are easy to change. Don't be the one who misses opportunities or is bypassed simply because it's easier to stay the way you are.

Participants are not always as enthused as their managers are about a workshop that addresses the personal and sensitive issues of appearance, behavior, and attitude.

Invariably, there are at least three categories most people fall into. There are the people who are excited about any opportunity to learn something new and are eager to pick up a few new ideas and learn more about themselves. These people attend workshops with a good attitude and an open mind, and they participate enthusiastically. They usually pick up a few new ideas and are able to implement them into their lives.

There are also people who attend, but aren't sure if it's a worthy investment of their time because they believe they already are successful, know about professionalism, and would rather be doing something else they consider more productive. The people in this category usually say they picked up a few good pointers, and it was a good reminder and refresher course.

And finally there are the people who attend only because they have to. They don't want to be there and can't understand why their company would waste its money and time having such a workshop in the first place. These people are sure they won't learn anything new or gain anything from the session, and they generally refuse to participate. They expend most of their energy resisting anything that takes place, and ultimately they fulfill their prophecy.

Most of us fall into one of these three categories. Maybe someone gave you this book and you wonder why. It could be required reading by your manager or teacher. Or maybe you are interested in picking up any new ideas you can and are reading this because you chose to. No matter what the reason, you can benefit from reading this book.

POLISH YOURSELF

There was a time when there was a mentality of "anything goes." There were more jobs than people to fill them, and skills were all that mattered. Silicon Valley, famous for its unconventional business environment, has changed. The computer "nerds" who led us to casual dress and a more casual work environment overall have had to change their ways. They've transformed into businesspeople like you and I, who recognize the need for finesse and polish.

Since I began my research in 1989, I've seen trends come and go, the jobless rate rise and fall, and have spoken and worked with scores of business owners, company leaders, career counselors, teachers, professors, and individuals. I've listened to their frustrations and concerns about the people they teach, employ, and guide.

I've received and read thousands of letters and questions generated through my syndicated newspaper column. I've heard from students, parents, employers, employees, and entrepreneurs who took the time to write, to seek, or to share advice. Every letter and every conversation has helped me gain a better understanding of the challenges we *all* face and, as a result, has broadened my perspective. My opinions have been shaped, reshaped, and reinforced.

The information in this book is not simply a reflection of my own opinions; it is time-tested and true. It is filled with knowledge you need in order to have an advantage in business today. I once read a saying that sums it all up, and much more effectively than I ever could. I wish I could give credit to its author, who remains anonymous: People, like diamonds, have a basic market value, but it is only after they have been polished that the world will pay its real value.

No matter what stage of your career you are in, you can improve. When you strive to be your best, you'll have every advantage to succeed. Like a brilliant, sparkling diamond, you too can shine. Polish yourself and see the difference it can make in your relationships, your income, your potential, and the value you bring to everything you do.

> **People, like diamonds, have a basic market value, but it is only after they have been polished that the world will pay its real value.**

PROFESSIONALISM DEFINED

If I were to ask you for your definition of a professional, what would it be? Are *you* a professional? What does it take to be someone with the *professional edge?*

I frequently ask this question, and I hear a variety of answers. Most people define a professional person the same way they describe a successful person: Someone who holds an important position with an impressive title, earns a high salary, wears expensive clothes, drives a nice car, and occupies a large office.

When I think of professionalism, I think of all the people I have met over the years who exemplified this quality, and many of the people who impressed me the most were far from the images described.

There is one person in particular who impressed me, and he didn't have a big title under his name, earn a lot of money, or wear expensive clothing. He made a lasting impression because he *exceeded* my expectations and exemplified my interpretation of a true professional.

He held what some of you may consider a menial position, but he acted as though it was the most important one there was. I first encountered him many years ago as I was on my way to work. I went to the drive-through of a local Burger King to get a muffin and cup of coffee. This was prior to the influx of coffee shops, and the Burger King near my office was the closest thing to a Starbucks at the time. If you've ever ordered food drive-through style, I am sure you will agree it is not usually an overwhelmingly positive experience. It hadn't been for me until that day.

A vibrant, enthusiastic, pleasant voice boomed over the intercom as he said, "Good morning, and welcome to Burger King. How may I help you?" I was a bit taken with this unusually perky greeting and immediately drew the conclusion that a manager was filling in for an employee. I ordered my coffee, drove to the window to pay, and got a good look at the young man who moved briskly and whistled as he worked. He smiled as he looked me in the eyes and sincerely thanked me for my business. I was impressed. How refreshing it was to encounter someone who was such a day-brightener. I paused for a moment and wondered why he was so unusually pleasant; what was he so happy about? What could be so great about working at the drive-through window of a fast-food restaurant?

It turned out that he was not the manager but an employee who took his job very seriously. I began to look forward to my morning drive-through trips and continued to receive the same fabulous treatment. Sam and I knew each other on a first name basis, and he always remembered my name and the fact that I took cream with my coffee. He even recognized my voice over the speaker.

One day, back at my office, I noticed an 800 number on the bag my food came in. It solicited feedback about the customer service I received. I was so moved by Sam's attitude and the level of service he provided that I took the time to call the number to tell the main office all about him. Now I, much like you, am a busy person and rarely take the time to call with a complaint, let alone a compliment, but I was so impressed by Sam's service and character that I wanted to do something to show my appreciation so he might benefit from it. I made the call simply to say how great he was.

It wasn't too long after I made that call that I pulled up to the speaker at the Burger King, expecting to hear that unusually perky greeting from Sam, but he wasn't there. I don't know who took my order that day or any day after. I never got the chance to tell Sam how impressed I was with him, and I didn't get to wish him well or even say goodbye. I can only assume he was promoted or moved on to fulfill whatever career goals he desired.

People often ask me why I didn't try to find out where he went or what he did with his life—they want to know the end of the story. I did try to find him several years ago, but I was unsuccessful in locating him. Even though I do not know where he went or what he's doing now, I am sure he is successful. After all, with an attitude like his, how could he possibly fail?

I first encountered Sam more than 15 years ago, and I still tell this story. Sam left a lasting impression on me, perhaps because so few people exceed my expectations the way he did. He performed the same job duties as others in his position, but he did it with more zest, more pride, and more enthusiasm than anyone I'd ever seen. Sam didn't have bad days, or if he did, he didn't let it show; he was consistent and predictable. For a period of time, I always knew what to expect when I pulled into the Burger King near my office, and I went there more often because of him.

Sam affected me because of the way he was, and also because of the way *I* was each time I encountered him. With each interaction, *I* sat up taller, smiled broader, and improved *my* attitude because of *his*. I began to wonder what effect I had on other people and if anything I did caused people to pause, think, or act any differently.

What about you? Do you ever cause people to pause, think, or act any differently? Do you meet the expectations of others, or do you *exceed* them? If a trip to a fast-food restaurant can be so awe-inspiring for me, imagine what you can accomplish by becoming an inspiration to the people you see every day.

You don't need to have a prestigious position or oodles of money to impress the people you meet. You don't need credentials or experience to make someone's day a little brighter. You can hold any position in any industry and do much more than what's expected.

Whether you are a seasoned professional or newcomer to the business world, you can gain the professional edge. Developing yourself professionally is an ongoing process and something that comes naturally to very few people. The people you see who are polished and professional work at it, just as they work at improving any other aspect of their job. No matter where you are in your life or career, it's important to step back and evaluate yourself every now and then. After you finish reading this book, your awareness of yourself and others will increase. This is the beginning of the ongoing process of change and personal growth.

As you read this book, you can learn to take control of yourself and your career; you can give yourself every advantage to succeed. You are already on your way toward a greater understanding about what works in business and what those extra qualities are that will show you how you can *gain the professional edge!*

POINTS TO REMEMBER

1. **Utilize resources to further your career.** Take classes, find a mentor, and ask for help. People won't know you need help unless you ask.

2. **Don't leave the odds of your success up to chance.** Take the time to think about what you want. Identify your goals and create a plan to reach them.

3. **Focus on your strengths.** When you focus on what you aren't, you're missing out on all that you are. When you portray yourself in a positive manner, others will view you positively too.

4. **Make something happen.** If you're hoping for a better opportunity, stop wishing and start taking action; if you want something to happen, make it happen.

5. **Polish yourself.** Like a diamond, it is only when you are polished that you will shine. Know what it takes to be a polished professional; polish yourself.

6. **Exceed expectations.** Work at exceeding expectations, not just meeting them. See what happens when you cause people to pause, think, and act differently.

7. **Be an inspiration.** Imagine what you can accomplish by becoming an inspiration to the people you see every day.

8. **Evaluate yourself.** Decide if you want to be an employee or entrepreneur. Know what you're good at and where you need to improve. It's important to step back and evaluate yourself every now and then. Begin today!

Chapter 2

Defining Your Success

True or False?

1. The more money you make, the more successful you are.

2. If you work hard, you will be successful.

3. The most successful people achieve their success quickly.

4. Everyone is motivated by money.

5. The smarter you are, the more successful you will be.

MOTIVATING FACTORS OF SUCCESS

Leon was energetic, hardworking, and driven to succeed. His family immigrated to America shortly after he was born, and his parents pushed him to excel. They encouraged him to do his best academically and told him he could accomplish anything, as long as he set his mind to it. He excelled in school and was the first member of his family to graduate from college.

Shortly after he graduated, he accepted a position with an office-equipment manufacturer and was instrumental in increasing the company's market share. Leon was a natural salesperson and an astute businessman. He sought outside investors and managed to raise enough money to fulfill his dream of starting his own firm. He worked diligently to build a thriving business, and by the time I met him, I could see his efforts had paid off. His business was flourishing and he enjoyed his financial success. He owned three homes, financially supported his parents, and made sure his nieces and nephews had enough money for a college education.

Leon went to great lengths to hire the best salespeople he could find, and he placed no limits on the amount of money each one could earn. "I don't understand," he told me over lunch one day. "The sky's the limit for my salespeople;

they could earn two to three times the income they are earning now. I've told them what it will take for them to make more money, but they don't push themselves to do it. When they've finished their work for the day, they could look for new business or make one more call, but they're more interested in walking out the door."

Leon was troubled. He struggled to understand how his salespeople could turn their backs on an opportunity to earn more money. Money motivated him; the more he had, the more he wanted.

I had the opportunity to work with some of Leon's employees. I expected to meet a group of unmotivated salespeople, but I did not. They were talented and ambitious and had a good understanding of the business they were in. Most of them were in sales for similar reasons, and all were attracted by the personal and financial independence they could achieve. Contrary to what Leon led me to believe, his people *were* motivated by money.

Mike, who had been with Leon the longest, showed pride in his accomplishments. "Leon is a great guy to work for, and I owe him a lot. He wants all of us to have what he has, but the truth is that most of us don't want or need that much money." Mike leaned forward and spoke quietly as he continued, "This business is everything to Leon. He never married or had children, and this business is his baby. Most of us have families, and those who don't have outside interests." Mike's face lit up as he talked about his family. "I've got a terrific wife and two beautiful kids, a house I just remodeled, and a cabin we go to on the weekends. I'm able to coach my daughter's softball team, and work out with my son. I work hard, and I'm paid well for what I do. The amount I earn may not be enough for Leon, but it *is* enough for me. If I worked as much as Leon, I wouldn't have a life!"

Mike didn't need to say another word; I understood what he was telling me. He *was* motivated by money, but other things motivated him as well. He *was* working long hours. Working additional hours would make it difficult for him to coach his daughter's softball team or find the time to work out with his son. He'd thought about moving to a bigger house but couldn't imagine leaving the one he'd just remodeled or leaving his neighbors who were his friends.

Leon was successful; he was a self-made man, took care of his family, and was proud of his accomplishments. Mike was successful too; he had a great job, a better-than-average income, a family he adored, and plenty of things to keep him happy. Both men were driven to succeed. Mike's feeling of contentment was a measure of his success; Leon's monetary value was a measure of his.

I could see that Leon's salespeople had ambition. Some were competitive and did their best work when competing for a bonus or award; *winning* was their motivation. Quotas drove others to produce; *reaching a goal* was their motivation. Once Leon understood what motivated each one, he was able to get the results he wanted.

HIDDEN MOTIVES

Do you know what motivates *you?* Are you working to fulfill someone else's needs or your own? Do you work because you *want* to or because you *have* to? Sometimes the answers can be difficult to find. People work for a variety of reasons. Many people feel they must work in order to survive and pay their bills. For them, getting a paycheck is the motivation. There are many ways to earn money, yet some people feel stuck in dead-end jobs—they are unable to see other options or a way out of a job they dislike.

Ann, a senior account executive, managed some of the largest accounts of her advertising firm, and was one of its top producers. She resented her boss for the added accounts he asked her to manage while her coworker was on maternity leave. She didn't appreciate the extra workload she was given, and felt she was being taken advantage of. She was not motivated and wondered how she could feel good about doing the extra work she resented.

In an effort to help her find a motivating factor, I asked Ann what would happen if she refused to manage the additional accounts. Our conversation went something like this:

Ann: "My boss would be upset with me."
Me: "What would happen if your boss was upset with you?"
Ann: "I guess it would be a problem; I may even lose my job."
Me: "What would happen if you lost your job?"
Ann: "I'd be upset—and unemployed!"
Me: "What would you do if you were unemployed?"
Ann: "I'd have to put together a résumé and start looking for a job."
Me: "How do you think you'd feel about looking for a job?"
Ann: "I don't think I'd like it—I'm not sure I'd find a job I want."
Me: "If you didn't find a job you wanted, what would you do?"
Ann: "I'd be miserable, and wouldn't be able to pay my bills."
Me: "And if you didn't pay your bills?"
Ann: "I'd lose my house—I'd have to move and . . ."

As a result of our conversation, Ann realized she *was* motivated after all; she was motivated to *keep her job*. She realized it was easier for her to manage the accounts than to resist. The consequences of refusing were too severe.

Whether you are self-employed or work for someone else, you will be faced with tasks you'd rather not do. The more you resist, the more difficult the task will become. If you can find a *reason* to do the thing you resist, it will make it easier for you to do. The motive may not always be apparent, but if you ask yourself enough questions, you will find your hidden motivation.

PERSONAL AND PROFESSIONAL SUCCESS

Ira was a successful litigation attorney. He was known for his shrewd tactics and aggressive manner. Although he succeeded in winning the cases he tried, he was not as successful in other areas of his life. His reputation was less than exemplary, both in and out of the courtroom. He had three failed marriages, numerous romantic affairs, and was known for his arrogant and sometimes lewd behavior. Ira didn't care about his relationships or what other people thought of him, but he did care about winning—at *any* cost.

What price are you willing to pay for your success? Are power, fame, and fortune something you'd want if they were all you had? Do you view your personal and professional successes independently or together?

Think about some of your personal and professional goals and the things you'd like to accomplish in each area of your life. If the time it takes you to accomplish your professional goals *at work* takes time away from your ability to accomplish your personal goals *at home,* will you feel you've been successful? Do you need to achieve both to fulfill your definition of success, or will you be satisfied achieving one or the other? It is important to consider *all areas* of your life as you define your goals and, ultimately, your success.

When will you consider yourself a *professional* success? At what point will you be satisfied with where you are in your career? Will it be when you earn a specific amount of money, receive a degree, work for a particular organization, own your own business, get a promotion, work from home, reach retirement, or something else?

When will you consider yourself a *personal* success? Will the things you accomplish *professionally* be an influence? Are you more concerned about your *achievements* or about the *kind of person* you become? There is no right or wrong answer; people view success differently.

You may think you know what success is all about, but if you are following someone else's standards or definition, you may end up working toward something that is of no value to you. Don't compare yourself to others—find *your* meaning of success.

I didn't stop to think about my definition of personal or professional success until I had been working for some time. As I look back, I can see I was trying to please others and reach a generic description of success. I believed if I had a good job, was paid well, and met my goals, I was successful. When I won an award or received a compliment, it was an added bonus, and I felt even more successful.

When my oldest daughter, Stephanie, was born, I began to question my success—and all of the obligations that came with it. In addition to fulfilling the expectations of my job, my boss, and my customers, I longed to fulfill my expectations of being a good mother. When my boss dropped off work for me to do at my home just two weeks after I gave birth, I was overwhelmed. I no longer enjoyed the travel or the time away from home my job required. What used to make me feel successful in my career was making me feel unsuccessful as a mother. Eventually, I made changes that made it easier for me to meet both my personal and professional goals and expectations.

I started my consulting and speaking business when my children were young. Spending time with my three daughters was important to me, and so was doing work I valued. It took time for me to build my business, and there were times I questioned my success. Based on what I'd learned from *others* about success, I felt I wasn't progressing fast enough.

For years, most of the money I made went into developing my business. At times, I looked at my income and felt like a failure. I considered giving up but hesitated because I knew I was making progress. I looked at my accomplishments and saw a number of small successes. I was working on new projects, had satisfied customers, and people thanked me for changing the direction of their lives. These accomplishments brought me tremendous satisfaction. I asked myself over and over again: *Does the amount of money I make determine my success, or is my success determined by my momentum and the difference I make in people's lives?*

I valued financial success, and I still wanted it, but my priorities were changing. I was becoming a better person as a result of my work. For the first time in my life, I felt I was doing work I was meant to do. I believed I had found my calling. Yet I felt torn because I knew I was capable of contributing more financially to my family. There were times I came close to closing my doors and finding another job.

When I finally trusted myself enough to work toward my own definition of success, I was motivated to carry on. Whenever I allowed myself to question my success or compare myself to others, I lost my focus and determination. I had to be sure I acknowledged every success I achieved, no matter how small, and continue to work toward my goals, even when reaching them seemed unlikely.

My definition of success has changed over the years. Perhaps yours has too. You will never know what your success really means to you until you take the time to find out.

How do you see *yourself* right now? Are you where you want to be?

Read the following four statements and select the one that most closely resembles your thoughts about your success.

1. **I have been successful.**

2. **I am successful.**

3. **I will be successful.**

4. **I want to be successful.**

Respond to the questions that follow the statement you selected.

1. **I have been successful.** *If you have been successful, identify your success; what have you accomplished? How did you do it? If you have reached success before, you can reach it again. What do you need to do to achieve success now or in the future?*

2. **I am successful.** *If you are successful, define your success; what have you accomplished? How did you do it? What do you need to do to continue to be successful now and in the future?*

3. **I will be successful.** *If you believe you will be successful, what are the indicators of your success; what successes (large or small) have you had so far? Define your success. What must you accomplish to believe you are successful? What do you need to do to achieve the success you envision?*

4. **I want to be successful.** *If you want to be successful, what will be the indicators of your success? What do you need to accomplish to be successful? What do you need to do to achieve the success you want?*

Regardless of where you are right now, it is important to "see" your success. You need to identify what you want to *accomplish* and determine the things you need *to do* to be successful. Anticipating or wanting success is not enough to achieve it; it's what you *do* that makes the difference.

DEFINING YOUR SUCCESS

Jan's class reunion was two months away. She was exercising and eating well, and she was in the best shape she'd been in years. She'd already lost 30 pounds, and people told her she looked fantastic. Jan wasn't satisfied. She was determined to attend the reunion weighing the same amount she weighed in high school; anything less was unacceptable. Although she had already succeeded at losing a substantial amount of weight, Jan didn't consider her weight loss a success because she hadn't met her goal.

When Tim's wife was diagnosed with breast cancer, he was determined to do all he could to save her life. He accompanied her on all of her appointments, sought second and third opinions, and spent endless hours researching treatment options. When his wife passed away, he felt responsible; although he did what he could, he thought he failed because he couldn't save her life. When Tim heard about the "Race for the Cure," he decided to participate. With the race just weeks away, he did what he could to prepare for the run. He was not in his best shape and knew it would be tough. Although he only managed to run a third of the distance, Tim felt he succeeded. His goal never was to *complete* the race; it was to honor his wife by *participating* in the race, and he did accomplish that.

Henry and Marc met at an outplacement firm shortly after losing their jobs. They became close friends and were a source of support for each other. When Marc received a job offer just two months after he began his search, he accepted it. Henry chose to decline the offers he received and wait to find exactly what he was looking for. After nine long months, Henry received an offer he enthusiastically accepted. Marc's goal was to find a job; Henry's goal was to find a specific type of job. Both men succeeded in accomplishing their goals.

Jan, Tim, Henry, and Marc all had specific and desired outcomes; accepting anything else was too much of a compromise. Jan's goal was to lose 40 pounds by her class reunion. It didn't matter that people thought Jan looked great, as long as she had her sights set on looking *better*. Tim wanted to honor his wife. Other runners were disappointed when they failed to *complete* the race, but it didn't matter to Tim, because his goal was simply to *run* the race. Marc's goal was to find a job, while Henry was searching for his *ideal* job. Henry wasn't willing to take a job he didn't want, and Marc wasn't willing to wait to get back to work.

Each person defined success differently. The one thing they all had in common was that each of them was motivated for personal reasons to reach their goal.

You need to know what you intend to do; you need to know what motivates you. You need to know *your* definition of success. Perhaps the definition from *Webster's Dictionary* will help:

Success: Achievement of something intended or desired. This definition may help you as you try to better understand your own success; the key is to know what you want and what you intend *to do* to achieve it. Success rarely happens overnight; it is a result of staying focused on the results you want.

The following questions will help you define your success and your motivating factors. Be specific in your answers.

> **Define your success. What are you striving for professionally?** (*The growth of your business, self-employment, a particular position, financial independence, an advanced degree, a specific income, a challenge, or retirement?*)

> **What do you need in order to feel good about your success?** (*A specific title or position, additional skills or knowledge, praise or acknowledgement, increase in revenue, new clients, independence, or flexibility?*)

> **What do you want as a result of reaching your goal?** (*Do you want a new title or position, more money, respect, or flexible hours?*)

> **What are you striving for personally?** (*Material possessions, free time, hobbies, travel, relationships, time with family, home improvements, community service, or additional education?*)

> **What motivates you to reach your goals?** (*Sense of accomplishment, personal commitment and responsibility, advancement opportunities, increase in income, or financial security?*)

STEPS TO SUCCESS

Many of your first successes happened early in your life. You may not remember the day you took your first step, but that first step was one of many that prepared you to walk on your own. You stood up, you fell down, you took a step, you fell down, you took two steps, you took three; every step you took, and every fall you had, prepared you to walk on your own. We don't scold the child who falls while making an attempt to walk, we cheer for him! We encourage him to try again and again and again!

As you work toward your goals, you may fall many times. We may marvel at the successful people we read and hear about and envy the success that looks so easy to obtain. But behind the success stories of many successful people are stories of struggle and failure. Few people reach success all at once; success is a series of steps, taken one at a time. The struggles and challenges we find so difficult to bear often help us build character and strength. Reaching success is not always easy.

Bruce was devastated when his position was eliminated. He had been instrumental in the growth of the company he worked for and contributed to the buyout that resulted in his layoff. He couldn't imagine working anywhere else and hadn't looked for work in years. His age and seniority had been a benefit until now. He feared his age would make it difficult for him to find a full-time job, so he offered to help out a friend who was struggling to build a small business.

Bruce never found another job, because he stopped looking for one. He and his friend became partners, built up the business, and sold it for millions of dollars. When Bruce lost his job he was devastated. However, what was a terrible loss at the time ended up being one of the best things that ever happened to him.

It's not always apparent when it happens, but many of the challenges we face are opportunities in disguise. When you look for the lesson and learn to move on, your challenges can make you a better and more successful person.

There are many levels of success. Setting your sights on a big goal is fine, but don't overlook all of the small successes you have along the way. If you're waiting to feel successful until you reach your highest goal, you may be limiting yourself.

A goal is a guide; *guide* your life, but don't forget to *live* your life. Goals evolve and change. Be flexible and be open to the direction your life moves you. You will make it easier on yourself if you do.

Do you remember the day you got your driver's license? In order to obtain your license, you needed to do a number of things. You needed to take driver's education, obtain your permit, complete behind-the-wheel instruction, and, depending on where you lived, fulfill a specific number of hours of practice driving before you could take your test. Each step you completed led you closer to your goal. You were probably elated when you got your permit. You didn't view practice driving as a waste of time because you knew it would help you reach your goal. The moment you're likely to remember most was the day you got your license, but it wouldn't have happened unless you completed *every step* along the way. Success happens in steps so step up to your success!

SKILL VS. ABILITY

Throughout this chapter, little has been mentioned about the skills you need to reach your goals. Skills and knowledge are essential, but they're not the only indicators of your success. There are many straight-A students who pass their classes with flying colors but fail in their attempts to hold a job or sustain successful relationships.

Some professions require more skill than ability, but more often than not, your *ability to learn* is more important than the skills you have. Skills can be limiting if you rely on them, but your *potential* is unlimited when you have the ability and the motivation to do something.

When I began interviewing for my first job, shortly after leaving college, I had few skills and no relevant experience. However, that didn't stop me from applying for open positions. I may not have had the skills or qualifications I needed, but I knew I had the ability to do well. "You don't have exactly what we are looking for," I'd often hear, "but you do have something." I'd listen intently as they tried to define that "something" they saw. "You've got confidence and enthusiasm. I'm sure you'll be successful."

It wasn't easy convincing someone to give me a chance. The only thing I offered was intangible: my ability to reach my potential. Even though other candidates may have had more knowledge, skill or expertise, I'm not sure they all had the ability to excel.

When people rely on their skills, they often miss out on opportunities. I didn't have skills to rely on, so I had to look for them. I needed a chance to prove myself. I will never forget the people who believed in me early on, the people who gave me my first opportunities. I will be forever grateful to those who trusted my ability to learn, develop skills, and become successful.

Believe in yourself. Never underestimate your ability or limit yourself with your current skills. Continue to learn and develop new skills for the rest of your life. Know what you are capable of and push yourself to the best of your ability.

PICTURE YOUR SUCCESS

There is power in positive affirmation. Knowing what you want and envisioning your success is more than wishful thinking. You increase your chances of success when you see what you want and believe you can and will have it. Self-doubt and negativity rob you of your strength. Conviction and positive affirmation are your most powerful assets.

Imagine you are successful; you've reached your goals and are living the life you've wanted. One day, you receive a call from an old friend you haven't seen since high school. He tells you he's gone through a difficult period in his life and would like to rekindle some of his old friendships. He's asks to see you, so you decide to meet him for lunch.

He tells you all about the rise and fall of his business and marriage, and now he wants to hear all about you. The following are the questions he asks you as you visit over lunch. As you record your responses, answer each question in the present tense as if you have already achieved your goals.

What have you been doing since high school?

Do you still see any of your old friends?

What kind of work do you do?

How did you end up doing that?

Tell me about your family: Do you have children? Where do you live?

What do you do when you aren't working?

How have you managed to accomplish so much? What's the secret to your success?

What accomplishments are you most proud of?

I'm struggling right now and trying to figure out what to do next. Do you have any advice for me?

Having an imaginary conversation may seem silly to you, but don't be too quick to judge. Every idea and every success begins with a thought and a vision. Hundreds of thoughts and ideas cross your mind every day, but they'll come and go unless you capture some and allow them to materialize. If you've had thoughts about doing something, you can continue to *think* about it or start *to do* something about it—it's up to you.

If you didn't answer all of the questions, review them again and finish answering now. Write your life story today and create whatever you'd like it to be. It's *your* life story, and no one else can write it for you.

True or False?

1. The more money you make, the more successful you are.

FALSE.

Making a lot of money is one aspect of success, but it's not always the most important one. You can earn a high salary and still feel unsuccessful if you haven't reached your goals.

2. If you work hard, you will be successful.

FALSE.

If you work hard, you will have a good chance of being successful, but it takes more than hard work to do well. Many people spend their entire lives working hard but never feel successful. Success means different things to different people. Once you define the success you want, you will be able to determine what you must do to achieve it.

3. The most successful people achieve their success quickly.

FALSE.

Success rarely happens quickly. There are exceptions, but it takes time for most people to reach the success they are after. Success is a reflection of plans and goals and is often a result of many smaller successes and failures over time.

4. Everyone is motivated by money.

FALSE.

*Money does motivate people and is one of the primary motivators of success; however, it is not the only one. Everyone is motivated differently, and people vary in the amount of money they need. Lifestyle, contributing to society, and personal achievement can be just as motivating as money to some people. It's important to determine what motivates **you**.*

5. The smarter you are, the more successful you will be.

FALSE.

The smarter you are, the more capable you are, but there is no guarantee that you will be successful. If you rely on your knowledge or skill, you may miss out on other opportunities. Your ability to adapt and do well in many different areas is the key to your success. It's not what you know now that will make you a success, it's who you know you can be.

Give yourself permission to be whomever and whatever you want. Allow yourself to achieve whatever you want to achieve. Once you create a picture of your success, look at it every day. Your picture can be in the form of a statement, a mental image, a collage, or something else. If you want your story to become reality, positive affirmation is the only way.

POINTS TO REMEMBER

1. **Define your success.** Create your definition of success both personally and professionally. Know what kind of person you want to become.

2. **Measure your success.** Identify ways to measure and recognize your success.

3. **Motivate yourself.** Know what motivates you and ask yourself questions to find your hidden motives.

4. **Identify your goals.** A goal is a guide; *guide* your life. Know what you're striving for and what you need *to do* to achieve your goals.

5. **Focus on your ability.** Continue to develop your skills, but don't rely on them. Your ability to learn new skills is your greatest asset.

6. **Step up to your success.** Success rarely happens overnight. Your overall success will be a result of the many smaller successes you'll have along the way.

7. **View challenges as opportunities.** Every challenge you face is an opportunity to learn and grow. If you're knocked down, pick yourself back up. Each stumble and fall you take brings you closer to success.

8. **Write your life story.** You can create the life you want. Once you have a picture of your success, remember to reinforce it everyday.

Chapter 3

Critical First Impressions

True or False?

1. You never have a second chance to make a first impression.
2. We draw long-lasting conclusions about people within the first few seconds of meeting them.
3. You cannot control the kind of impression you make.
4. First impressions are not always accurate.
5. Initial impressions are instinctive.
6. In a job interview, the decision to hire someone is often made within the first few moments of the interview.
7. A person's physical appearance is the strongest factor in a first impression.

YOU NEVER HAVE A SECOND CHANCE TO MAKE A FIRST IMPRESSION

It was Administrative Professionals Day, and I was the keynote speaker for the entire administration of a local college. The topic: "Professionalism and the Critical First Impression."

I felt especially confident and well prepared that morning, and I left myself plenty of time to arrive at the conference center at least 30 to 40 minutes prior to the 8:00 A.M. meeting time.

I'd been to the conference center only once before and had requested directions, which I made sure I followed exactly. As I was driving, I was listening to the radio and taking in the scenery of the beautiful sunny April morning, but I became a bit concerned when, after a left turn, nothing looked familiar. I pulled over and called my contact. When I told her where I was and the directions I had been given, she informed me the directions I'd received were wrong. I should have turned *right* where I had been told to turn *left*.

I traveled a great distance in the wrong direction, and now I had to back-track. I turned down the radio as I merged back on the highway. Traffic had picked up and moved very slowly. I looked at the clock and feared I wouldn't make it to the center on time. It was close to 7:30, the time I had planned to arrive, and I was miles away, stuck in rush-hour traffic.

I tried to convince myself that everything would be ok. After all, I thought, there will be rolls and coffee, and people will enjoy the chance to relax, eat breakfast, and visit with one another. Not everyone shows up on time, I ration-alized, and maybe they will be glad to have a few extra minutes before the pro-gram begins. As I continued to prepare myself for my embarrassingly late entrance, I considered explaining to the group that my tardiness was part of the program, that I planned it this way to reinforce the impact of first impressions, but I didn't know if I could pull off the facade I was considering. What if no one believed me?

I finally drove into the parking lot at 10 minutes *after* eight. A large picture window in the conference room faced the parking lot, and through it I saw a group of the most humorless-looking people I'd ever seen, each of them watch-ing my every move. They weren't eating breakfast, visiting with each other, or hurrying to take a seat; everyone was seated and waiting for me. I got out of the car, gathered my belongings, and proceeded to the door.

I suddenly faced a feat to accomplish for which, in all my diligent planning, I had *not* prepared—overcoming the very negative first impression this room full of people had of me.

I held my head high as I entered the conference center, and smiled as I rushed to the podium. I looked at the scowling faces whose eyes were all on me, took a deep breath, and with as much confidence and enthusiasm as I could muster, I said "Good morning! I'm here today to talk about profession-alism and first impressions!" Silence.

I wanted to find a way to connect with this audience, but I could see they had no desire to connect with me. I knew they were not impressed with me, and I was desperate to find a way to restore myself.

"What impression do you all have of me right now?" I went on bravely. A few faces started to loosen up, not in smiles, exactly, but not scowls either.

"Have you ever had something go wrong, in spite of careful planning and preparation?" Some heads started to nod.

"Have you ever made a mistake or had a problem get in your way?" Most of the faces were with me by now.

"I made a wrong turn on my way here this morning," I continued. "And that one wrong turn turned my whole morning upside down. I could let it destroy me, I could complain, I could let it get me down. But, wait a minute, isn't that exactly what we're here to talk about—how to work with problems while remaining professional?"

I continued on as I made every attempt to relate to all of the people in that room, and I encouraged them to relate to me. I could have complained, denied responsibility, or blamed the person who gave me the wrong directions, but what good would it do? It certainly wouldn't make me look any better, and it might make me look worse. Instead, I was honest, vulnerable, and humble. Most important, I communicated the message that professionalism isn't being something you're not; *it's being the best of who you are.*

By being honest and open with the audience and admitting I had made a mistake, I believe I actually helped create a bond between us. I wasn't preaching to the group, but I was sharing a part of myself with them. My frankness reinforced the fact that people like to deal with other *people,* not with people who act like robots. I took responsibility for what happened and didn't blame anyone but myself. People can be very forgiving and accepting when you admit a mistake. Finally, the experience reminded me how important it is to leave plenty of time to spare so I will always be early and never have to go through an experience like that again.

We all have things that get in our way, surprise us, or alter our expectations. How we *deal* with the problems and the surprises is the test. I *did* manage to overcome the negative first impression my audience had of me that day, and I delivered a program that was well received. However, it took some quick thinking, a lot of work, and a little luck. And you can be sure that no one in that room will ever forget the first impression they had of me.

FIRST IMPRESSIONS ARE LASTING IMPRESSIONS

When you fail to make a good impression in an initial meeting, you create more work for yourself in subsequent meetings. If you work hard enough, you can overcome a negative first impression, but it takes time to convince someone you are different than you first appear. Most people have learned to rely on their initial reactions, and letting them go isn't easy.

I was working on a project when I first met Patty. I'd heard a lot of great things about her and envisioned someone very different from the woman I met.

We had a brief encounter, and after that initial meeting, I was concerned. I understood Patty would be my primary contact for the project, and I anticipated working with someone who would stay on top of things and help move the project along. Patty seemed too laid-back.

On the day I met her, I immediately noticed how lethargic she seemed; it was early in the morning, yet she seemed burned out. She didn't *look* like someone capable of managing a big project; she wore a simple white shirt, which was hanging outside her pants. She made sarcastic remarks I didn't know how to interpret, and although I sensed she was a nice person, she was not what I expected.

I wondered if she could be trusted to follow through. Would she take this project seriously? Could I count on her to move things along? Although I worried, I didn't have a choice. I was going to have to work with her.

Over the next few months, as I got to know Patty better, I saw a very different woman from the one I saw the day I met her. I later discovered that when we met, she was in the early stages of her fifth pregnancy. As we became better acquainted, she told me how sick she had been the morning I met her. Her clothes were too snug, and her pants wouldn't zip, so she was forced to wear her shirt outside her pants to cover the zipper.

"I was so embarrassed about the way I looked the day I met you," she told me one day. "I wanted people to know why my clothes didn't fit, but my husband and I agreed we wouldn't announce my pregnancy until I was further along." She proceeded to tell me about a previous pregnancy that resulted in a miscarriage. Her eyes filled with tears as she talked about her loss, her regret for announcing the pregnancy too soon, and her reasons for delaying her announcement this time.

Patty and I became dear friends. The more I got to know her, the more I liked and trusted her. Her sarcastic remarks always came at the perfect time and would make me laugh. I was amazed at her ability to keep things under control. She was pregnant, working full-time, and had three other children at home.

Patty managed the project beautifully and kept things moving along. The only thing that bothered me was how wrong I had been about her when we first met. I've never forgotten my first impression of her or how I misjudged her.

First impressions are lasting impressions, but they are not always accurate. We have a brief amount of time in which we make important decisions about people we meet, and there are times those initial assumptions are incorrect.

You *can* overcome a negative first impression. However, research shows it will take at least *seven additional encounters* before letting go of that first impression. *Seven times* until you are able to view someone differently than you did the very first time.

Every time you greet someone, you reinforce or negate the impression you made the time before. When you are consistent, or *better* than the time before, you have an advantage. When you are inconsistent, or not as good as you were the time before, people will change their opinion about you. First impressions are critical, but they're not the only impression to pay attention to.

I've known Patty for over 10 years, and although I rarely see her now, when I do, I am always reminded of the negative first impression I had of her. I am over it, but I can't forget it. First impressions are lasting impressions; first impressions are powerful impressions. Save yourself time and effort; focus on making a good impression the first time and *every* time thereafter.

YOU HAVE ONLY 10 SECONDS

Have you ever met anyone you immediately disliked? How long did it take you to make your decision? Did it take hours, minutes, or seconds? How did you *know* you didn't like this person, and what did you base your assumptions on?

It doesn't take much time to draw conclusions about the people we meet. Consider it a survival skill; the need to assess people and situations quickly is often vital, and at times our lives may depend upon our ability to do so.

Imagine you are a visitor in the downtown area of a city you've never been to before. You decide to walk around and get a bite to eat at a restaurant that was recommended to you. You're chatting on your phone as you take in your new surroundings, but because you aren't paying attention to where you're going, you have difficulty finding the restaurant. As you stop to look around, you realize you are lost. You don't recognize any of the buildings and aren't sure which way to go. There's hardly a soul in sight, and as you contemplate your next move, you see three men walking toward you. They are engaged in a quiet conversation, and you can see they are well dressed; all are wearing business suits and appear well groomed.

What would you do, and how long do you think it would take to make your decision? You could follow them, turn the other way, or ask them for directions.

Picture yourself again: You are a visitor in the downtown area of a city you've never been to before. You are walking around, talking on the phone, and about to get a bite to eat. When you realize you are lost, you also realize you are in an isolated area. As you are deciding what to do, you see three men walking toward you. You hope they can help you and wonder if you should follow them or ask for directions. As they approach you, you can see they are in tattered clothes, have long, shaggy hair, and are unkempt. The men are disorderly and talking loudly.

What do you think you would do, and how long do you think it would take to make your decision? Would you walk toward them and ask for directions or turn the other way? What conclusions can you draw about these men?

I've used similar scenarios in my workshops, and with little to go on, people manage to conjure up the most intrinsic details. Even though the scenarios are fiction, we can relate; we are used to assessing the situations we are in and the people we meet, because we do it all the time.

Picture this: You are entering the elevator of the office building where you work. As the door begins to close, you see a woman running toward the elevator. You hold the door and wait for her. She struggles as she runs in her high-heeled boots and pushes back her long, wavy bleached-blond hair. She's buttoning up her black leather jacket as she tugs at the matching tight leather miniskirt. She thanks you for holding the door and asks you to press the button for the 16th floor. You work on the 16th floor and learn she is interviewing for a job within your company. You are aware of only two available positions; one is for chief financial officer and the other for a receptionist.

Which position do you assume this woman is applying for? How long will it take you to decide, and on what will you base your decision?

With each scenario you had little to go on, but you were able to make a decision based on the visual images described and your perception of those images. The information I gave you may be superficial, but it is telling. If you had a gut reaction as you read the information, it happened in a matter of seconds.

It's not fair, but it is true—impressions are formed within *seconds* of meeting someone. Our initial assumption, or "gut feeling," can be helpful and informative. Our reaction provides us with the critical information we need to assess people quickly and efficiently, often helping us distinguish a threatening situation from a nonthreatening one.

INGREDIENTS OF IMPRESSIONS

Many theories explain that the way you present yourself affects perceived job performance and career success. In a job interview, for instance, the interviewer often decides *within moments* whether or not you are a serious candidate for the job. You don't have much time to establish your credibility or your expertise.

A stellar résumé, years of experience, even the right contacts may not be enough to help you overcome the weak handshake, the inappropriate attire, or the awkward comment made during these critical moments of initial judgment.

If credentials were all that mattered, why would an interview take place at all? Why not hire someone based on his or her résumé? An employer can quickly scan a résumé to gather information about you and determine if you are qualified for a position, so why bother meeting with you?

Résumés are based on *facts*; interviews are based on *feelings*. Résumés are strictly informational; interviews are much more personal. You may prefer to believe that facts are what's important, but the truth is, people choose other *people* to work with, not the facts on a piece of paper.

Michelle and Peter graduated at the top of their class. Both had impressive letters of recommendation, carefully crafted résumés and relevant job experience. They pursued similar companies, and interviewed for a few of the same positions. Every time they competed for a job, Michelle was called back for a second interview but Peter was not. Michelle accepted a position and began working immediately after graduation. Peter interviewed for two more months before he was offered a job.

Hundreds of people often apply for one position. A company representative may interview 10, 20 or more people for one position. Employers are too busy and too hurried to take the time to really get to know someone in an interview. In an interview, an employer is looking for reasons *not* to hire you.

You may have an impressive résumé, but if you have an *unimpressive* interview, chances are you won't get the job. The first few moments of an interview often provide enough information for an experienced hiring manager to make a decision.

Michelle made an impressive and positive first impression, but Peter didn't warm up until the second or third meeting. Because they both had similar qualifications, interviewers relied on other factors when deciding which candidate to pursue. The *impressions* Michelle and Peter made were the determining factor.

Many qualified people have equal skills and ability, but in an interview each person is assessed for how he or she looks, acts, speaks, reacts, and, ultimately, how he or she will fit the culture of the company. In an interview, *who you are* becomes more important than *what you are* on paper.

You don't have to let simple mistakes in your personal presentation obscure your ability or natural gifts and talents. You don't have to give an employer a superficial reason not to hire or promote you.

It's not always easy to make a positive impression when you're feeling stressed or nervous, but failure to do so can result in the failure to get the results you want. When you make a negative impression, you have to work much harder to overcome it.

We make first impressions through both verbal and nonverbal communication. That part is fairly obvious. But you might be surprised by how many factors combined convey an impression that is registered in just a few seconds:

INGREDIENTS OF IMPRESSIONS

Verbal	Nonverbal
Tone of voice	Overall appearance
Choice of words	Posture
Attitude	Facial expressions
Rate of speech	Gestures
Enunciation	Clothing
	Hair

As you look over the ingredients of impressions, how many do you think are within your control? Can you control what you say and how you say it? Can you control how you appear? Who decides what you wear, how you stand, or what gestures you make? Many people believe that the impression they make is out of their control, but it is not. Each of the ingredients listed above is within your control and can be analyzed, practiced, and, ultimately, changed. Yes, we all have "bad hair days," but *what we do about them* is within our control.

Think about your objectives when you are meeting someone for the first time. If you were interviewing or making a presentation to the board of directors or a potential client, what kind of impression would you like to make? Once you know how you'd like to come across, you can decide how you will do it. The more prepared you are, the better your chances of success.

NOTICE WHAT YOU NOTICE

You may agree that first impressions are crucial in an interview but find it difficult to believe that first impressions have the same degree of importance for someone who is already established. You may think that someone who has experience and credentials shouldn't have to put forth as much effort as a younger person who's just starting out.

First impressions are formed so quickly that there's little time to gather information about someone. You don't have a chance to talk about yourself or boast of your accomplishments. Experience and credentials are not always obvious, and age can work for or against you. No matter what stage of your career you are in, your first impression matters.

I've had people tell me they will *never* try to impress *anyone*. They want to believe that appearance doesn't matter. They tell me they don't look for superficial clues; they look for depth. And because they don't focus on their own appearance, they believe no one else does either.

People focus on different things. Clothing and appearance are important to some people and insignificant to others. Whether it is important to you or not, the way you *appear* is the single most influential factor in the impression you make.

Ed was the scholarly type; he drove the same car he'd driven for years. He wore the same jacket he'd worn for years. His long, full beard was his trademark, and he hadn't shaved it since the day he grew it. A high school English teacher, image wasn't important to him. He said he'd never waste his time on such trivial matters.

When Ed met someone for the first time, he didn't pay attention to the person's clothing or style. Instead, he listened intently to every word the person said. The only thing that bothered Ed was when someone used poor grammar, mispronounced or misused words, or had poor sentence structure, because those things stuck out like a sore thumb to him. Ed was always correcting his students, both in and out of the classroom. "When you open your mouth, you expose your mind," he always said. Ed knew the importance of grammar— *grammar was his focus.*

Kate was a personal shopper and a wardrobe consultant. Her client list consisted of high-level executives, physicians, attorneys, and television news anchors. "Image is everything," Kate frequently said. Kate and I were eating lunch one day when she abruptly interrupted our conversation. "Now that's a great look," she said as she pointed to the woman wearing a long red jacket. A few moments later, she grabbed my arm as she discreetly pointed out a man in a great-looking sweater.

Kate was in the right business. She loved clothes and loved helping people create their image. She never held back; if she thought she could help someone look better, she made a suggestion. Kate always noticed clothing and image details—*image was her focus.*

Matt loved cars. He collected cars, read about cars, and worked on cars. I was always amazed with his ability to spot a car and identify the model name and year within a matter of seconds. To Matt, people and their cars went hand in hand. Once Matt knew you and your car, he'd never forget either.

It had been several years since I'd seen Matt. One of the first things he asked me after we said hello was if I was still driving the same car. I don't even remember what car it was, but he knew the color, the year, the make, and the model. Matt loved cars—*cars were his focus.*

Someone has to make a fairly big mistake for me to get worked up about grammar. I don't think I've ever been distracted by clothing in the middle of a conversation, and I couldn't tell you the make or year of a car if I tried.

It's not where I place my focus. It's important to *notice what you notice.*

Marti cuts hair; she notices hairstyles. Al is a dermatologist; he notices skin. Jim is an architect; he notices buildings. Leslie is an interior designer; she notices decor. Sherry is an organizational consultant; she notices disorganization. Harold sells jewelry; he notices jewelry.

What's your focus, and what do you notice?

No one is right or wrong, or better or worse, for where they put their focus. However, we tend to pay attention to the things that are important to *us,* the things we *notice.* As a result, we notice things other people overlook, and overlook things other people notice.

Imagine you've just eaten the chewiest and tastiest chocolate-chip cookie you've ever had. You obtain the recipe and several weeks later, you get a craving for the cookies. You pull out the recipe and decide to make the cookies for the first time.

As you gather the ingredients, you see that you need a stick of butter. You don't like to use butter and decide to make the recipe a little healthier, so you use olive oil instead. You omit the oatmeal, because you don't have enough, and you use one egg instead of two. You substitute skim milk for whole and white sugar for brown. You don't have a lot of time, so you increase the oven temperature to bake the cookies faster. When you take the cookies out of the oven, they look different than you expected. You take a bite, and although they are edible, they are not as good as you expected. You acknowledge the few minor changes you made, but you can't understand why the cookies don't taste better.

When you make cookies, the closer you follow the recipe, the better the chance they will turn out as expected. You may not see the value or importance in the oatmeal or butter, but there is a reason each ingredient is listed.

If you want to increase your chances of making a positive first impression, follow the "recipe," and include all 11 ingredients mentioned earlier in this chapter. When you pick and choose the ingredients only *you* think are important, you neglect the ingredients that are important to someone else.

When we meet someone, we make important decisions quickly. Our initial judgments are based solely on image and perception. If you fail to make the kind of impression you want, you'll have to work much harder at convincing people to take you seriously. Why work any harder than you have to?

THE PROCESS

What process do you go through as you get ready for each day? Most of us have a routine—take a shower, brush our teeth, eat our breakfast, read the paper, get dressed, and go. If you're like most people, you don't even *think* about your routine; you function on automatic.

I recommend you add a step to your routine and implement this process: As you prepare yourself for each day, ask (and answer) the following four questions:

1. Who do I expect to see and meet today?

2. What do I want to accomplish—what are my objectives?

3. What kind of impression do I need to make to achieve my objectives?

4. How will I convey that impression?

These four simple questions are not as simplistic as they seem. Practice the process:

1. **Who do I expect to see and meet today?**
   You are meeting with a prospective client today.

2. **What do I want to accomplish—what are my objectives?**
   Your objective is to help her solve her staffing problem and ultimately gain her trust and her business.

3. **What kind of impression do I want or need to make to achieve my objectives?**
   You decide you need to appear confident and friendly.

4. **How will I convey that impression?**

It won't take you long to answer the first three questions. The challenge is figuring out how you will put it all together. We may know what we want to do but lack the skills to do it. What if you want to *appear* confident but don't *feel* confident?

First, you need to figure out what **confidence** *looks like.* When I think of a confident person, I think of someone who is self-assured; someone who moves about with purpose; someone who stands tall, sits tall, and has focused eye contact. I see someone who is polished and put together, someone who speaks accurately and calmly, someone who is in control.

What do you see?

Once you *see it,* you need to *be it!* But what if you *do* see it, know what you need to do, but are nervous and not sure you can pull it off?

You'll need to focus more on what you *do* and less on how you *feel.* You'll need to take a deep breath, stand tall, hold your head high, and do all the things a confident person would do. You can *act* confidently even when you feel a lack of confidence. When you *appear* confident, people believe you *are* confident. What's so amazing is that eventually even *you* believe it because you are getting the results you want.

Everyone can see your actions, but unless you choose to let your feelings show, no one has to know how you really feel.

What does **friendly** *look like?* How do you appear friendly in a matter of seconds? When I think of a friendly person, I think of someone who is happy and smiling. I picture someone with a hearty handshake; someone with a sparkle in his eye. What does friendly look like to *you?* You have to *see* it before you can *be* it.

Finally, you need to make conscious decisions that support your objectives as you prepare for the day. Select something to wear that will help you feel and appear more confident and friendly. It may be your favorite suit or a colorful tie. Prepare, practice, and do all you can to become more confident. Focus on projecting friendliness; remind yourself to smile and be genuinely excited when you meet someone.

Developing and projecting your ideal impression is a learned skill, and it's something you must work at, like any other skill. Don't leave it up to chance; take time to plan the kind of impression you want to make.

COME TO YOUR SENSES

We make judgments and draw long-lasting conclusions about people quickly and often subconsciously. We don't have enough time to analyze the information we take in, so we rely on our feelings and instincts.

Within a matter of seconds, we begin to make decisions about the people we meet. We quickly determine how successful, trustworthy, or credible someone is, and we make assumptions about their economic status, their education level and their social status—all within a matter of *seconds*. Our response, which is instinctive, is a result of paying close attention to our senses. In an instant, we take in information and draw conclusions based on what we *see*, what we *hear*, and what we *smell*.

What We See: Clothing, shoes, hair, face, posture, gestures, expressions

What We Hear: Pitch, tone, volume, accent, words, dialect

What We Smell: Body scent/odor, breath, perfume, cigarette smoke, food odors

Our senses are reliable and provide us with enough information to generate a response to someone. Our senses do the work, requiring little or no conscious effort on our part. Our sight is the strongest of the senses, making what we *see* most influential.

The way you *appear* to others creates either a positive or negative reaction. Your ability to convey a positive impression is within your control. It is not determined by the amount of money you make or how much money you spend on your clothes. The impression you make is a result of your *overall appearance*—the way you stand, sit, walk, and carry yourself, as well as your clothing, grooming, mannerisms, behavior, and attitude.

You can make a positive impression any time you choose to; however, it won't happen without a little planning and effort. When you focus on your objectives and become more aware of yourself and others, you will be able to determine the kind of impression you want to make. With proper planning and a little practice, you can achieve your desired impression in no time at all.

POSITIVE AND NEGATIVE RESPONSES

When we meet someone or walk into an environment, we have a positive or negative response. Our responses are often a result of the expectations we have. When you meet with your accountant or attorney, do you expect the same type of impression as you do from your doctor or dentist? What about the waiting areas—have you come to expect comfortable chairs, magazines to read, or quiet music to listen to as you wait for your appointment? What would your reaction be if you walked into an office expecting these things and they weren't there? What if your accountant showed up in a lab coat or your doctor was dressed in a T-shirt and cutoffs? What would your impression be?

Every atmosphere creates a mood and an impression, and so does every person. When people meet our expectations, we respond favorably. When they do not, we respond negatively. What we see, hear, and smell will generate either a positive or a negative response.

The following is a breakdown of the things we notice when we meet someone in a professional environment. Each category lists both the positive and negative aspects of what we see, hear, and smell. This is a generic list to use as a guide; however, there will always be exceptions.

Sight

Clothing

Positive: Age- and industry-appropriate style, clean, pressed, proper fit, good condition, matching patterns, coordinating colors, clean shoes in good condition.

Negative: Sloppy, dirty, stained, ripped, missing buttons, mismatched patterns, unusual or odd colors, anything outdated, too big, too small, too long, too short, inappropriate style for occasion or position, too youthful, too revealing, scuffed and unpolished shoes.

Hair

Positive: Clean, updated style, good condition, blended roots that match rest of hair, age- and industry-appropriate style.

Negative: Hair in face or covering eyes, obvious looking toupee, unnatural color, faded color, color in need of touch up, messy, outdated style, big or wild, oily, dirty, dandruff.

Face

Positive: Smile, steady eye contact, positive expressions, blended makeup for women, clean-shaven for men, twinkling eyes, clean teeth.

Negative: Frowning, wrinkled brow, darting eyes, looking away, squinting, expressionless, too much or unblended makeup, unshaven, food in teeth, bad teeth, chewing gum.

Posture and gestures

Positive: Head held high, shoulders back, steady stride, strong and smooth gestures, open arms, sitting upright, firm handshake.
Negative: Slouching, looking down, weak handshake, jerky movements, hands in pockets, nervousness, nail biting, hangnail picking, cracking knuckles.

Sound

Positive: Fluent, medium-low pitch, medium-deep tone, medium volume, smooth speech pattern, command of language, articulate.
Negative: Speech fillers, poor grammar, too loud, mumbling, whining or negative tone, high or squeaky pitch, elevated inflection at end of statement, fast-paced talking or very slow speech.

Smell

Positive: No smell.
Negative: Body odor, cigarette smoke, alcohol, coffee breath, food odors, strong breath mint, overpowering perfume.

If our perception of what we see, hear, and smell is positive, we will draw positive conclusions. If our perceptions are negative, we will draw negative conclusions. There will be additional information about clothing, gestures, and smell in the following chapters.

As we attempt to make our final decision about someone we have just met, we rapidly ask ourselves a series of questions:

- Should I trust you?
- Do I feel safe with you?
- Are you credible?
- Do you know what you are talking about?
- Are you intelligent?
- Are you interesting?
- Are you successful?
- Do I want to get to know you?
- Are you worthy of my time?

- Are you worthy or my attention?

- Should I pay attention to you or ignore you?

Based on our answers, we then either engage or disengage. It is not a perfect system. Sometimes we make inaccurate assumptions, and the more we get to know someone, the more we begin to see that person differently. The first 10

True or False?

1. You never have a second chance to make a first impression.

TRUE.

*First impressions are **lasting** impressions. Though it is possible to overcome a negative first impression sooner or later, it takes twice as much effort and as many as seven encounters with someone to change a bad first impression.*

2. We draw long-lasting conclusions about people within the first few seconds of meeting them.

TRUE.

It only takes a few seconds to make judgments about the people we meet. Although we draw conclusions quickly, our impressions last much longer. Of course, you want to be valued for who you are, and over time it will happen, but you might never get the chance if you fail to connect up front. Even when you do, the first impression will never be forgotten. Get it right the first time!

3. You cannot control the kind of impression you make.

FALSE.

*You **can** control the kind of impression you make, but it won't happen without planning and effort. As you prepare to get ready each day, think about the people you expect to meet and the kind of impression you'd like to make. Once you determine the type of impression want to make, you can do what's necessary to achieve your objectives.*

4. First impressions are not always accurate.

TRUE.

Initial impressions are formed quickly and without enough time to obtain all the information we need to make an accurate assessment. Our first impression of seconds speed up the process, but it is up to you to make the final decision. However, if you cannot find a reason to take the time to get to know someone, you probably won't.

It is much easier to see what others are doing wrong than it is to see it in ourselves. Watching yourself on video is a good example. When you see yourself on video, do you like what you see? I've yet to meet someone who says yes. Most people shun the TV when they are on it. Most people take issue with the way they look and sound. It may not reflect the way you see yourself, but it does reflect the way others see you.

someone is our reality. Even when we have proof that the impression was inaccurate, it takes time to let go of our initial assumptions. By the time we realize we were wrong, it may be too late to do anything about it.

5. Initial impressions are instinctive.
TRUE.
The initial impression or "gut feeling" we have about someone is instinctive. Our feelings are a result of the information we gather from our senses: what we see, what we hear, and what we smell. In an initial meeting, we don't have enough time to process the information we take in, so we rely on our feelings instead of logic.

6. In a job interview, the decision to hire someone is often made within the first few moments of the interview.
TRUE.
An interviewer looks for ways to determine the best person for the job, often relying on the initial impression. The better the impression you make at the start of an interview, the better your chances of getting an offer. Don't give someone a reason to disqualify you—your first impression is key.

7. A person's physical appearance is the strongest factor in a first impression.
TRUE.
Our sight is the strongest of our senses, and it provides us with enough information to determine how we feel about a person we've just met. What we see influences us and is a combination of a person's clothing, grooming, posture, carriage, mannerisms, and attitude.

You know what your intentions are, but the people you meet do not. They have but one thing to go on: the initial impression. You can take advantage of this knowledge. Use the information in this book as you continue to craft your image.

POINTS TO REMEMBER

1. **First impressions are lasting impressions.** You never have a second chance to make a first impression. Make the most of the only chance you get.

2. **Get it right the first time.** When you fail to make a positive impression, you create more work for yourself. While the first impression can be altered, it is seldom forgotten. Make it easier by getting it right the first time.

3. **Implement a process.** As you get ready each day, make sure you know who you plan to meet, what your objectives for the day are, and what you need to do to accomplish your objectives.

4. **Notice what you notice.** Know where you place your focus, but don't assume everyone else is focusing on the same things you are.

5. **Follow the recipe for making a good impression.** There are 11 "Ingredients of Impressions," both verbal and nonverbal, that affect the first impression you make.

6. **Pay attention to your senses.** We make impressions based on what we see, what we hear, and what we smell. Be aware of the way you look, the way you sound, and how you smell. The safest smell is no smell at all.

Chapter 4

The Impact of Image

True or False?

1. Your image determines how people respond to you.

2. The more money you have, the better your chances of having a good image.

3. People who are physically attractive have an advantage over those who are not.

4. Your image is a reflection of how you feel about yourself and your organization.

5. A positive image gives you a competitive advantage.

6. People with good images are more productive.

EXTREME MAKEOVERS

My family and I had just finished dinner. The television was on in the adjoining room, and although I wasn't watching closely, when I realized the program on was the one I'd heard so much about, I decided to pay attention. With a dishtowel in my hand, I moved closer to the television to get a glimpse of program that was on. I'd heard *Extreme Makeover* was generating hundreds of letters from viewers, all pleading for an extreme image change.

Unlike most television programs, which typically feature above average-looking people, this one was different. On this program, good looks were a *disadvantage*. The less attractive you were, the better your chances of getting on the show. If you were out of shape or could benefit from cosmetic surgery, you were a likely candidate.

After years of seeing and comparing ourselves to the better-than-average-looking people on every channel we surfed, we finally got a chance to see people worse off than ourselves. *Extreme Makeover* is atypical; the featured "stars" are people who typically *avoid* the spotlight.

Two women were featured on the show that night, and both had numerous image challenges. Each one spoke of the negative impact her image had on her life. Both were more than willing to go through months of surgery, recovery, and misery in order to have a better image.

I was captivated. With my towel still in hand, I moved even closer to the TV. With dishes still piled in the sink, I plopped myself on the couch, got comfortable, and decided to watch the entire show.

One of the women made her transformed debut on her wedding day. This woman, who had laser eye surgery, a nose job, a face-lift, chin reconstruction, dental work, liposuction and more, turned heads as she walked down the aisle. It wasn't simply because she was a pretty bride; it was because she had been transformed into someone no one recognized. The cameras captured the shocked expressions of the man she was marrying, her friends and family.

The other woman featured on the show that night spoke of the way she used to control her laughter and conceal her smile. In an attempt to hide her crooked teeth, she never reacted too exuberantly—always controlled and close-mouthed. Her son, who said he hadn't seen her smile in years, marveled at her new set of teeth and her magnificent smile, which she proudly displayed. Her negative self-image affected her entire personality.

It's difficult to determine the long-term results of these extreme makeovers, but the short-term results are astonishing. As I watched the *outer image* of these women change, I saw their *inner image* change as well. At the start of the show, these women appeared inhibited, introverted, and self-conscious. By the end of the show, they looked vibrant, daring, and confident. These really were *extreme* makeovers.

I could see why the show was a hit. After all, everyone can find *something* they'd like to change about their image, but most of us don't want or need such extreme makeovers. As critical as we tend to be with our images, I find it interesting that I encounter as many people as I do who *resist* making any changes to their image.

Image can be a touchy subject. There are people willing to change their image in front of millions of people on television and people who won't even acknowledge their image, let alone how it impacts their lives. It's an interesting phenomenon.

Of the many issues I address in my seminars and consulting, *personal image* is the most volatile. The issues surrounding image generate the strongest reaction and the most opposition. Image is a sensitive subject. Image is an intimate and personal matter.

No one wants to be informed that their *image* is holding them back. It's easier to be told to take a class or work longer hours than it is to be told to change your image. Often small and subtle changes can make a difference to someone's image, and I've worked with people who were able to tweak their image easily and painlessly. I've never had to recommend an extreme makeover to anyone.

IT'S NOT FAIR!

I've witnessed firsthand the negative reaction people have toward the topic of image. I've been engaged in conversations with people who seemed interested in self-improvement but uninterested in image improvement. People are willing to accept new facts and data but won't accept information about image. They'll be open to new ideas for enhancing communication but closed to suggestions about personal presentation. I've seen rational people become irrational when talking about the subject of image.

Image is *personal.* People are willing to go to great lengths to protect their image, because it's so personal and such a sensitive subject. I've heard many reasons (see the list below) people object to focusing on one's image, and I typically agree—the issue of image is not fair. Perhaps you'll agree with some of the following statements I commonly hear:

- It's not right to judge people on their images.
  I agree: It isn't right.

- Too much emphasis is placed on image.
  I agree: Too much emphasis is placed on image.

- Pressure to conform to a specific or cloned image is unwarranted.
  I agree: It's unwarranted.

- People should be valued for who they *are,* not how they *appear.* It's not fair.
  I agree: It's not fair.

- People can have a good image but be shallow. Image is superficial.
  I agree: Image is superficial.

- People should be accepted regardless of their image. It's discriminating.
  I agree: It's discriminating.

I agree with the objections I hear. It *isn't* fair that image is as influential as it is. There's enough pressure in life without the added stress of worrying about image.

Image. You love it, you hate it, or you misunderstand it. You can challenge it, but you'll have to face up to it; image and success go hand in hand. It may not be fair, but it is a reality—image is important. Your image matters more than you realize. The impact of image is well known and well documented. We all make judgments based on image, and we've been doing it for thousands of years.

There is a positive side to image. Image can be an asset; it distinguishes one person from another. It's not as bad as it seems. You are not born with a particular image or stuck with an image you do not like. Your image is not based on inherited features or good looks. *You can create the image you want;* your image is totally within your control.

A MATTER OF PERCEPTION

Image doesn't have to be confusing. You have more control over your image than you think you do. You can manage your image the same way you manage everything else you do. *Your image is your choice.*

When I speak of image, I am not speaking about natural beauty, age, nationality, or size. These are aspects of image over which we have little control. Anyone can create a positive image, but it's what you do with what you have that matters. I've met people with extremely positive images who do not fit the "norm" of attractiveness. I've also met people who have beautiful images (on the outside) who lack substance on the inside, which changes my image, or perception, of them.

Image extends beyond people and appearances. Many of the decisions you make each day are influenced by image. The clothes you wear, the car you drive, and the products you buy have images too. So do the restaurants you frequent, the stores you shop in and the neighborhood you live in.

Companies and manufacturers spend a tremendous amount of time and money creating images, which can make or break a business or a product. The next time you make a purchase, think about the reasons you selected the particular product you did. Chances are it had something to do with the *image* of that product. You may not be aware of it or even like it, but there's a very good chance you *are* image conscious.

Have you ever thought about the foods you eat and the beverages you drink? Which products do you buy, and why do you select the products you do? What influences you to buy the products you do?

We all need water and have many choices when deciding what type of water we will drink. Do you drink tap water, fluoridated water, bottled water, sparkling water, spring water, artesian water, purified water, or flavored water? Do you buy your water or get it for free? I'm sure you have your own opinions about the water you drink.

Drinking water has become big business, and bottles of water line the shelves or grocery stores and fill the space in vending machines. If you've never considered buying water, you may wonder why anyone would be willing to pay for something they can get for free. After all, you reason, it doesn't cost a dime to turn on the faucet. Yet some people refuse to drink tap water because they believe it is toxic; they have a negative *image* of the water that comes from the faucet. They'd rather pay for what they *perceive* to be clean drinking water.

Who's to say who is right and who is wrong? It's a matter of *perception*. You may not think about your perceptions, but you have them. Your perceptions influence every decision you make. The following exercise will help you become more aware of your perceptions.

There are six groups listed below, and each group has eight items listed. Each group represents a different category. Work with one group at a time. First, read each item in the group. Next, rate your perception of each item on a scale of one to eight. Number one will go to the item that has the best image and perception, and number eight will go to the item with the worst image and perception. Rate each item in the group, but don't overanalyze your responses. Your initial reaction is your most honest one.

There is no right or wrong answer; it's all based on *your* perception.

Age/Gender:

25–35 year-old male

25–35 year-old female

35–45 year-old male

35–45 year-old female

45–55 year-old male

45–55 year-old female

55–65 year-old male

55–65 year-old female

Automobiles:

Cadillac	Lexus
Chevrolet	Mercedes
Ford	Rolls Royce
Honda	Volkswagen

Cities:

Chicago	Paris
Detroit	Baghdad
Hong Kong	New York
Las Vegas	Orlando

People:

Britney Spears	Michael Jackson
Hillary Clinton	Oprah Winfrey
Jerry Springer	Tiger Woods
Martha Stewart	Tom Cruise

Profession:

Accountant	Government employee
Attorney	Politician
Car salesperson	Psychic
Engineer	Small business owner

Size:

Overweight male	Tall male
Overweight female	Tall female
Short male	Underweight male
Short female	Underweight female

How long did it take you to make your decisions? You took time to think about your perceptions as you did the exercise, which made you more aware of them. Now take some time to think about other perceptions you have. What judgments do you make every day based on image and perception?

When you meet someone, what determines whether you will have a positive or negative perception? Is it based on circumstance, appearance, personal belongings, or something else? If you discover that someone drives the kind of car you view most positively, will it change your perception?

What if you were a hiring manager who had a negative perception of people who were taller than you? What impact would it have on the qualified but tall candidate who interviewed with you for a job?

Be aware of your preconceived perceptions, and pay attention to your reaction to the images of others. As you increase your awareness, make sure you understand the norms and standards in your industry or work environment. What perceptions about successful and unsuccessful people exist? Do you meet or exceed these expectations? If not, what price are you paying as a result?

You cannot change the perceptions of others. You can, however, increase your chances of others perceiving your image positively. No one is born with a perfect image. A positive image is the result of careful planning, preparation, and an honest assessment of your personal image.

WHAT'S *YOUR* IMAGE?

Have you thought about *your* image? What do you see when you look in the mirror? Do you like what you see? Do you think your image is helping or hurting you in reaching your objectives?

The perception you have of yourself influences the perception others have of you. Ultimately, your image, or the way in which you present yourself, influences the way other people respond to you and the way people treat you.

When we fail to get the responses we want, we tend to look outside of ourselves for the reason. If you aren't getting the response you want from other people, it may have more to do with *you,* and the image you project, than someone else.

Paula was an attractive 32-year-old pharmaceutical sales representative. She was recently divorced and working to support herself and her young son. She was feeling good about herself and was ready to date again.

Paula was a bright and bubbly woman who attracted men easily. She was flattered by the attention she got, but she wasn't sure how to respond to the suggestive and sometimes sexual comments she received.

Paula assumed all women dealt with this type of harassment and never considered she was part of the "problem." She didn't realize that her tight and revealing clothes were attracting the type of attention she sought to avoid. Her image reflected her wish to meet new men but did nothing to reinforce her desire to be seen as a serious and successful pharmaceutical sales representative.

Your image, and the way you present yourself, can be an asset or a detriment. The response you receive from others is a reflection of your image and expectations. More often than not, people will treat you the way you expect to be treated.

Paula *expected* men to comment on her appearance; although she found it irritating, she assumed it was out of her control. When she began to dress less provocatively, the number of comments and looks she received declined significantly. Changing her image changed the way people responded to her.

At the beginning of this chapter, you evaluated and rated the image you have of various people, places, and things. Now it's your turn to evaluate yourself. The following questions will help you gain a better understanding of the image you project to others. Read each question and respond.

1. Are you dissatisfied with your image?   Yes/No

2. Do you often apologize for your appearance?   Yes/No

3. Do you often apologize for your actions?   Yes/No

4. When you pass a mirror, do you avoid looking, because you don't like what you see?   Yes/No

5. Do you feel people underestimate your ability?   Yes/No

6. Do you wish people responded differently to you?   Yes/No

7. Are you dissatisfied with your current weight?   Yes/No

8. Are you shy?   Yes/No

9. Do you feel awkward in new situations?   Yes/No

10. Do you become uptight under pressure?   Yes/No

11. Do you feel rushed and stressed much of the time?   Yes/No

12. Do people frequently misunderstand your intentions?   Yes/No

13. Do you ever regret something you've said?   Yes/No

14. Do you ever rethink ways in which you could have handled a situation more effectively?   Yes/No

15. Do you try to please others?   Yes/No

As you review your responses, pay attention to your positive, or "yes," responses. These responses indicate that you might not be comfortable with yourself. Any behavior can occur occasionally, with little reason for concern. We all have good days and bad days; however, it is the frequent recurrence of problem behavior that you'll want to watch out for. Read through the questions again, and then read the explanations that follow.

1. Are you dissatisfied with your image?

If you said yes, what aspect of your image are you dissatisfied with? Are you willing to change your image? You can change your image, and small changes can make a big difference. Identify the specific areas of your image that you are dissatisfied with. Then determine what changes you need to or are willing to make to feel better about your image.

2. Do you often apologize for your appearance?

Why do you apologize and to whom? Do you apologize because you didn't take the time you needed to feel you look as good as you should? Do you opt for sweats or other laid-back styles, rather than wear clothes that are more flattering and businesslike? If you frequently comment on your appearance, chances are you are not happy with it, and you risk appearing unsure of yourself. The next time you feel you need to apologize for your appearance, stop and think about what it would take for you to feel better about yourself. Apologizing does nothing to help you or your image.

3. Do you often apologize for your actions?

If you frequently apologize for your actions, what are you apologizing for? Is it because you've reacted in haste and regret something you did? If you tend to act without thinking, slow down. You'll save yourself a lot of time if you get things right the first time.

4. When you pass a mirror, do you avoid looking, because you don't like what you see?

If you don't look at yourself in the mirror, what is it that you don't want to see? What do you need to do to feel more comfortable with your image? You can avoid looking in a mirror, but you can't avoid the negative feelings you have about your image. Determine what you need to do to feel more comfortable with your image and make the necessary changes. Spend time in front of the mirror and make whatever changes you need to feel better about what you see. The more comfortable you are with yourself, the more comfortable you will be with others.

5. Do you feel people underestimate your ability?

If people underestimate your ability, there is a reason why. Do you underestimate your ability too? If you want others to view you as competent and capable, you need to project competence and capability. Watch your words because if you question yourself or negate your ability, people will pick up on it and question you too.

6. Do you wish people responded differently to you?

When you fail to get the response you want, it may have more to do with you than the other person. Take a good look at the responses you are getting. Is there a common theme or reaction? Then take a good look at your image. Is there anything about your image that invites the responses you are getting? Pay close attention to the messages you are receiving. Make small changes in your attempt to determine what makes a difference. And if you are ready to hear the truth, ask for feedback.

7. Are you dissatisfied with your current weight?

If you are dissatisfied with your weight, are you dissatisfied with your image too? If you are, what are you willing to do about it? Have you held off buying new clothes until you get to a weight you're happier with? If so, you're taking a chance with your image. People see you every day. No matter what you weigh, take pride in your appearance. You can and should look your best, no matter what you weigh.

8. Are you shy?

Pay attention to the successful people you meet. The more successful the person, the less likely you will see someone who is shy. Shyness can be overcome. Many people who appear confident and extroverted haven't always been that way. You'll need to build your confidence over time, but meanwhile, do what you can to avoid labeling yourself as someone who is shy; it won't do a thing to help boost your image or your career.

9. Do you feel awkward in new situations?

If you feel awkward, others feel it too. If you are uncomfortable, you make those around you uncomfortable. Try looking at new situations differently; rather than viewing new experiences as threatening, view them as exciting opportunities. Do you want the image of someone who's stuck in a rut or someone who embraces challenge and change?

10. Do you become uptight under pressure?
Your ability to handle pressure is paramount to achieving a successful image. There are few jobs that are stress-free. If you crumble under pressure, people may wrongly assume you can't handle much of anything. Learn to manage the pressure you feel.

11. Do you feel rushed and stressed much of the time?
Is it because you're too busy or too disorganized? The more rushed you are, the more out of control you appear. It doesn't look good to be rushed, and people will make incorrect assumptions about you if you are stressed all the time. They will assume you are out of control, which is definitely not good for your image. Take time to get organized and slow down.

12. Do people frequently misunderstand your intentions?
If you mean well and try hard but people don't know that about you, it's up to you to set the record straight. It's up to you to make your intentions known and to communicate directly and clearly. Minor misunderstandings can create big problems. Communication is key; don't be afraid to ask questions or to volunteer information.

13. Do you ever regret something you've said?
It's good to be on a path of constant self-improvement, but if you find you are second-guessing yourself or spending too much time reviewing past conversations, it's time to move on. Learn from your mistakes, but don't dwell on them.

14. Do you ever rethink ways in which you could have handled a situation more effectively?
What's done is done. It doesn't do you any good to spend time thinking about the things you could have, would have, or should have done. If you spend too much time reliving the past, you will never enjoy the present or move into the future.

15. Do you try to please others?
No matter how hard you try, you'll never please everyone. The person you should be most concerned about pleasing is yourself. If you're overly consumed with pleasing others, you will eventually disappoint yourself.

Make it your goal to turn some of your yesses into noes. Defining your image will help you **refine** your image. You will be better able to manage the message you send to others when you learn how to manage yourself. You are the one who manages your thoughts and actions and, ultimately, the image you project.

WEIGHT: A SIZEABLE ISSUE?

Few people look like the models gracing the covers of magazines or the mannequins wearing the latest fashions. Although many view these images as the ideal size to strive for, it is not possible for most people. According to the Centers for Disease Control, 64 percent of American adults are overweight and 23 percent of adults are considered obese. The number of overweight and obese Americans is increasing at an epidemic rate and unfortunately, so is discrimination against them.

If you have ever felt your size has worked for or against you, it probably has. A public opinion survey conducted by the Employment Law Alliance found nearly one-half (47 percent) of American workers surveyed believes that plus-size workers are being discriminated against in the workplace by their co-workers and supervisors.

When Ann Johnston, vice president of ProGroup, Inc., a workplace diversity consultancy delivered the seminar, "Size: A Diversity Undiscussable" for the first time, she never expected the standing-room-only crowd it attracted. The seminar was the first of its kind to delve into America's increasing obsession with appearance and the country's growing overweight problem. The seminar was a huge success and led to greater awareness for both the attendees and for Ann. Ann, who wears a size 18 or 20 and refers to herself as a "big gal," was shocked by the e-mail she received from an angry participant who chastised her for not being large enough to fully understand the issue or present on the topic.

Typically, the kinds of comments a larger individual is likely to hear are not so blatant. Public remarks tend to be much subtler, making it difficult to prove size discrimination exists.

Large-sized women are often viewed more negatively than their husky male counterparts, but anyone is subject to discrimination because of his or her size. The overweight are frequently and inaccurately accused of being lazy, lacking motivation, and discipline. According to the National Association to Advance Fat Acceptance, those who are overweight earn salaries 10 percent to

20 percent lower than their thinner colleagues and are less likely to receive promotions than slim people, regardless of their job performance.

While some of these statistics are distressing, if you are overweight you are not doomed to failure. The key is to strive to be your best and present yourself professionally no matter what size you are. There is no perfect size. Some people say they are discriminated against because they are too small; others feel being average can be a disadvantage. What you perceive to be a disadvantage can work for you rather than against you. You can either reinforce or destroy the myths people have through what you do. Start by being more aware of your own prejudices and assumptions.

Give yourself every advantage to succeed and don't be too hard on yourself because of your size. I've talked with people who tell me they won't buy nice clothes because of their size or want to wait until they fit into a smaller size to invest in a new wardrobe. Few people find shopping or creating a wardrobe easy. Keep in mind that everyone has personal image challenges to deal with.

There is no reason for you to postpone looking or feeling your best. It is essential to *being* your best. The tips in this chapter are for *you*. No matter what size you are, you can have a positive image and present yourself professionally.

IMAGE DEFINED

World Book Dictionary states image as: *The impression that a person, group, or organization presents to the public.*

Everything and everyone has an image. *You* have an image and impression that comes to mind when people think of you. Many people believe the image they project simply *is* and exists independently of who they really are. They assume their image is out of their direct control. This book will prove that *nothing could be further from the truth*. You can create the image you want just as you can create the impression you want.

Your image is your reputation; your image is who you *are* to other people.

Whether consciously or unconsciously, each of us sends a message about who we are every time we interact with another human being. When you are cognizant of the messages you send, every interaction you have will be more effective. As you learn how to consciously manage the message you send to others, you will notice a difference in your relationships and the results you are able to achieve.

What image do you want to project? What image do you need to project for your career? Define your image before your image defines you.

COMPONENTS OF IMAGE

Your professional IMAGE is made up of five key components:

Impression

Movement

Attitude

Grooming

Etiquette

The *I* in IMAGE is for *Impression:* In Chapter 3, the importance of first impressions was stressed; you only have a few seconds to make a lasting impression. We make and leave impressions with everyone we come into contact with. Immediately establishing yourself as a credible and valuable resource saves you time and effort. You shouldn't have to work harder than you need to in an attempt to convince people of your value and worth. A strong image reflects your capabilities, which should be apparent to everyone you meet. Make your first impression a positive impression.

The *M* in IMAGE is for *Movement.* The way you move and carry yourself speaks volumes about you. It's a language more honest than your spoken words. It may be easy to lie verbally, but our bodies have a very difficult time with deception. If you want to know the truth about someone, pay attention to his or her body language.

The *A* in IMAGE is for *Attitude.* There are hundreds of things that are out of our control, but the one thing we can control is our response to what happens. You can choose to be happy, sad, positive, or negative. There's an old saying: People won't long remember what you do or what you say, but they'll always remember how you made them feel. If you make people feel good, you'll be welcome most anywhere.

The *G* in IMAGE is for *Grooming.* Your clothing and appearance is one of the first things noticed about you. Being well groomed and wearing appropriate clothing is evidence that you take yourself and your job seriously. Don't give people a reason to underestimate your ability. Look your best and pay attention to your grooming.

The *E* in IMAGE is for *Etiquette.* Knowing how to handle yourself at a business meeting, over dinner, or at a company party is crucial to your success. It isn't only job performance that can make or break a career; understanding the many unspoken rules of etiquette can save you time and embarrassment.

Each image component is critical to your success. It doesn't do you any good to select just one or two to master; each component is supported by the next. It's essential for you to grasp each one of the five components, because they all work together to help you convey a positive and professional image. It's not enough to simply dress well and look great; you need to carry yourself with confidence, too. Throughout this book, you will have a chance to learn more about each component and the necessary steps you'll need to take to achieve *your* desired image.

BEYOND APPEARANCES

Several years ago, I presented a workshop to the sales associates of a temporary-help agency. During the session, I noticed a well-dressed male participant who was listening intently to everything I had to say as he diligently took notes.

After the session ended, he came up to me to tell me he agreed with the principles I was teaching, and that he too believed appearance was critical to success. It was obvious that he did. He wore an expensive-looking charcoal-gray designer suit with a crisp starched shirt and a beautiful silk tie. He looked as though he'd walked off the pages of a fashion magazine.

The problem he was having, he said, was that since he had become a sales manager, he was getting negative feedback from customers who found him aloof and uncaring. He was very concerned, because he did care about his clients and felt his business was suffering as a result of this false perception.

I looked at this handsome, serious man and responded with the first thought that came into my mind. "Do you ever smile?" I asked. He looked me straight in the eyes, and with no expression at all, he replied, "I take my work very seriously, and I'm not the type to waste time or get too personal with my clients. I don't chitchat or goof around—I prefer to get right down to business."

"You didn't answer my question," I said politely. I smiled a big, toothy smile as I repeated the question again, "Do you ever smile?" He was dumbfounded, and so was I. I wondered how someone could place so much emphasis on clothing while neglecting something as basic as a smile and a friendly appearance.

After talking with him for just a few minutes, I concluded that the reason his clients found him uncaring and aloof was probably because of his own discomfort. Sure, he looked good, but his good looks simply weren't enough. In fact, he may have taken his grooming a bit too far—he looked *too* good. I suggested he take off his jacket, loosen his tie and roll up his sleeves. He needed to smile, engage in social conversation, and learn to relate better with his clients. These were not skills that came easily to him, but he realized he needed to refine his overall image.

Perfection can harm an image too. A good image is not necessarily a *perfect* image; perfection can be threatening. The best image is one other people respond favorably to. Create an image others will relate to.

Chances are that you too have certain areas of your image you tend to focus on. We are drawn to the things that interest us and stay away from areas that do not. The problem is that when you focus heavily on one area, you tend to neglect the others. Don't limit yourself to the areas that come easily to you. An effective image is a well-rounded image. You don't have to wait for a problem to arise to enhance your image. Do it now, *before* you encounter problems.

BENEFITS OF A POSITIVE IMAGE

A positive image has many advantages. If you are serious about your career and want unlimited opportunity, you need to pay attention to and carefully plan your image. Here are some facts about the benefits of a positive image:

- The image you project is directly attributed to your product or service.

- Productivity can be increased 20 percent or more by presenting an effective professional image.

- Your visual appearance and your professional manner are among your most powerful and accessible business skills.

- A positive self-image leads to a positive attitude.

- Visual appearance, in particular, plays a leading role in presenting a positive image.

- Your effectiveness and confidence increase when you are consistently well dressed.

- A positive image is necessary at all times but especially critical during periods of anxiety.

- A positive image is a competitive advantage.

- A positive image leads to an increase in advancement opportunities.

- A positive image correlates with higher earnings.

- Your image is within your control; you can change and improve your image any time you want.

- Your image is your reputation; an ideal image will lead to an ideal reputation.

PERILS OF A NEGATIVE IMAGE

Despite the proof that a positive image is an asset, there still are people who resist. I've had people tell me they refuse to play the "image game." You have an image whether you acknowledge it or not. You can't escape image. If you rebel, you'll have a rebellious image. Think about this:

- If your image is perceived negatively, your products and services are likely to be viewed negatively as well.

- Appearance matters; if you don't care about your appearance, people may assume you don't care about your work, either.

- A poor self-image leads to a poor attitude.

- Appearance is the first thing others notice about a person. An inappropriate or sloppy appearance can create a negative first impression.

- The less effective your image, the less effective you will be.

- An ineffective image can lead to lost business and opportunities; when competing for a job or opportunity, image is often the determining factor.

- Your image is within your control; if your image is outdated, you will appear outdated.

- People with negative images have to work harder to prove their value.

- An odd or unusual image creates barriers; people are more likely to trust someone who fits an anticipated image.

- A positive and predictable image inspires positive and predictable performance. A carefree and unpredictable image inspires carefree and unpredictable performance.

- Money is no guarantee; you can't buy a positive image. Your image must be earned; it is the result of careful planning, consideration, and effort.

- Your image is your reputation; settle for a less-than-perfect image and you will have a less-than-perfect reputation.

POINTS TO REMEMBER

1. **You *can* control the image you project.** Learn to manage your message through IMAGE—Impression, Movement, Attitude, Grooming, and Etiquette.

2. **Your image is who you are to other people.** Your image reflects the way you feel about yourself, your job, and others. When people think of you, it is your image that comes to mind; your image is your reputation.

3. **Take the time to create your image.** A positive image is the result of careful consideration and planning. Take time to plan the image you want.

4. **You can create the image you want.** Your image is within your control; only *you* can decide and determine the type of image you want. Your image is your choice.

5. **Image goes beyond appearance.** The image you project is a result of your clothing, behavior, and actions. Your image is directly attributed to your product or service, as well as your chances of landing a job, keeping a job, or moving ahead in a job.

6. **Image expectations will vary.** Every company in every industry has image expectations. Know what is expected in your company and industry. Straying too far from the norm can make people question your ability.

True or False?

1. Your image determines how people respond to you.

TRUE.

People gather information about you from your image and treat you accordingly. If you aren't getting the response you want from others, take a good look at your image. Small changes in your image can lead to big results.

2. The more money you have, the better your chances of having a good image.
FALSE.

You can have a positive image with or without a lot of money. The image you project is a sum of more than money can buy. It is important to look good and be well groomed but is not the only factor in your overall image. You can wear expensive clothes and look classy, but it won't help at all if your talk is cheap and brassy.

3. People who are physically attractive have an advantage over those who are not.
FALSE.

Remember that image is the impression that a person, group, or organization presents to the public. When it comes to the impression you make, you need more than attractiveness to make a good one. It's what you do with what you have that's most important.

4. Your image is a reflection of how you feel about yourself and your organization.
TRUE.

Your image makes a statement about how you feel about yourself, your job, and the organization you represent. When you take pride in your image and choose it consciously, it is apparent. Every industry and every organization has an image. Make sure your image fits the industry you are in and reflects the image of the company you work for.

5. A positive image gives you a competitive advantage.
TRUE.

All things being equal, image often is the determining factor. It's why you shop where you shop, dine where you dine, and buy the products you buy. Image is important; the more positive your image, the greater the advantage you will have.

6. People with good images are more productive.
TRUE.

Your image affects the way you feel about yourself and your job. When you feel good about yourself, you feel better about everything you do. Studies show that people with positive images are more effective and productive.

Chapter 5

Do You Hear What You Are *Not* Saying?

True or False?

1. How you come across is more important than what you say.

2. Controlled, smooth movements communicate confidence.

3. You should avoid looking people in the eyes.

4. It is difficult to hide our true feelings and reactions.

5. Less than 10 percent of communication is through the spoken word.

6. Nervous gestures are distracting to your message.

ACTIONS SPEAK LOUDER THAN WORDS

The seminar

The workshop I was teaching began promptly at 8:00 A.M. A man and a woman entered the room at 9:15 A.M., over an hour late. They moved about the crowded room, huffing and puffing as they attempted to find two seats together. They grunted and groaned when they were unsuccessful, and each found a seat at opposite ends of the room. Moments later, I heard the clanking of cups, and looked up to see the woman pouring coffee in the back of the room. I watched her set it on the table in front of her seat, go back to get more, and walk across the room to bring a cup of coffee to the man. Moments later, the man, who was seated in the front of the room, got up. He bumped against the people seated in his row, and walked to the back of the room to get sweetener for his coffee. Neither the man nor the woman uttered a word, but it was obvious to me that everyone in the room could hear them loud and clear.

66

The presenter

I arrived in Denver in just enough time to get to my hotel, grab a bite to eat, and attend the afternoon session of the conference. When I decided which session to attend, I walked into the room and sat down. The presenter sat at the front of the room and was working on her computer. I watched her scratch her head, rub the back of her neck, and tap her foot on the floor. She looked at her watch, rolled her eyes, and shook her head. Without a glance or a smile, she raised her hand high to signal she needed five more minutes. She hadn't spoken a word, but before the session even began, I felt I knew a lot about her.

The dinner

My husband and I were celebrating our anniversary at our favorite restaurant. We were enjoying good food and conversation, until the couple at the table beside us became a distraction. The woman abruptly stood up, threw her napkin on the table, and turned to walk away. The man, who had a sad look on his face, gently grabbed her arm, pulled her closer to the table, and motioned to her to sit down. She sat back down, cupped her face in her hands, and dropped her head. The man reached across the table and placed his hand under her chin. He gently lifted her chin until they were looking into each other's eyes. He shrugged his shoulders, tilted his head to the side, dropped his chin, and wiped a tear from his eye. I couldn't hear a word they said, but was sure I knew what he was saying.

In each situation, I heard what other people were saying without ever hearing anything at all. I had no direct contact or communication with any of the people in my stories. As you read each scenario, perhaps you too could hear what was being said. Actions speak much louder than words.

We hear what people are saying *without words* all the time. Sometimes we pay attention, and at times we don't even notice. All you have to do is sit in an airport, or the lobby of a busy building, and watch people. You can hear what they have to say as they walk by, greet friends, or talk on the phone. People can hear you too; you may not be aware of it, but at any given moment you could be communicating something to someone unknowingly.

VERBAL VERSUS NONVERBAL COMMUNICATION

It takes more skill than most people realize to comprehend everything we hear, see, and do. Communication is complex; most conversations require an immediate response, giving us little time to think through what we want to say or *how* we want to say it.

How much of your message do you think you convey through your body language, tone of voice, and words? Some of us believe the content of conversation is most important, but when we communicate, we rely on what we hear through vocal tone, rate, and pitch, and what we see in terms of expression, gestures, and posture much more than the actual words we use.

Our messages are conveyed visually, vocally and verbally:

Visually (what we see): Eyes, expression, posture, gestures, and overall appearance

Vocally (what we hear): Tone, pitch, volume, and rate of speech

Verbally (what we say): Words spoken

Extensive research conducted by Dr. Albert Mehrabian of UCLA determined the breakdown in communication as such:

55 percent of your message comes from your body language.

38 percent of your message comes from your tone of voice.

7 percent of your message comes from the words you speak.

The results of his findings take some people by surprise. If only 7 percent of our overall communication is a result of what we say, that means 93 percent of our communication is a result of everything we *don't* say. Our primary form of communication is *nonverbal communication*—communication *without words.*

Although our nonverbal communication is silent, don't be fooled—the messages you send nonverbally come through loud and clear.

Your tone of voice, inflection, pitch, and rate, combined with your movements, expressions, posture, and actions add *context* to the *content* of your conversation.

As we struggle for ways to communicate more effectively, it's easier and less time-consuming when we think about the *words* we use than it is to think about the many additional aspects of our communication. When you start focusing on your nonverbal communication, you may become overwhelmed—it's a lot to think about! Thinking about your nonverbal messages gives you a chance to become aware of many things you do automatically.

SIMON SAYS

Have you ever sensed someone's anger or frustration? Think of a time you were with a family member, coworker, or friend when you had a feeling something was wrong. What did you do? That feeling that something isn't right can be strong and difficult to dismiss. Sometimes we try to find out if our hunches are right, but even when we do, we may not get the answers we are looking for.

Imagine you are with a friend when you sense something is wrong. You decide to check in with your friend, so you say, *"You seem upset—is everything all right?"* Your friend tells you she's fine, but the way she says it leaves you feeling unsure. You want to believe her words, but you don't, because her tone was sharp and her manner abrupt. Her message was confusing and contradictory.

If you've ever been misunderstood (and chances are, you have), what happened? Most *misunderstandings* are a result of *miscommunication*. You have a message, which you try to convey, but you are misunderstood because something got in the way. Simply put, a misunderstanding takes place when you *say* one thing but *do* another.

Have you ever played the game Simon Says? Simon Says can be played with two or more people. One person plays Simon and leads the game while everyone else follows Simon's commands and actions. For example, Simon will stand before the players, and as he places his hands on his head will say, "Simon says, put your hands on your head" and everyone proceeds to put their hands on their heads, just like Simon. He'll continue to give a variety of commands; he might tell you to turn around, touch the ground, tap your toes, or scratch your nose. He'll start out giving commands slowly but eventually will speed up in an effort to confuse you and, ultimately, force you out of the game.

In order to win when playing Simon Says, you must pay close attention to *everything* Simon tells you to do. If he claps his hands and tells you to clap your hands but doesn't first say, "Simon says clap your hands," you don't do it. If you do, you are *out*.

The secret to the game, which is also the most difficult part to do, is to listen very closely to everything Simon says and follow his *verbal* commands rather than his nonverbal commands. In theory, the game is fairly simple, however, in practice, it is not. When we receive a mixed message, we tend to believe what we *see* over what we *hear.*

Several years ago, I was a guest on a television show the same day a *professional* Simon was a guest too. He was so good at his game that he was paid thousands of dollars to perform at company functions and celebrations. He played a round of Simon Says with the studio audience, which I was able to watch from the stage. Adult men and women enthusiastically leaped to their feet to play the game but were quickly out of the game and told to sit back down within the first few moments. People were so intent on watching and following him that they forgot to listen to him. Even when they *heard* his words, *his actions spoke louder;* they "listened" to his actions.

There are other versions of Simon Says, and they are played at home, at work, and at play. We play it when we send mixed messages by saying one thing and doing another. It is frequently called *ineffective communication.*

If you want to communicate more effectively, make sure the things you *do* coincide with the things you *say;* people may not always listen to everything you have to say, but they will hear you loud and clear because they'll be watching everything you do.

LISTEN TO YOUR BODY TALK

Through our body language and nonverbal messages, we communicate our *true* feelings and reactions to people, places, and things. Our bodies "talk" and transmit messages, whether we are aware of it or not.

Think about what happens when you're standing in the beverage aisle of the grocery store and you can't decide if you want plain or flavored coffee. You probably stand there looking at both products. You might put your hand to your mouth, squint your eyes, or frown, as you concentrate on making a decision. Then you move first toward one product, and then reach for the other. If someone were watching you, what would your actions convey? Most likely, nothing but indecision!

Smooth, well-paced movements immediately convey an attitude that says, "I know what I want and where to go to get it; in fact, I'm on my way there now." Graceful movements without hesitation, combined with upright, confident posture, say it nonverbally so you don't have to say anything verbally.

Make it your goal to have fluid, natural movements that are well paced. You don't want to move too fast or too slow. When you think of someone who has no sense of urgency, whose pace is overly relaxed, what do you decide about that person? You'll probably decide this person is lazy, not feeling well, or not very bright.

Now imagine someone who is always in a hurry—dropping things, apologizing, and never composed. You'd probably think he or she is unprepared, disorganized, or having a bad day—all negatives.

Something as simple as pacing your movements can help you convey either a positive or a negative message. You can develop smooth and controlled body movements by being aware of how you move. Catch yourself when you're moving too fast, too slow, or with hesitancy, and when you do, make a change.

DO YOU SEE WHAT OTHERS SEE?

How do you see yourself? Do you think you view yourself objectively? What's your reaction when you watch yourself on video? Do you like what you see? Most of us do not. We tend to see ourselves differently than others do, and when we receive feedback, we tend to dismiss it if it isn't on par with what we see or expect.

It isn't unusual for someone to come up to me after a seminar I've given and solicit feedback about his or her image. I'm frequently asked, "How am I doing? How do you think I come across to others?" I'm sure I disappoint people when I refuse to deliver the feedback they've requested. I could respond, but my opinion isn't nearly as important as the feedback they receive every day. They may not pick up on it, but it is there.

Feedback is abundant. You and I receive feedback all the time, although we may not pay attention. Your *results* are your feedback. Your feedback comes in the way people *respond* to you.

When you don't get the results or response you want, what do you do? If you look outside yourself for the reason, you may not find it. You've got to look *inside yourself* first.

Think of someone you love to be around, someone who brings energy to you and others. This person is upbeat and vibrant; every time you're with this person, you feel better as a result. Can you think of someone who literally lights up a room by being in it?

Now think of someone you'd prefer to avoid, someone whose presence *drains* you. This person is dreary and dull; every time you're with this person, you feel worse as a result. Can you think of someone who darkens a room by being in it? This person lights up a room when he or she *leaves* it!

There's a good chance you aren't the only one who responds as you do to these different types of people. Chances are, they generate the same response wherever they go. The upbeat person finds others to be upbeat, while the dreary person sees everyone as dreary as he is.

When we are willing to pay attention to the feedback we receive, we can determine how we are doing. I'll bet the upbeat person you thought of receives positive feedback, and the draining, dreary person you thought of hasn't a clue.

The next time you enter a room, pay attention to what *you create*. What kind of response do you get from others when you enter a room? If you're not satisfied with your results, take a good look at yourself.

TURN ON THE TV

Early in my speaking career, I decided to videotape myself as a way of improving my presentations. Although I was getting positive feedback, it was still scary to see myself on tape. I put off watching it for over a week. The night I decided to watch it, I waited until I was sure everyone was asleep. It was after midnight when I put the tape in the VCR. I turned the volume down low to make sure no one else could hear. I took a deep breath, pressed the play button, and watched.

As it turned out, getting up the courage to watch that tape was one of the most important and powerful steps I've taken as a professional speaker. I noticed things I didn't like, of course, but I also saw things I *did* like, although not right away. The first time I watched it, I was horrified. I didn't like the way I looked, what I did with my hands, or the sound of my voice. Then I made myself watch it again and again. After watching the tape several times, I didn't need to hide from myself any longer. As a result, I came up with new ideas about aspects of my presentation, and I identified ways in which I could improve my style.

I still don't like watching myself, but I make sure I videotape my presentations at least two times a year. I always wait until it's after midnight and everyone is asleep, as I prefer to watch it by myself. It is the only way for me to check in with myself and honestly evaluate how I am doing. I recognize the need to see what others see.

I've realized that as hard as it is for me to watch myself on video, I am not alone. Most people avoid watching themselves on video, and when they do, they don't like what they see. I find it most interesting: We see ourselves in the mirror every day, and we hear ourselves talk every day, yet when we see and listen to ourselves on tape, we cringe!

It is important to see yourself as others do, and the only way to do that is to view yourself objectively. Ask someone you trust to videotape you in a variety of situations—working at your desk, talking on the telephone, or standing in front of a group of people making a presentation. Then watch yourself several times.

The first time, you'll likely think what we all think—that you look awful. So get through the first run and watch it again. Then watch it again and again until you can objectively view what you see.

Then take out the tape and turn on the TV. Select a show and watch it *without* sound. Try to determine what's going on. Who do you think the good guy is? Can you tell who the bad guy is? Notice who's sad and who's angry.

Then put *your* tape back in, and this time, watch it without sound. Observe your body language and movements. What are you communicating *without* words? Do you seem hesitant? Confident? Bold? It will be right there for you to see.

Take your new awareness and begin to use it in your life. Think about the way you communicate nonverbally. Become acutely aware of the way your body talks and the way others talk to you.

ACCENTUATE THE POSITIVE

Think of yourself as a gift that needs packaging. You're smart, skilled, competent, creative, and highly motivated. You're willing to do a great job, and you have the talent to do it. That's the gift. But you're the only one who knows these positive things about you; telling others how wonderful you are in so many words just isn't the right approach. You can *think* it, but you probably shouldn't verbalize it!

So what is a good approach? Present yourself in a way that lets others know you're in charge. You want people to perceive you as more than just competent; you want people to know you're able to handle any situation and are in control.

Before you begin to work on using nonverbal communication to improve your image, consider the image you *don't* want to convey. Can you think of someone you've never felt comfortable with, someone you don't trust? Perhaps it's the way that person puts others down or monopolizes the conversation. You may sense there's a hidden agenda replacing openness and honesty.

Now think of someone you admire. What qualities does this person possess? Try to picture the person in your mind.

If you want others to think of you as diplomatic, assertive, and calm when handling problems, everything you do needs to support your intentions. The messages you send through your body language can be viewed either positively or negatively. Look at the list of responses through body language and decide which you convey and which you might need to work on.

Positive Responses

Consistent eye contact

Smiling

Confident, upright posture

Relaxed, controlled body movements

Expressive face

Uncrossed arms and legs

Tilted head

Open hands

Nodding head

Head held high

Negative Responses

Avoiding eye contact

Frowning, squinting

Slouched, hunched posture

Nervous, jerky body movements

Lack of expression

Crossed arms and legs

Rigid posture and movement

Hands clenched

Shaking head

Looking down

Next, read the following statements and rate yourself in each area. Respond by selecting *Always, Sometimes,* or *Never.*

	Always	*Sometimes*	*Never*
People respond favorably to me.	*1*	*2*	*3*
My handshake is firm and brief.	*1*	*2*	*3*
I sit upright with my feet on the floor.	*1*	*2*	*3*
I make eye contact at least 90 percent of the time.	*1*	*2*	*3*
I smile often and with sincerity.	*1*	*2*	*3*
I hold myself in an open and approachable way.	*1*	*2*	*3*
I carry myself with confidence.	*1*	*2*	*3*
I am aware of the expression on my face at all times.	*1*	*2*	*3*
I am aware of the response I generate from other people.	*1*	*2*	*3*

Now that you've analyzed some of your body language, look for areas you consider your strengths—areas that will help you convey your message positively. Then look for areas where you can improve. How many times did you respond with the number 2 (*sometimes*) or 3 (*never*)? What do you need to do to increase your focus in these areas?

What you send out to others is received and sent back again. When you present yourself positively, you will generate a positive response from other people. Continue to increase your awareness of your communication, both verbally and nonverbally, and you will see the difference it can make.

NONVERBAL CUES THAT SAY IT ALL

The image you convey can and should be controlled by you at all times, although it is impossible to control completely. If your face turns red when you're embarrassed or you perspire when you are stressed, there's not a lot you can do when it happens. However, you can reduce the amount of stress you have, and you can build your confidence so you're not so easily embarrassed.

Nonverbal cues are more effective than words. For example, standing up and reaching out your hand to shake the other person's hand is a sure way to end a meeting. Gathering up papers on the conference table in front of you and placing them in your briefcase, standing up, or sliding your coat on are other nonverbal ways of indicating that you are moving on to your next task.

Nervous hand gestures or other repetitive movements can be very distracting to an audience of one person or 200 people. On the other hand, when used effectively and in moderation, gestures can add impact to what you say. The key is to control your gestures and movements and use them to add color and interest to what you have to say. Use gestures to emphasize a point, but don't overuse them.

I'll never forget the time I was on the local news. After being interviewed for a story, the producer thanked me and told me I did a great job. When I watched the broadcast later that night, I saw nothing but my hands. When the camera was on me, my hands took on a life of their own! They were flailing all over the place; it looked as if I were swatting a fly. It was very distracting and the only thing I remember about what I saw. I never realized how exaggerated hand gestures could appear, especially on TV.

We don't always know what to do with our hands, or how our gestures will be perceived, so we fumble around trying to figure out where to place our hands. I've learned to establish a home base for my hands, and you should too. When your hands begin to feel bigger than you, or you don't know what to do with them, bring them back home. Many people find comfort when clasping their hands together. Your home base can be folded or clasped in front of you, on your lap if you are in a chair, or on the table if you are seated at one. You're free to gesture as you speak, but as soon as you are done with your hands, you should bring them home.

Here's some additional advice about hands:

1. **Keep your hands out of your pockets.** It's too tempting to jiggle your change and too distracting to others.

2. **Keep your hands to yourself.** You may be a touchy, feely person, but not everyone is. There is good touch and bad touch in business. Good touch is a good handshake. Bad touch is any touch perceived as an intrusion into personal space; not everyone wants a hug or a pat on the back.

3. **Keep your hands away from your face.** Don't fuss with your glasses, play with your hair, or put your hands to your mouth. These gestures are distracting and prevent others from seeing your facial expressions.

4. **Keep your hands on the table.** Don't hide your hands or put them under the table. People might wonder what you're doing with them, what you're hiding, or if you feel uncomfortable.

5. **Keep your hands in good condition.** Your hands will be seen; keep your nails a reasonable length, and make sure your hands are clean and well manicured. The better your hands look, the better you look.

6. **Keep your hands above your waist.** People will look at your hands and follow them. You are better off drawing attention toward your face than below your waist.

Some gestures will help you convey your message while other gestures will be distracting. When you are feeling impatient, insecure, stressed, or nervous, the tension you feel manifests in many different ways. The more pressure or uncertainty you feel, the more likely you are to display it.

Nervous and distracting gestures include:

Biting fingernails

Wringing hands

Twisting rings

Playing with hair

Rubbing nose or ear

Stroking body

Excessive doodling

Tapping fingers

Swinging legs

Fidgeting

Twiddling thumbs

Scratching head

Acceptable gestures that convey a *positive* message include:

Nodding in agreement

Tilting head

Leaning forward

Hands clasped in front of you

Hands together in a pyramid or steeple formation

Broad, controlled gestures

Chin on your hand or fingers (thought position)

Resting open hands on a table

Holding pen without playing with it

Arms on arms of chair

Gestures that convey a negative reaction include:

Finger pointing

Pulling or turning away

Crossed arms

Hands on hips

Looking over glasses

Pounding fist or hand on table or desk

As you watch for the signals people are sending, pay attention to everything they do; your real clues come through their series of movements. One negative gesture will not provide you with enough information to make an assessment about someone. Look for repetitive gestures and series of movements. You wouldn't isolate one word in a sentence to understand what you are hearing, and you shouldn't isolate one gesture of many in an attempt to understand what you are seeing.

Now that you know what to watch out for, watch yourself too. You will enhance your communication when you use gestures that are perceived positively. Gaining control over your movements will be an advantage even under pressure. Most people don't notice every little gesture you use, but when any gesture is used repeatedly, it will get noticed. Pushing the hair out of your eyes is fine, but if the hair keeps falling back into your eyes and you continually push it away, it will be noticed and become distracting to those around you. You may need to clear your throat every now and then, and nobody will notice, but if you are into the habit of clearing it continually, it will become very distracting.

NOTIFY YOUR FACE

I was at a party mingling about when I noticed a woman standing by herself a few feet away. She didn't look as though she was having much fun, so I walked over and introduced myself to her. I asked her how she was doing and she told me she was great and having a wonderful time. Her enthusiastic response took me by surprise. Although she said she was having fun, the expression on her face told me she wasn't enjoying herself at all.

Your facial expressions convey a great deal about you. Studies indicate that we are viewed from the neck up over 85 percent of the time. Because we can't see ourselves, we are unaware of our expressions. However, others see us and pick up messages from our faces.

I am certain the woman I met at the party had no idea what her face said about her. I wanted to tell her to notify her face that she was having a wonderful time!

If people ever say you look sick or seem upset when you are not, look in the mirror! You may have been deep in thought or thinking of nothing at all, yet you look as though you are feeling ill, bored, sad, or mad. Any expression can have multiple meanings.

One of my favorite workshop exercises to observe is one in which participants show their interpretation of different facial expressions. I have everyone select a partner. First I ask them to make eye contact and just look at each other. It never fails; they all break out into laughter. So we try again and again.

I tell them to listen to the words I speak and to respond to them without using words or their bodies; to just show a reaction with their face. I usually start by telling them to show anger. Some pout, others squint their eyes, and eventually everyone breaks into laughter. In a group of 30 people I will see 30 different interpretations of each emotion I mention, yet each expression effectively conveys that emotion. Everyone perceives and displays emotions differently; it takes a lot of practice to be able to read the expressions of others effectively.

Sometimes we think of a person as cold or aloof when, in fact, they are uneasy or shy. It takes more than a glance to understand someone, but by becoming more observant of others, you increase your ability to read the messages they send.

Listed below are five commonly used expressions that can be interpreted in a variety of ways. Make a note of the words that best reflect what you think these facial expressions convey.

No expression: shy, neutral, bored, disinterested

Smile: deceptive, friendly, happy, outgoing

Tight, set lips: rigid, cautious, uptight, confused

Squinted eyes: thinking, tired, worried, unsure

Raised eyebrows: surprised, flirtatious, angry, interested

Each expression has several possible meanings. The message? Vary your facial expressions! Take a moment to think about the messages you convey to others.

How do you rate your facial expressiveness?

_____ Good. I vary my facial expressions, smile frequently, and control my expressions when necessary to mask true feelings. (For example, you are in a meeting and someone makes a comment you consider to be ridiculous. Your inclination may be to laugh, roll your eyes, or snicker, but instead you remain expressionless. Or perhaps you've just met with a customer who is demanding and irritating. You may feel tense and frustrated, yet you know you need to keep smiling and act in a pleasant manner without showing your irritation.)

_____ Fair. I have an open, confident expression, but I'm frequently not aware of what I'm conveying through my facial expression. (There are times when a neutral expression is important. The key is in recognizing those times. Perhaps you have confidential information someone wants from you, or people are talking about a subject in which you don't wish to get involved. A neutral expression can be an advantage in some situations.)

_____ Needs work. I'm not aware of what my facial expressions convey. (Perhaps people misunderstand you. You can't figure out why you need to defend what you say, or you feel people don't take you seriously. It could be that your facial expression contradicts your words and causes confusion to your listener.)

Which specific areas do you need to improve?

_____ Smile: Not smiling or smiling too much.

_____ Neutral expression: Not showing any expression at all, which can convey a lack of interest or even hostility.

_____ Unvaried expression: Forgetting to show response to people via expression.

_____ Tight, set lips, squinted eyes or raised eyebrows: Can convey anger, distrust, or confusion.

What specific areas will you work on?

_____

_____

_____

Start to become more aware of your expressions by thinking about them. Ask people for clarification when you sense a lack of understanding. If you think it will help to practice, sit or stand in front of a mirror and practice making different facial expressions. Look happy, then sad, then frustrated, but do it where no one can see you or you'll have some explaining to do!

POINTS TO REMEMBER

1. **Ninety-three percent of what we communicate is nonverbal.** Only 7 percent of what you communicate comes from the words you use. Focus less on *what* you say and more on *how* you say it.

2. **Think of yourself as a gift that needs packaging.** No one will know how wonderful you are unless you present yourself in a way that lets others know what you are capable of.

3. **Listen to the silent language of communication.** You may rely on words, but you don't always need them to understand what someone is telling you.

True or False?

1. How you come across is more important than what you say.

TRUE.

You are believed more visually than verbally. Your tone of voice and mannerisms will add to, or distract from, your overall message.

2. Controlled, smooth movements communicate confidence.

TRUE.

The more fluid your movements are, the more natural and confident you will appear.

3. You should avoid looking people in the eyes.

FALSE.

When you avoid eye contact, you avoid connecting with another person. Maintain eye contact at least 90 percent of the time when in conversation with someone.

4. It is difficult to hide our true feelings and reactions.

TRUE.

It may be easy to lie verbally, but our bodies have a difficult time masking the truth. If you want to get a true sense of what someone is telling you, watch his or her body language.

5. Less than 10 percent of communication is through the spoken word.

TRUE.

Based on Dr. Albert Mehrabian's study, 7 percent of verbal communication is made through the spoken word. The balance of communication comes from nonverbal communication.

6. Nervous gestures are distracting to your message.

TRUE.

Any repeated gesture is likely to be noticed and irritating. In fact, such habits can overshadow anything you say, because they become the focus of others' attention. Controlled gestures put you in a better position to convey your intended message and add an impact to what you say.

4. **Turn on the TV.** Have someone videotape you and then watch the tape several times to see yourself as others do. Become more aware of yourself and others.

5. **Be open to feedback.** Feedback comes from the way people respond to you. Pay attention to the feedback you receive.

6. **Accentuate the positive.** Present yourself positively and focus on the positive aspects of your communication. The more effective your presentation, the more effective you will be overall.

7. **Control your hands and gestures.** Use your hands and gestures to add interest when you speak, but beware of the messages your gestures send.

Chapter 6

Every Interaction Is Important

True or False?

1. An effective handshake should involve at least four to five pumps up and down.

2. Smiling can make you appear friendly or influential.

3. Never look someone directly in the eyes or you risk being threatening or invading personal space.

4. Men should shake hands more gently with women than with other men.

5. Always introduce the oldest person first.

6. Eye contact should be maintained 90 percent of the time when talking with someone.

ALL INTERACTIONS ARE IMPORTANT

Think of each interaction you have on the job, including business social functions, as an important opportunity to build relationships. Whether you're greeting the office receptionist in the morning, returning a phone message to a not-so-key potential client, or presenting a top priority report to the board of directors, any exchange could be the most important one you're going to have today.

Why this emphasis on every little interaction? First, any business situation represents an opportunity of some kind. Second, it is essential for you to build relationships with others and create a strong network of contacts. Also, each interaction builds a larger sense of your overall capabilities and your reputation. When you have a reputation for treating others well, regardless of position or status, and for handling all situations competently, you become known very quickly as a person of quality, reliability, and professionalism.

When I received the call from a prominent surgeon looking to enhance his image, I was intrigued. Here was a man capable of performing complex surgery, yet he was concerned with his image and his ability to be at ease in social situations. He said he was awkward and desperately wanted to gain control over his behavior and reputation.

Sometimes the more skilled we are in our technical or product expertise, the more we rely on that knowledge, rather than our ability to interact with others. The surgeon is typical of other people I've worked with: people who have advanced academic or technical knowledge, but don't have a clue when it comes to communication and social interaction. Sometimes people hide behind their degrees, awards, and certificates of achievement, never fully feeling capable in any other arena. The key is in finding balance and being comfortable in a variety of situations.

MAKE A CONNECTION

The ability to feel comfortable and make others feel comfortable quickly is helpful in any situation. It is natural to feel some apprehension when you are about to enter a room full of strangers or are thrown into a new situation with little time to prepare. When you know you can handle all your interactions smoothly, you'll feel sure of yourself and convey a clear sense of competence and reliability. You'll be free to concentrate on the people you are with rather than being consumed with yourself. As a result, your relationships with others will strengthen.

So often during the course of the day, we're so engrossed in ourselves that we fail to acknowledge others. It doesn't take long to make a connection, but the rewards are long lasting. Sometimes we need to remind ourselves to slow down, concentrate, and make an effort to really connect with people.

Think of all the people you meet and greet throughout the course of a day. Have you ever gone through the act of meeting someone without actually meeting him or her at all? And if you had to introduce him or her to someone else, you couldn't because you didn't even hear the person's name? It happens all the time. Instead of taking the time to get to know people, we gloss over them.

When you take the time to connect with another person, something magical happens. Instead of simply going through the motions by shaking hands and saying hello, you allow yourself to become involved and emotionally connected. You stop only looking at people and start seeing them for who they really are.

I once heard the saying, "When the student is ready, the teacher will appear," and I've tried to live by that philosophy by always being ready to learn. I do believe we can learn something from everyone. When I remind myself of this, I find value in everything that happens and with everyone I meet.

After finalizing a program with a company, the man who hired me wanted to introduce me to the people I'd soon be working with. I met 12 people. With each one, we shook hands and exchanged greetings. Yet only one of these people had an impact on me. I left thinking about this person, trying to figure out why he'd made me feel so welcome, appreciated, and connected to him. Did I know him from somewhere else? Why did he seem so familiar? The more I thought about it, the more I realized it was the connection we made when we said hello that made all the difference. With everyone else, the introduction was routine, but with him, the interaction felt *important*; it felt personal and real. Instead of the usual one-to three-second glance, we held our eye contact for three to six seconds. We stopped long enough to do more than just look at each other; we sincerely *acknowledged* each other. As a result, we established a *real* connection. Just a few seconds made all the difference. Try it next time and see for yourself.

SAY WHAT YOU MEAN AND MEAN WHAT YOU SAY

People can only count on you when you're reliable. Think about all of the times we say things we might not really mean or we tell others what we think they want to hear. How often do you say "I'll call you tomorrow" but never do, or say something like, "Let's get together soon," and allow months to go by before you make an effort to call? Though little comments are rarely taken verbatim, you don't want your words to be taken lightly.

How often do you tell people what you think they want to hear? How often are you truly accountable for what you say? When was the last time you said you'd be somewhere at 2 o'clock and showed up at 2:15? How often do you say you'll return a call but don't?

It's the little comments that make or break trust. It's the little things that eat away at your reputation. Other people need to believe that what you say is what you will do. When you give your word, you give people reason to trust in you. When you break your word, you give people reason to lose faith in you. Listen to what you say. When you commit to something, be sure to do it.

INTRO TO INTRODUCTIONS

I like to keep my workshops interactive, and I often include exercises throughout. In order to help people relax and get acquainted with others in the room, I will ask each person to introduce himself or herself to someone else in the group. Sometimes I'll provide a topic to discuss, but I rarely allow more than two to three minutes for people to get acquainted, which surprisingly has always been more than enough time. Once participants are back in their seats, I ask them to take out paper and pen and write down three things:

1. The first and last name of the person they just met.

2. The color of his or her eyes.

3. The rating of the handshake exchanged.

The response is often laughter mixed with sighs, moans, and groans. People realize right away these are things they should know and pay attention to, but most do not. I review the questions one at a time and usually see results similar to this:

1. Remember names. Very few people remember both the first and last name, and less than half remember the first name of the person they met just minutes before. It is important for you to remember the names of the people you meet. People respond to the sound of their own name, and when you can address others personally, you make them feel important. Repeating a name immediately after hearing it, and using it in your conversation, will increase your ability to remember it, but the most important thing you can do to remember a name is to listen.

2. Make eye contact. Less than half of the people can name the eye color correctly. Since there are only a few eye colors to choose from, I ask how many people guessed at their answers, and generally more than half of the people admit they did. Look at people when you say hello, and pay attention to their eye color. When you look at someone long enough to remember the color of their eyes, you allow enough time to make a connection.

3. Offer a firm handshake. Very few people receive a high rating on their handshake, and many admit they didn't shake hands at all. Handshakes and introductions go hand in hand. The topic of handshakes always leads to some of the most interesting discussions: Men think they should shake hands differently with women, women think men shake too gently, and the debate goes on. There are many misconceptions about handshakes. Many people underestimate the value of a good shake. When it comes to introductions, a little bit of effort can go a long way toward creating a lasting connection.

When you're introduced to others, whether you are male or female, offer your hand immediately, and shake hands firmly. Make eye contact while shaking hands, and smile warmly. Say something in your greeting that's general, but gracious and noncommittal, such as, "I'm very pleased to meet you." Here are some examples of appropriate and inappropriate responses used during introductions:

Say . . .	Not . . .
It's nice to meet you.	It's nice to know you. (You don't.)
How do you do?	Charmed. (Are you?)
I've heard many good things about you.	I've heard about you. (Leaves the person wondering what you heard.)

If you're introduced to several people at once, shake hands with each just after the introduction. You don't have to wait until all have been introduced. That way you can acknowledge and make contact with each in turn, rather than making a collective gesture of greeting.

If you're confused about the proper way to introduce someone, the general rule of thumb in a business situation is: the person who is most honored or who has the higher rank is mentioned *first,* while the other person (or people) is presented to him or her. For example, "Ms. President, I'd like to introduce you to John Doe." Generally, the host or hostess is responsible for introductions. In a business setting, that means the person in whose office the meeting takes place, the person who called the meeting, or the most senior member of the group, if he or she had some responsibility for calling the gathering together. If two people are equally responsible for calling a meeting, then they should determine in advance who is going to do the introductions.

It is also appropriate for whomever knows both parties to introduce those who don't know each other. Introductions should be done immediately. There's nothing more awkward than standing around without being introduced while others are talking and laughing together. So, rule number one: Immediately introduce people who don't know each other! And remember, you can always introduce yourself if no one is there to make an introduction.

If you do find yourself in the awkward position of introducing someone whose name you've forgotten, you can admit it, or you can encourage others to introduce themselves. For example, if you are holding a meeting with people who don't know each other well, it is appropriate for you to introduce yourself, brief everyone on why you've brought them together, and allow each person to introduce him or herself. You'll want to structure this self-introduction, though, by saying something like, "I'd like each of you to introduce yourself, telling us your name, the company or organization you represent, and your primary interest for attending this meeting." This gives each person time to mentally prepare before being asked to speak, and you will minimize the time introductions take by structuring what you want each person to say.

When you know you will be in a position of introducing people, it helps to know the names of the people you are introducing—another good reason to remember names! When you are introducing people, provide additional information such as the company or organization the person is associated with, or other information that may be of interest. This information will give others a basis for conversation, and might help someone who can't quite place the person being introduced.

You may be used to dealing with people on a first-name basis, but don't ever assume it's OK to be on a first-name basis with someone. Wait until it is requested, or ask how someone prefers to be addressed. If you're not at the same rank, use the other person's professional title (i.e., Judge, Doctor, Professor). It's always appropriate to tell others how you'd like to be addressed: "Please call me Sue. What do you wish to be called?"

Finally, always rise when meeting someone; it shows respect and interest.

LOOK 'EM IN THE EYES

Maintaining eye contact is another important aspect of nonverbal communication, and it's critical in connecting with someone. As I mentioned earlier, it's important to take the time to connect by using your eyes. When you say hello to people, hold your gaze for several seconds. You can communicate with your eyes, and your willingness to make eye contact helps you communicate more effectively.

Avoiding eye contact or shifting, darting eyes can send several negative messages, among them: "I'm not interested," "I'm bored," "I have something else to do," "I don't like you," or "I don't like what you're saying." Because you aren't actually saying anything, the person you are with will draw his own conclusions.

When you are talking to someone, you should maintain eye contact up to 90 percent of the time. It is natural to glance away occasionally, especially when you are gathering your thoughts, but your focus should be on the person you're talking with. If you are uncomfortable looking directly into someone's eyes, make face contact instead by focusing on other areas of the person's face.

Connecting with people through eye contact can be more difficult when you are speaking with several people at once or addressing a large group. The key is to make contact with everyone you can, scanning your eyes slowly around the room, rather than glossing over a group of people with your eyes. The larger the audience, the more challenging it is to connect with your audience, but it can be done.

When you are in front of a large group, if you look at one person too much or for too long, you will make that person feel uncomfortable and singled out. Instead, look for a few friendly faces in different parts of the room and make contact with them. Hold the glance three to five seconds before you move on. If you don't look at people, you won't connect with them. Though you may feel self-conscious in front of people, try to appear relaxed and be yourself.

SMILE!

A smile is one of your most valuable business tools. It is also easy to use, easy to read, and doesn't cost a dime! Anyone, speaking any language, understands a smile. When you smile at someone, they will usually smile back at you. A smile makes you appear pleasant, upbeat, and friendly. One of the biggest benefits is that it's good for you to smile!

Smiling can make you seem approachable, genuine, and influential. It can elevate your mood, make you look younger and happier, and even prevent wrinkles! It takes over 70 muscles to frown, but only 14 to smile! You don't want to overdo a smile and walk around with a phony grin, but don't be afraid to smile big and let your teeth show!

TAKE HOLD OF YOUR HANDSHAKE

One of the most important and underestimated gestures you make when greeting and of meeting others is your handshake. Handshakes are an integral part of our greetings, and because impressions are formed in only seconds, your handshake is very important. Most interactions begin and end with a handshake, but the type of handshake you give is critical. Just because you've been offering your hand and shaking with others does not guarantee you've been doing it right. Men are taught at an early age to shake "like a man" and, while

I believe things are slowly changing, there are many women I know of who were never taught to shake hands at all.

There are many misconceptions surrounding the handshake. The rules of etiquette used to require a man to wait for a woman to offer her hand before offering his, but there is no longer a need to wait—either party can offer his or her hand first. A handshake is a gesture of friendliness and acceptance of the other person.

I often ask men if they think they should shake hands differently with women than they do with other men, and the majority of men say they think they should. When I ask them *why,* it's usually because they think women have petite hands and worry about shaking them too hard. This is simply not true. Gender need not be an issue when it comes to handshakes. Women, like men, can and *should* offer a strong grip and shake hands firmly.

Be generous with your handshake: It's a good way of creating a link with the other person. So shake hands often and do it in a firm, warm, and gracious manner. Offer your hand when:

- Being introduced or saying hello

- Leaving or saying goodbye

- Greeting someone from your business, company, or organization

- Greeting a client, customer, or acquaintance

An effective and impressive handshake is the result of more than extending your hand. You can pull off the ideal handshake by doing the following when you greet someone:

- Step forward

- Make eye contact

- Smile

- Extend your arm and hand

- Try to match the web of your hand with that of the person you're greeting

- Give as much of your hand as possible in a firm, confident grasp

- Grasp the hand firmly (without crushing) and give a little squeeze

- Keep smiling and maintain eye contact

- Pump up and down once or twice; then let go

If you've ever had a handshake last too long, you know how awkward it can be. A handshake is meant to be brief, which is why it is so important to get it right. If you think I'm making too much out of a simple handshake, let me explain: A handshake is an important aspect of the impression you make and leave with the people you meet. Handshakes have been around since ancient times and originated as a gesture of peace. Today, a handshake is a gesture of friendliness, and it's generally the only physical contact you will have with someone, as most touching in business has become taboo.

STAND BY ME

Your stance also conveys a great deal about you. Even when you're standing or sitting still, the way you hold your body says something about your presence in a business interaction or meeting. For example, do you shift your weight from foot to foot or put all your weight on one foot while standing? Do you lean back in your chair when sitting? Do you shuffle your feet back and forth, cross and uncross your legs, or make other repetitive movements?

All of these habits take away from the image you want to portray. Holding your body still and upright conveys: "I'm interested in what you have to say," "I'm in control," and "I know exactly what I'm going to do with the information you're imparting to me at this moment."

There is a fine line, however, and while you don't want to slouch, you don't want to stand too rigidly either. Slouching conveys boredom, lack of confidence, or laziness. A rigid stance makes you appear uncomfortable, formal, or otherwise ill at ease. You don't want to look like a soldier or a scarecrow. Develop an upright but natural stance.

When you stand, stand solidly with your weight evenly distributed on both feet. Don't sway back and forth. Keep your shoulders back and your spine straight. When sitting, lean forward a bit to prevent rounding your back by allowing your lower back to rest against the chair. Keep your feet flat on the floor with one foot just ahead of the other. Keep your hands and body in an open position; you'll appear positive and approachable. Practice these sitting and standing stances until you find yourself naturally assuming these positions at all times.

Reminding yourself to sit up straight during the day, with your head high and your shoulders back, is all you need to do to look and feel more energetic and professional. I've read many books on making presentations, and I've sought the advice of experts in an attempt to improve my speaking skills. Yet some of the techniques I tried felt unnatural. One coach told me I moved around too much, and when I am speaking before a group I should stand still. Yet when I speak in front of a group, my adrenaline starts pumping, and I need to walk around to use my energy efficiently. When I stood still, I felt I didn't communicate as effectively and was constrained.

If I were to tell someone who was more comfortable standing behind a lectern to get out from behind it and pace back and forth, it would be unnatural for him or her. Stay true to your natural style as you do what you can to add to your overall presentation. Most of the ideas and principles in this book are just as effective one-on-one as they are in front of a large group.

DON'T BE A SPACE INVADER

Everyone has an unconscious but powerful inner sense of personal space. Generally, most of us are comfortable with another person when separated by at least three feet. This general rule about personal space distance varies from person to person and culture to culture. The key thing to remember is that invading someone's personal space will make him or her feel threatened and uncomfortable.

When you're with someone you don't know at all, keep at least an arm's length between you. A distance of three feet or more is generally reserved for strangers or those you don't know well. By controlling the distance, you can control the encounter by making people feel more or less comfortable. We tend to have less touching and greater distance in the North American culture, while other cultures tend to be more intimate.

Nino, a Russian foreign-exchange student, told me that one of the most difficult things for her to adjust to during the year she spent in the United States was the lack of kissing and hugging. In her country, it's customary to hug and kiss on both cheeks when greeting anyone. In the U.S., touching or other displays of affection aren't a part of most interpersonal interactions, unless they occur within an intimate relationship.

Each culture observes varying degrees of touch and personal-space boundaries. In some European cultures, if you don't stand close enough to smell the breath of the person you're talking to, you might offend him or her. By contrast, North Americans tend to back away from close encounters and feel threatened when our space is invaded. An example that illustrates North American personal-space considerations is an elevator encounter. We have an unwritten rule that if somebody is in the elevator and another person gets on, we automatically stand far away from that person, not side by side. We go to the other end of the elevator because that gives us the space and the distance we need to feel comfortable. If you stand too closely or "invade someone's space," you will be able to tell by his or her response, which is likely to include moving away from you. The key is to observe comfort—theirs and yours!

DO YOU HEAR WHAT I HEAR?

Joan had just begun her career as a motivational speaker when we were invited to share the platform at a conference. As she got up to speak, she became overwhelmed by the crowd and wasn't sure how to begin. She shrugged her shoulders, raised her eyebrows, and merely opened with a high-pitched, "H-I-I-I-I?" She knew instantly she had made a mistake. She struggled to get back on track. The minute you open your mouth to speak, your sound, volume, and pitch all play together to create a message. Know how you want to sound, and see to it that you sound just that way!

As a speaker, my voice is my business. When I was preparing to tape my second video, I was struggling with hoarseness. Because the taping was just two weeks away, I went to a doctor specializing in ear, nose, and throat medicine. After examining me, he told me I had nodules on my vocal cords formed from years of misusing them. He referred me to a speech pathologist, where I first learned to rest my voice (no talking for three days) to get it back for my videotaping. I continued to work with my speech pathologist for over a year to learn correct breathing, posture, and delivery skills. It was one of the most difficult and challenging things I ever did, but it made a world of difference. I hadn't realized how raspy my voice had become or how unpleasant it must have been to listen to. It wasn't until I healed and protected my voice that I could hear the difference.

How do *you* sound? To find out, record yourself. Capture yourself everywhere—on the phone, in your own office, at lunch. Considering asking permission to tape a meeting of a group you belong to so you can hear yourself as you respond to others. Then listen. You'll find, perhaps much to your amazement, that you don't sound at all like yourself! Why? Because ears, placed at the side of the head, pick up the sound of your own voice only peripherally—you never hear yourself directly. The result? How you sound to yourself and how you sound to others are *very* different.

People who have a unique and pleasing voice quality can market their voices, and sometimes a voice becomes a trademark. Think of James Earl Jones. His deep, soothing voice has been his trademark. And what about Demi Moore? You can recognize her voice easily, and she is often described by the sound of her voice. Fran Drescher, known for her role in *The Nanny,* is another example of an actress who is well-known for her voice. She has continued to play many similar roles, possibly because her voice limits her. Many women speak in a pitch higher than they need to and could enhance their sound and credibility by lowering it.

When you listen to yourself, look for the following and note your answers, yes or no:

- **Diction.** Do you pronounce letters and sounds correctly?

- **Clarity.** Do you speak clearly without mumbling?

- **Grammar.** Is your speech grammatically correct?

- **Slang.** Do you avoid using slang, jargon, or swear words?

- **Repetitive speech.** Do you speak clearly and directly without clearing your throat, coughing repeatedly, or using filler phrases such as "you know," "um," or "ah"?

- **Inflection.** Do you vary your tone and strive to sound animated and interested?

- **Volume.** Do you speak audibly but not too loudly?

- **Pitch.** Do you speak with a soothing, mellow pitch, neither too low nor too high, with no nasal, rough, or squeaky tones?

- **Listening.** Do you listen, without interrupting, more than you talk?

Based on your answers, what areas do you need to work on?

Once you've identified how you sound to others, you can take some simple steps to improve your voice. First, think about how you'd like to sound to others. Most of us want to sound confident, assertive, in control, and sure of ourselves.

If you think you need to, consult with voice experts to help you identify problems, and work to develop or change your speaking voice. For example, a communications specialist can help you improve your public speaking. A professional media consultant can help with television, film, video, radio, and press conference appearances, as well as speaking opportunities. And a speech pathologist can help with specific speech or voice problems.

To summarize, this is what you want to achieve in voice quality:

1. **Using good diction** so you'll be easily understood in all speaking situations, in public or one-on-one.

2. **Conveying warmth and strength** to show a sense of competence and confidence.

3. **Varying pitch and rhythm** to convey your interest, energy, and grasp of the subject matter.

4. **Modulating volume and rate of speech** so you're not too loud, soft, fast, or slow.

5. **Using appropriate grammar and vocabulary** to convey your knowledge and competence. Remember that an extensive vocabulary and complex sentences might be difficult for some of your listeners to follow. Instead of sounding intelligent and knowledgeable, you could come off as pompous, perhaps even arrogant.

6. **Avoiding repetitive words or phrases** that makes you appear nervous, unimaginative, or boring.

Here is a list of words and phrases to watch for and the unflattering messages they suggest:

Word or Phrase	Message Conveyed
You always/never/only/ever	Blaming, exaggerating
Everybody or anybody	Grandiosity, refusal to take responsibility
I don't know/care	No ownership, indecision
It doesn't matter	No conviction, no involvement
You know?/OK?/I mean	Uncertainty, nervous filler
Um/Ah/Yup/Nope/Uh-huh/Yeah	Lack of sophistication

7. **Being sure to use proper intonation,** in which your voice drops at the end of each sentence. A new and unfortunate trend in speech is raised intonation at the end of every sentence. The net effect is each sentence sounds like a question: "I'll attend the meeting? But I can't stay long? So could you take notes for me?" If you haven't heard this yet, listen more closely to general conversation, and you're apt to hear it soon. When you do, train your ear to find such intonation distasteful

and remind yourself not to do it. Making a statement that sounds like you're asking a question takes away your power by making you sound as if you're seeking approval.

POINTS TO REMEMBER

1. **Sit and stand with upright posture.** Remembering to sit up straight during the day, with your head high and your shoulders back, is all you need to do to look and feel more energetic and professional.

2. **Get connected.** Make a point to really connect with people. Don't just go through the motions—*connect* with your emotions.

3. **Control your hands and gestures.** Use strong, purposeful gestures, but use them sparingly, and find a home base for your hands.

4. **Use a vocabulary that communicates clearly.** Avoid complex words or sentences in an attempt to impress your audience.

5. **Listen to yourself.** Work with your voice to control its warmth, strength, and resonance.

6. **Remember names.** When you meet someone, repeat his or her name and make sure you understand it. The sweetest sound to most people is the sound of their own name.

True or False?

1. An effective handshake should involve at least four to five pumps up and down.
FALSE.
A handshake should be short, sweet, and to the point. You only need one to two pumps.

2. Smiling can make you appear friendly or influential.
TRUE.
A smile can make you appear friendly, approachable, and influential. A smile is a valuable asset. It puts others at ease. The least expensive gift you can share with another is a smile.

3. Never look someone directly in the eyes or you risk being threatening or invading personal space.

FALSE.

Eye contact is essential to good communication. When you avoid eye contact, you avoid making a connection. You don't want to have a stare down, but it's a good idea to maintain eye contact when conversing. It's natural to look away for a brief moment to collect your thoughts, but if more than a few seconds is spent looking away, your message might indicate disinterest, insecurity, or insincerity. If you find it hard to look at someone's eyes, make face contact by looking somewhere on the person's face.

4. Men should shake hands more gently with women than with other men.

FALSE.

Gender shouldn't be a consideration when offering your hand or determining how to shake hands. Handshakes in business have become universal. The type of handshake you give sends a message to those with whom you shake hands. A firm handshake rates well among both men and women.

5. Always introduce the oldest person first.

FALSE.

Introduce the most honored person first. Honor comes before age.

6. Eye contact should be maintained 90 percent of the time when talking with someone.

TRUE.

Other than occasional glances to gather your thoughts, your eyes should be focused on the person you are talking to. Eye contact should be maintained at least 90 percent of the time.

Chapter 7

You Are What You Wear

True or False?

1. Your clothing is the first thing others notice about you.
2. Shoes should always be the same color or darker than the color of your slacks or skirt.
3. The fit of your clothing is more important than the style or the quality.
4. You do not need to wear socks during the summer months.
5. Darker colors convey strength, power, and authority.
6. A solid, dark color will make you appear thinner.
7. Flip-flops are acceptable to wear in a casual atmosphere.
8. The most professional and formal choice in business attire is the two-piece matching suit.

APPEARANCES ARE REVEALING

Many facets of image are covered in this book, and each one is important. However, your appearance is the most visible and influential aspect of all. While you cannot change some aspects of your appearance, you have more control over it than you might think.

The link between appearance and self-esteem is significant. The more satisfied you are with your image, the higher your self-esteem is likely to be. Of 21,000 women who participated in Avon's 2003 Global Women's Survey, the majority agreed that the way they look is important to their self-esteem and their definition of who they are.

Image does not affect only women. Increasing numbers of men are recognizing the importance of a strong image, and many are seeking help and making self-improvements.

Placing an emphasis on appearance may seem unfair, especially to those who struggle or are unhappy with theirs, but a successful business image can be achieved by anyone. If you dress professionally and appropriately, take pride in your appearance, and keep your image updated, you will have every advantage to succeed.

Clothing is a great equalizer and a key factor in the impression you make. Fair or not, we are often judged by our clothing before we have a chance to speak. Select your clothing very carefully; what you wear should suit your workplace, your personality, and your personal style. You don't have to pretend to be someone you're not to look and be successful.

Scott, a salesman in his first job out of college, wanted to be successful. Heeding the advice of a fashion consultant, Scott wore European-cut designer suits in unique colors and was known for his wild ties. Although he never felt totally comfortable dressed in such a trendy, fashion-conscious way, he trusted the advice of his consultant.

When I met Scott, his eager attitude and willingness to please had gotten the best of him. "I work 10 hours a day. I'm trying so hard, and yet something isn't working. I don't know if I should be dressed like this. Sometimes I could swear people are making comments about my clothes behind my back," Scott told me. "Maybe this isn't the business for me."

The fashion consultant Scott worked with had failed to understand Scott's personal style and workplace environment before recommending a look for him. She was putting him in the latest fashions, but because he wasn't in the fashion industry, he was dressing in a manner that was too trendy and, therefore, inappropriate.

Scott thought his clients might relate to him better if he took off his jacket, rolled up his sleeves, and looked more like he was on their level. I encouraged him to speak with his supervisor and ask if it would be appropriate to dress more casually.

Scott did just that and ended up going to work every day wearing slacks, a button-down shirt, and a conservative tie. He felt much more comfortable with this change, and therefore more confident. And his sales results began to reflect it.

We all need to find the look that is right for us. What might be a great look for one person is not necessarily right, appropriate, or even attractive for someone else. What works in one industry doesn't always fit another. Staying true to your personal likes, dislikes, and comfort zone is essential in determining your personal style.

WHAT DOES YOUR IMAGE SAY ABOUT YOU?

It's important to stop and think about what you wear and what your clothing communicates about you. When presenting workshops, I often ask the participants why they wore the clothing they did that particular day. I find it interesting to hear how they made their clothing decisions and what they think their clothing communicates about them. I ask them, Did you wear these clothes:

- Because they were clean?
- Because they fit well?
- Because it's what you wear every Monday?
- Because someone else selected your outfit for you?
- Because of the weather? Did you want to be warm or cool?

People often laugh because, odd as it may seem, most didn't give their clothing choices much thought prior to the moment I asked them about it. What you choose to wear says so much about you, and it often indicates how you feel about yourself. The style, color, and fit communicate your intentions, attitude, and level of professionalism. Select styles that enhance your intentions and professionalism.

Assess your personal style

1. What colors/types of clothing do you wear most often?

2. What colors/types of clothing do you feel best in?

3. What colors/types of clothing do you avoid? Why?

4. If you were to dress for an important meeting and select your "best" or favorite clothing, what would it be? (Describe in detail, including tie, watch, socks/hose, and shoes.)

5. If you could select an acceptable, comfortable daily uniform, what would it be?

6. Think of someone in your field whom you consider to be particularly successful. What does that person wear? (Be as specific as possible.)

7. Which articles or styles of clothing would you *never* wear? Why not?

Review your responses and think about what your clothing choices communicate about your attitude and intentions. Since it's a good idea to dress for the type of job you want to have, not necessarily the one you currently have, pay particular attention to your answer to number six; perhaps this person can serve as a role model. If you wish to be perceived as successful or ready for a promotion, you have to *look* successful and *look* ready!

CASUAL CAN BE CONFUSING

In the early 1990s, dressing casually was a trend. Before long it became the norm. You can call it whatever you want: business casual, dressing down, casual dress, smart casual, or a relaxed dress code. You can do it once a week, once a month, or every day of the week. Whether you like it or not (and many people do not), chances are, casual attire has made its mark in your workplace. "Business casual" is "business as usual" for many.

Although dressing casually for work began as a once-a-week occurrence, it didn't take long before people were dressing casually every day of the week. Viewed as a benefit for employees and a perk employers could afford to provide, casual dress infiltrated companies coast to coast. As soon as the business climate began to change, thinking about dress did too. Fearing that relaxed attitudes toward dress would lead to relaxed attitudes about work, company executives reconsidered their clothing strategies. Concerns about customers' perceptions and maintaining the competitive edge led to stricter dress-code policies in many companies. More and more companies are reversing their dress code policies entirely. A return to more formal dress codes is on the rise.

When you think about your clothing options, there are many factors to consider: How much face-to-face contact do you have with others? What are the industry standards? Are you working in a conservative environment in which traditional attire is the norm, or in a more creative environment with fewer restrictions? How do your competitors dress? What image will help you remain competitive?

Think less about what *you* want and more about what your *customers, clients, and employer* want. What do *they* expect?

Seventy percent of the executives responding to a national survey conducted by No nonsense, the second largest manufacturer of legwear in the U.S., agreed that workplace attire affects an employee's state of mind and behavior. Two-thirds agreed that employees who wear more professional attire advance faster in their careers.

No matter where you work, having a casual dress code is not the equivalent of not having any dress code. If you aren't sure what to wear, ask. Always dress better than you need to. *Don't dress for the job you have today; dress for the position you dream of having tomorrow.*

Do you want to be noticed? Do you hope to advance quickly? Do you want others to take you seriously? If so, then take yourself seriously. *Look* sloppy and you *are* sloppy. *Look* like a pro and you *are* one. It's that simple. You are what you wear.

Always look your best. Make sure your clothes are clean, pressed, mended, and fit well. Keep your shoes clean and in good condition, and always wear socks. You may be thinking, "All of this is obvious." That's what a client of mine thought too, until she found herself in the embarrassing position of actually sending her front-desk person home to change her clothes, because casual-dress day to her meant dressing like Annie Oakley—right down to the leather, fringe, and ankle-length skirt—while greeting corporate customers in a law office.

Each company should put together its own dress policy, but casual dress can be dictated by four simple rules:

1. Consider your customer.

2. A casual environment doesn't mean anything goes. Ask for and follow the company policy.

3. Wear traditional business attire if you prefer. Never feel you must dress casually.

4. Place your emphasis on *business* first, *casual* second.

Be grateful if you are given a dress code policy. Although you may not like being told what you can and cannot wear, a policy makes it easier for you to decide what to wear. When expectations are clearly communicated confusion about what is acceptable is significantly reduced.

BUSINESS AND CASUAL DRESS DEFINED

It isn't always easy deciding what to wear. It can be especially difficult when you are attending a meeting or function outside of your office. Even events declared "business casual" leave many people wondering what is acceptable. When you are not sure what to wear, consider this: If you're questioning whether you should wear something, *don't wear it—when in doubt, leave it out!* And keep in mind the following: You are always better off slightly *overdressed* than terribly underdressed.

If you have visitors coming to your facility and your company dress code is casual, let your visitors know in advance so they may dress accordingly. However, if you know they will be dressed in traditional business attire, it's best you dress in the same manner.

Even when you attend company parties, dinners, or other get-togethers that take place after business hours, they're still business events, so dress accordingly. Always represent yourself and your company in the best possible manner. Tasteful, simple apparel is your safest choice.

If you're in charge of planning such an event, provide guidelines in your memo or invitation for what is appropriate attire: sport coat, no tie, or slacks but no jeans. If you're attending such an event and are unsure what you should wear, call the person hosting the event and ask what "casual attire" means. Consider the following.

1. First and most important, know your company's dress code or guidelines regarding casual dress. If your company has no formal or stated policy, inquire about what is acceptable to wear. Make sure you know just how casual you can be in your particular workplace environment.

2. Choose a flattering style that fits well—don't wear anything that is too big, too small, or too revealing.

3. Wear colors and patterns that coordinate.

4. When it comes to dressing casually, remember: It's casual *dress,* not casual *attitude.* Never forget that business is still business, even when you are dressed casually.

5. It is better to err on the side of formality than it is to wear something too casual.

6. Shoes are an important aspect of your appearance, and they *will* be noticed.

7. Look to managers and corporate officers for ideas on what to wear if you're in doubt.

UNIVERSAL TABOOS

Though each workplace environment has distinct differences, similarities exist across all workplace environments regarding what are considered appropriate and inappropriate ways of dressing.

Across-the-board business dress taboos include:

- **Ripped clothing.** Any clothing that is torn or has holes, no matter how fashionable, is not a becoming choice for work—ever.

- **Sweats and terrycloth.** Sweatpants, sweatshirts, and terrycloth outfits are comfortable. They're perfect for exercising or lounging on your day off, but are too casual for work.

- **Printed T-shirts and sweatshirts.** *Any* shirt with potentially offensive slogans, pictures, or graphics is always taboo.

- **Spandex and other tight clothing.** "Second skin" clothing is a comfortable after-hours option. Whether flattering or unflattering, tight, clingy clothing draws attention to the body, and is therefore distracting and inappropriate.

- **Baggy, extremely loose-fitting tops and pants.** Clothing that is too big looks sloppy. It's not professional to go to work looking like you're ready to clean the garage or as though you can't afford clothing that fits.

- **Shorts.** Shorts are meant to be worn on a hot summer day when you are outside, not inside an air-conditioned office.

- **Sleeveless tops.** Most sleeveless tops simply expose too much skin. On women, they also tend to reveal undergarments. Many halter and tank tops are cut low enough to show cleavage—which, believe it or not, your coworkers don't want to see.

- **Sandals and sneakers.** For health reasons as well as appearance reasons, sandals shouldn't be worn to work. And while comfort is an important factor in footwear, any shoes that are dirty or worn-out will not make it, even on casual-dress day.

- **Sleepwear, loungewear, or swimwear.** Sleepwear is for sleeping, lounge wear is for lounging, and swimwear is for swimming. None of these are a substitute for businesswear.

- **Theme clothing.** Western, retro, and vintage clothing are too theatrical for the workplace.

- **Low-cut tops and bottoms.** Never reveal your undergarments, your cleavage (even a little!), or any part of your bust, and avoid low-riding pants. No one wants to see your underwear or thong. If you're not sure whether your pants are too low, try sitting in them before wearing them. If your thong or underwear shows when you do, find something else to wear.

- **Miniskirts and tiny crop tops.** Skirts should be no more than three inches above the knee, and tops should cover your chest and midsection, including your navel.

- **Jeans.** Unless your company says otherwise, jeans should not be worn to work. There are too many variables in style, color, and shading. "No jeans" topped the list of responses in the No nonsense survey when bosses were asked about what one thing they would change about their employees' attire.

- **Hats, caps, and visors.** Unless you work outside or must cover your head for health reasons, there is no reason you need to wear a hat, cap, or visor, so don't!

THE MOST PROFESSIONAL LOOK

Most people have an idea of what professional dress is. For men, it's usually a dark suit and tie, but for women it can be everything from a suit to a dress to a skirt or slacks. The media, retailers, and fashion magazines dictate their ideas about what professional dress should be, but rarely do these mediums pin down what works in *business*. The styles shown are often too tight, too short, or too trendy.

What works best is simple, well-tailored clothing in neutral colors. Because there is such a wide range of choices, it's often difficult to know what to wear. Here, in order of professional appearance, are the best options for women and men.

Women: (From most professional to most casual)

- Two-piece matching skirted suit

- Two-piece matching pantsuit

- Skirt with blouse/top and jacket

- Business dress with jacket

- Slacks with blouse/top and jacket

- Business dress with or without sweater

- Skirt and blouse or sweater set

- Slacks with blouse or sweater set

- Slacks with sweater

- Casual pants with casual shirt or sweater

Men: (From most professional to most casual)

- Two-piece matching suit, shirt, and tie

- Slacks with shirt, tie, and blazer

- Slacks with shirt, tie, and sport coat

- Slacks with shirt and tie

- Slacks with shirt, tie, and sweater

- Slacks, shirt, and sport coat

- Slacks with sweater

- Casual pants with sweater

- Casual pants with long-sleeved shirt

- Casual pants with short-sleeved shirt

Although women have more clothing styles and options available to them, it's safest to limit those options to the same ones men follow in the workplace. Never become careless or sloppy in your appearance. You can easily upgrade your image and your level of professionalism if you wear a jacket, which always adds a sense of completion and polish to an outfit. Invest in a good jacket that will mix with other items in your business wardrobe.

Shoes are an important aspect of your appearance. You can dress the part, but if it's not head to toe, you reveal a lack of attention to detail. In face-to-face encounters, our eyes meet the eyes of the other person, then they sweep down to the feet and back up to the face again. This happens so quickly, you may not be aware of it, but you do this with everyone you meet. So, avoid runs in your nylons or dirty, unpolished, down-at-the-heel shoes; they will be noticed. Shoes should always be the same color as, or darker than, the color of your slacks, skirt, socks, or hose. When lighter than the rest of your out-fit, your shoes stand out and draw attention to your feet. The more professional you look, the more you show (through your appearance and attention to detail) that you take pride in yourself and your work.

WHAT'S IN A COLOR?

While you might have your own preferences for color, it's important to understand the impact the colors you wear can have on others. Color presents a message of its own. Sometimes we subconsciously avoid people who are wearing a color we don't like. Conversely, others may avoid us if we're wearing a color they dislike. You're less likely to trust or buy from someone dressed in a color you find threatening or unappealing. Communication can be disrupted when you are surrounded by colors to which you react poorly.

Companies invest considerable time and money in choosing the appropriate color schemes for their offices and products. The color they choose must match the message they intend to send.

Color adds excitement and helps us express our style and taste in many areas of our lives. How appealing would a plain metal (colorless) car be to drive? How appetizing would gelatin be if all the flavors were clear? In clothing, neutral, basic colors such as black, brown, blue, white, beige, and gray are always safe. You might stand out and be remembered negatively as the one in the bright-orange suit, but rarely will you leave a negative impression for wearing a neutral, basic color.

In general, lighter shades have been found to communicate an approachable, nonthreatening image, while darker colors communicate authority and power. For example, to appear and feel more authoritative yet approachable, you could wear a dark suit (which says "authority") with a light blue or yellow shirt (a lighter, less threatening color). To appear and feel more authoritative, wear a white shirt instead. To appear neutral, wear a blue suit, which is less intimidating than a black one.

When making a presentation, consider both your audience and the message you intend to deliver. When speaking and acting from a position of authority, dress authoritatively. In our culture, that means wearing a dark suit without exception. On the other hand, when you are meeting with others in a more conciliatory or advisory capacity, tone down your color scheme. You want to be certain your clients or customers feel comfortable with you, so they feel free to open up.

The key here, of course, is to consider your audience. Are you applying for a job, making an important client presentation, conducting a performance review of an employee, prosecuting an accused criminal, defending an accused criminal, making a sales call, or waiting on customers in a department store? What message do you want to communicate in each of these situations? What image do you want to project? By taking a little time to think through the encounters you anticipate each day, you can use color to convey your intended message.

Color can also be used to enhance your silhouette and camouflage an imperfect physique. Since the eye is drawn to the lightest spot of the silhouette, it is important to place color strategically. A white shirt, for example, puts the focus on just the right area—the face. Light shoes or socks with dark slacks, however, will draw attention to your feet! Always wear the lightest colors next to the areas to which you want to draw attention.

A solid, dark color can make you look taller and thinner. A navy, charcoal gray, or black suit with dark socks and shoes creates a smooth, monochromatic line and is thus more slimming than a light-colored suit or a sport coat and slacks in contrasting colors, such as navy and tan. Following are some characteristics of colors. As you read through the list, pay attention to the colors you wear most often and what they communicate about you.

Characteristic	Colors
Assertive	Black, dark gray, red, navy
Creative/Artistic	Mauve, yellow, white
Traditional/Classic	Medium brown, taupe
Intuitive/Sensitive	Indigo blue, periwinkle blue, purple
Friendly	Peach, pale yellow, tan, grass green
Energetic	Red
Powerful	Black
Approachable	Peach, tan, pale or medium pink, coral, rust
Authoritative	Charcoal gray, navy, black
Inventive/Soothing	Teal, turquoise
Trustworthy/Organized	Navy
Conservative	Dark brown, medium gray
Sophisticated	Burgundy, forest green, black, plum, brick red

Clothing matters in business. It would be nice if we were all noticed for our hard work or honorable intentions alone. But your appearance sends a strong message that precedes your chance to impress with good work.

Remember, less than 10 percent of your message comes from the words you speak. The visual conveys the rest.

When you show up for work each day, how you look reflects how you feel about yourself, your job, your customers, and your coworkers. Even on tired, slow days, it's important to put effort into your appearance and behavior. Others will always seek out the person who appears eager to help, knowledgeable, and in possession of a positive attitude.

FABRIC SENSE: WHAT WORKS BEST

Fabric is one of the most important elements in determining the cost of a garment and how well it will wear. The best suit fabric to buy is wool. A good wool suit will drape beautifully, resist wrinkling, clean well without showing wear, and, in the long run, will last longer. It may cost more up front, but it's worth the investment.

You can test the fabric of any garment by subjecting it to the "feel and wrinkle" test. First, try it on. How does it feel to you? If it's comfortable, it passes the "feel" part of the test. Then take some of the garment's fabric in your hand and crumple or squeeze it. Let it go. Does the fabric retain the creases? The way it looks after crumpling is an indication of how it will look when you wear it. If it looks good after scrunching, it also sails by the "wrinkle" test. Darker colors tend to show less wrinkling. Linens and cottons tend to wrinkle the most. Always invest in the best clothing you can afford. *You're better off having fewer clothing items of better quality than a lot of cheap clothing.*

SHOPPING ON A BUDGET

You can save some money when purchasing your initial wardrobe and in maintaining it each year by waiting for sales in good quality retail clothing stores or shopping the discount and outlet stores. The key to doing this successfully, whether you're shopping the sales at your usual clothing store or searching the racks at a discount store, is to go in with a plan. *Know exactly what you need before you step foot in any store.* That great bargain will only be good for you if you can use and wear it. If you've shopped around enough, you should have enough knowledge about fabric, labels, and prices to know if what you're considering really is a bargain.

It's also a good idea to find a clerk in the store to work with you. A clerk who knows you can help you find what you're looking for and can call you when something you want goes on sale. You don't necessarily have to use a formal clothing consultant to do this. Just getting to know a clerk, seeking that person out whenever you shop in that store, and leaving your business card so he or she can let you know when particular items go on sale can save you both time and money.

Discount and outlet stores offer a good, sometimes even great, alternative to paying full price. You can find some great deals if you shop carefully. Watch for quality, fit, correct size, and be careful to watch for irregular or imperfect merchandise. Inspect all discount and outlet merchandise for flaws; look for color flaws, snags, tears, or mismatched patterns. Check for poor sewing. Is one sleeve longer than the other? Does the jacket or pant leg hang funny? Are there puckers in shirt seams, lapels, or jacket seams? Do the pants hang correctly from the pleat?

If the discount is substantial, if the clothing can be altered or fixed, and if it's still a value after your investment in tailoring, then consider buying it. Shopping for the clothing you need should be both fun and rewarding. If you have a plan before you go, you'll be more likely to come home with just the clothing you need.

More and more people are ordering from catalogs and the Internet. Some items look better in a photo than in person, so make sure the items you keep don't look cheap; always check for quality, and return any item that is questionable.

Shopping tips

- Look good when you shop; you'll receive better service.

- Wear the shoes you intend to wear with the item you're looking to buy. It's hard to get a sense of how a suit or pair of slacks will look when you're wearing sneakers.

- Plan your shopping to avoid impulse buying. Know exactly what you need before you enter a store.

- Shop on a weekday, when stores are less busy.

- Shop alone if you do better that way, or shop with someone you know will help you.

- Shop when you're feeling good.

- Avoid major sales if you don't do well with crowds, need personal attention, or tend to buy on impulse.

- Gain the support and help of a clerk to assist you with shopping, and encourage the salesperson to contact you if something you want goes on sale or comes in stock.

- Wear clothing that is easy to get in and out of so trying things on isn't a chore.

- Don't "shop until you drop." Take a break, have something to eat, and avoid getting exhausted—you'll make better decisions and be more likely to stick to your plan when you're feeling fresh.

HOW TO GET THE MOST FROM YOUR CLOTHING-DOLLAR INVESTMENT

When you have a special occasion, such as a class reunion or a wedding, you might find yourself shopping for the right clothes for that particular event, and you might spend a lot of money doing it. Yet the one item you find is worn only at that one occasion or perhaps a handful of times after. We often place less importance on the clothing we wear to work, shuddering at the thought of spending a lot of money on something for everyday wear. Well, we all know the special feeling that comes with dressing for a special occasion. Why do we only allow ourselves to feel that way just once in awhile? *Why not dress each day as if it were special?* The better and more special you feel each day, the more effective you will be. The investment you make in your image will be one of the safest and most gainful investments you will ever make.

Tips on what to buy

- **Buy quality garments.** Spend more upfront and make an investment in your work wardrobe.

- **Buy high-quality fabrics.** Since fabric determines how well a garment will wear, select fabrics that resist wrinkling. The better the fabric, the longer the garment should last.

- **Pay attention to fit and detail.** Check the fit of your clothing, making sure nothing pulls or shows. Buy only what looks good and fits well.

- **Select your clothes carefully.** Choose a style that is flattering and appropriate to your environment.

- **Read laundering instructions.** Many cottons and linens will look better if you launder them professionally; however, it will cost you more in upkeep. If you clean them yourself, follow the laundering instructions for each article to ensure they look their best.

TAILORING TRICKS

A perfectly good suit can look shabby, even obsolete, without attention to the finer details addressed by a good tailor. These small details distinguish an average suit, dress, slacks, or jacket from a high-quality one. Here are some examples of the kinds of details to pay attention to and things to look for:

- Does it hang nicely?

- Is it even?

- Is the skirt too long (lower than the bottom of your calf) or too short (more than three inches above your knee)?

- Are the slacks too long (touching the floor) or too short (above the top of the shoe)?

- Does the sleeve length break at the wrist?

- Do the seams/lines match?

- Are the buttons sewn tightly, so they don't hang loose or fall off?

- Do the vents of the jacket lie flat?

- Does anything pull?

- Can you move freely (i.e., can you lift your arms, bend, and sit comfortably)?

Additional factors to watch for to ensure good tailoring:

- The lining should never show.

- The color of the zipper should match the fabric color.

- Seams should be smooth and well-finished, with no puckers.

- Shoulder pads should be invisible.

- Snaps should be hidden.

- Hem should hang straight and evenly.

- Patterns should match at the seams.

- Undergarments should never show (bra straps, button gaps, slips, thongs, boxers, briefs, etc.).

- Pants should break at instep and cover the top of the shoe heel.

POINTS TO REMEMBER

1. **Check yourself over, from head to toe.** Before you leave the house each morning, look at yourself, fully clothed, in a full-length mirror to get the full effect of the image you project. Check yourself over, head to toe. Shoes polished? Underclothes invisible? Clothing lint-free?

2. **Invest in your best dress.** Always buy quality, not quantity.

3. **Wear clothes that fit.** Choose clothing in a flattering style that *fits* well—nothing too big, too small, or too revealing. Remember, the fit is more important than anything else. Hire a good tailor to ensure a great fit.

4. **Know your company's dress code.** Make sure you know just how casual you can be in your workplace.

5. **Coordinate.** Wear colors and patterns that coordinate—no crazy clashes.

6. **Think casual *dress,* not casual *attitude.*** When it comes to dressing casually, never forget that business is still business. Maintain your usual high standards of behavior and professionalism and you can't go wrong, whether you're in your power suit at the annual meeting or slacks and a shirt at a casual event.

True or False?

1. Your clothing is the first thing others notice about you.

TRUE.

No matter what you wear, it sends a message that tells others a lot about you. Whether you're dressed in athleticwear, business attire, high fashion, or even a '60s-era look, you are sending a message about who you are, what you like, and what you dislike. Why do you wear the clothing you do? Because it feels like it's you.

2. Shoes should always be the same color or darker than the color of your slacks or skirt.

TRUE.

Since the eyes are always drawn to light colors, it is important to place color strategically. A white shirt, for example, puts the focus on just the right area—the face. Light shoes with dark skirts, slacks, or stockings, however, will draw attention to your feet! Always wear the lightest colors near your face.

3. The fit of your clothing is more important than the style or the quality.

TRUE.

Even the most expensive garment won't look good if it's too tight, too loose, too short, too long, or doesn't fit well in other ways. Always make sure your clothing is tailored for you so the fit is good.

4. You do not need to wear socks during the summer months.

FALSE.

Unless you are instructed otherwise, you should always wear socks. Bare feet aren't sanitary or appealing in an office setting.

5. Darker colors convey strength, power, and authority.

TRUE.

Darker colors convey authority, which can sometimes mean that people will feel less comfortable communicating freely with you. Lighter colors, on the other hand, tend to make you appear approachable. Think about your objectives and the image you want to project when deciding what colors and tones to wear.

6. A solid, dark color will make you appear thinner.

TRUE.

A solid, dark color creates a smooth line and thus creates the illusion of thinness. Anytime the line is broken, attention is drawn to the point where the break in the eye flow occurs. For example, a navy blazer and khaki slacks chops up a look, while a solid-colored suit presents a smooth line.

7. Flip-flops are acceptable to wear in a casual atmosphere.

FALSE.

Flip-flops can only be worn without socks, and as stated in number four, you need to wear socks to work. Flip-flops are too casual and too noisy for most office environments.

8. The most professional and formal choice in business attire is the two-piece matching suit.

TRUE.

A business suit creates a polished look and communicates a serious attitude. You can never go wrong dressed in a business suit, unless you work in an environment where a suit is inappropriate.

Chapter 8

Details Make a Difference

True or False?

1. The safest smell in business is no smell at all.

2. A great way to camouflage a bald spot is to grow your hair long on one side and comb it over the area where hair is thinning.

3. Glasses can make you appear more knowledgeable and mature.

4. Don't spend a lot of money on a pen. It's a disposable item and is too easy to lose to justify a big investment.

5. Tattoos are fine as long as they aren't too big or too visible.

6. People become accustomed to their own smell very quickly.

LITTLE THINGS MAKE A BIG DIFFERENCE

I was a bit frazzled when I left for the airport on my way to Indianapolis. By the time I arrived at my hotel, it was almost 10 o'clock at night. I took a relaxing bath, organized my things, and reviewed my notes for the presentation I was giving the next day. As I finished unpacking my bags, I realized I was missing the skirt to my suit. I searched the room thoroughly, but it was nowhere in sight. The only bottoms I had were the capris I'd worn on the plane, and they were stained. I called the front desk and found out there was a Wal-Mart nearby. I got up early, went to the store, and bought the only black slacks in my size.

The style of pants didn't look good with the jacket, and the shades of black didn't match very well, but I had no other option. Considering I was speaking about clothing and image, I was feeling a bit self-conscious, knowing I'd be standing in front of a large group of people—I hoped no one would notice.

I wasn't sure if I should say anything to the group, but decided to mention it late in the day. When I asked if anyone noticed my outfit didn't match, several people raised their hands. A woman who studied textiles in college said she noticed it right away. She wondered why I would wear such a mismatched outfit. I was glad I had said something after all; at least she now knew why I wore what I did that day.

We never know who will notice what, or what the implications of them noticing will be. Too often we think we can get by wearing something we should have cleaned or repaired, assuming no one will notice the missing button or stain. But I can tell you from experience that sometimes it's the littlest things that make the biggest difference.

There's more to looking successful than choosing and wearing the appropriate clothing. Your overall grooming, the appearance of your hair and nails, the accessories you wear, the condition of your clothing, and even the eyeglasses you wear are part of your total look of success. Don't forget the details or the finishing touches.

There are a host of little details that can make or break even the most put-together professional ensemble. Imagine you're making an important sales call to a potential customer. You've dressed carefully to fit in with the appearance norms of your customer's company. Your shoes are polished, your hair is newly cut, and you feel great. But as you leave your office, you realize you spilled something on your shirt at lunch. You don't have an extra shirt with you, and you haven't left enough time to make an emergency stop to change into a new one.

Remember, in face-to-face encounters, eyes meet eyes, quickly sweep down to the feet, and go back up to the face again. The spot on your garment *will* be noticed.

You probably will make an effective sales pitch and land the account, but this sort of detail does register with the observer as a negative. When your image communicates something negative, you've lost control of the message you want to get across. When the details are wrong, your power and effectiveness are severely reduced.

When the printing salesman walked into my office, he came inside with his overshoes on and his tie flipped over his shoulder as if blown by the wind. As he stood there talking to me, all I could think about were the marks his dirty overshoes were making on my office carpet and how silly he looked with his twisted tie. No matter what he had to say, these two things said it all and—far louder than his words!

Details can contradict the message we intend to convey. No one should see your undergarments, whether it's your bra, the strap of your slip, or the lace on your underwear. Lace and straps may be in vogue in fashion magazines, but they are not fashionable in the office. Mishaps will occur; the best you can do to prevent problems is to plan for them. You can't predict a run in your nylons or a rip in the seams, but you can be prepared. It's a good idea to carry an emergency repair kit with you, which can include all or some of the following:

- Extra tie, shirt, or blouse

- Pair of shoes

- Needle and thread

- Cloth for wiping shoes or removing stains

- Panty hose

- Toothbrush, toothpaste, mouthwash, and floss

- Comb or brush

- Hair spray

- Lint remover

- Static spray

TAKE CARE OF YOUR CLOTHES

Keep your clothing in good condition. When you have good quality clothes and accessories, maintain them. Dry clean your suits, ties, jackets, and coats as needed, but not too often, because the process is hard on fabric. If you can afford it, use a professional laundering service to maintain your shirts; have them laundered and starched. Get rid of shirts that are frayed or yellowed. Use a fabric protector on ties. This will protect them from food spills and make them easier to clean.

Dry clean and launder your clothing regularly so you're never tempted to wear a soiled garment just because it's still hanging in your closet. Keep suits and jackets on their original hangers if possible. Other alternatives are wood, tubular or plastic-molded hangers. Curved hangers are best, because they help hold the shape of your jackets and prevent wrinkling or bulging in the shoulders.

Store your shoes in shoe boxes to keep them clean and free of dust. These boxes can either be the original cardboard ones the shoes came in or the plastic boxes sold in stores. Cedar shoe trees are advantageous for two reasons:

They maintain the correct shape of your shoes, and they absorb moisture, which will extend the life of your shoes. Keep your shoes well polished and in good condition.

In addition to clothing maintenance, don't forget *personal* maintenance. Bathe daily, use deodorant, brush your teeth, shave, wash, comb, and style your hair. Do these daily maintenance steps consistently. One of the most difficult things to have to tell someone is that they have poor personal hygiene. It can become an overriding distraction and, eventually, the only thing noticed about someone.

HANDLE YOUR HAIR WITH CARE

If you're still wearing the same hairstyle you wore five years ago, it's time for a change. People often keep the same hairstyle for years; it reminds them of their youth, or of happier times, or of being in fashion. But in fashion when? Styles change over the years; an outdated style will quickly outdate *you*.

Helen is an attractive woman. It's obvious she cares about her image. Everything about her speaks to perfection, with one exception: her hair. The color is unnaturally blond, and the style is about 20 years old.

You have a lot of room for personal taste when it comes to hairstyles. There isn't one particular look that works for everyone. When deciding on a style for your hair, you must take into consideration your hair type, your age, the business or industry you are in, and the amount of money and time you are willing to devote to maintaining your color and cut.

For men working in traditional or conservative industries, hair should be no longer than the nape of the neck in back. For women, hair length is more flattering and professional when it is at or above the shoulders.

Karen rarely cuts her hair. Her long hair was her trademark in high school, and it wasn't until after she was married that she trimmed the ends for the first time. Everywhere she goes, people comment on her hair and want to know how she manages to wash and dry it. Her hair has always been her claim to fame. Now in her fifties, her long hair has grayed and become damaged. It's not as flattering as it once was, but she still receives comments on it. Karen perceives the *comments* she receives as *compliments,* but they are not. People comment because her hair is so *unusual.* Karen's long hair outdates her and takes away from her other features. Her hair is all that's noticed.

Alan, who is a successful business owner, offered to read my first manuscript in its early stages. Because he's already quite successful, we both assumed he wouldn't learn anything new, but we were wrong. Not only did he pick up several new ideas he planned on using with clients, but he made the decision to change his hairstyle too.

Alan's hair had been thinning over the years, and he did what many men do when that happens: he created a part on the side and pulled the hair over to cover the balding area.

After reading the chapter on details, he was motivated to change his hairstyle. He said he never paid much attention to it before, but after changing it, he realized how many other people did notice hair. He found the responses he received to be very positive, and although most people notice he looks different, some can't figure out what has changed. When I saw him for the first time wearing his new style, I noticed how much more professional he appeared, and at the same time how much *younger* he looked.

It's interesting how often people stick with a style, assuming it keeps them looking younger, because it rarely does. When someone wears a particular style too long, or wears a style intended for someone younger, the result is someone who typically ends up looking *older*! If you're not sure if it's time for you to change your hairstyle, start paying attention to what you see at work, on television, and in magazines.

Find a good stylist; a stylist does more than just cut hair. He or she will consult with you about what you like and dislike and will consider your face shape, the amount of hair you have, and even the type of work you do before recommending a particular style. Many stylists offer a free consultation during which they ask questions. A good stylist needs to understand your lifestyle, the types of clothing you wear most often, and how much time you are willing to spend grooming your hair. Your answers will help the stylist develop the right cut and hairstyle for you.

Tips on hair include

- Avoid making drastic changes. Don't dramatically change your style and color all at once. It takes time for you to adjust, so take it slow.

- Never allow a stylist to do "whatever" he or she wants. What *you* want is most important. Ask for ideas, but the final decision should be yours.

- Use quality styling products in your hair, and styling it will be much easier. Your hair will be more manageable, and look healthier too.

- Use quality products to maintain healthy hair. The products you use make a difference. There are products for every type of hair; select the products suited for your hair type.

- Choose an easy-to-maintain style, unless you have extra time to spend on your hair each day.

- Ask your stylist to show you how to style your hair. If you've found the right stylist for you, you're going to love the way your hair looks when he or she styles it. Pay attention when it's being styled, and ask how you can achieve the same look. Consider a special appointment for a styling lesson; it will be worth your time.

- Follow your natural hairline. If your hair is thinning, there are many choices and styles. Select a style based on what *looks* best rather than what covers your bald spot best. If you opt for a toupee or a hairpiece, buy the best you can afford. Nothing is more obvious or distracting than a bad toupee. If your hair loss is a problem for you and you can afford a hair transplant, consider doing so. It is costly, but it may be just what you need.

- Consider coloring your hair. Coloring your hair can enhance highlights, make your hair look thicker and healthier, and make you appear years younger. Both men and women color their hair. One of the chief reasons is to cover gray. Whatever color you choose should be a color found in nature, so avoid pastels, jet black, or very bright colors. Try to select a natural-looking color.

Richard was becoming discouraged in his job search. When he discovered he had been the second choice for three different positions, he was willing to do whatever he had to to become number one. A distinguished-looking man, his gray hair never bothered him before, but after several people suggested he color his hair to see if helped him find a job, he decided to do it. Everyone commented on how much younger he appeared. Shortly after, he found out he was the number one choice for a job and received an offer.

Richard will never know for sure if washing away his gray was the reason, but he assumes it was. He says he plans to color his hair indefinitely, and he encourages others to do the same. "Why give away my age?" he said. "If there's an easy way to look younger, why make life difficult by looking older? Age is a barrier, and gray hair gives away age. Why give someone a reason *not* to hire you?"

Don't give anyone a reason to overlook you, because of your hair's style, condition, or color. Your hair shouldn't be a focal point. Think of your hair as a frame for your face. When you have a special photo you decide to frame, the frame you choose should compliment, not distract from, the photo. The same is true for you; color and style your hair in a way that enhances your face. Draw attention to your face rather than to your hair.

FACE YOURSELF

As discussed in Chapter 5, your face is seen more than any other part of your body. When in conversation with someone, we speak to the face. Your face is important.

If you are a woman and you use makeup, use it sparingly. When makeup is appropriately applied, it can help the old look younger, the young look older, and the tired appear rested. Most women agree they look better wearing some makeup, although many are hesitant to wear it every day. Makeup is a touchy issue. When I am asked why women have to wear makeup when men do not, I don't have a definitive answer. However, men do have to shave; perhaps men's "makeup" is their facial hair. Men shave or shape their faces with facial hair while women simply use makeup!

If you don't like the way you look in makeup, it may be because you haven't used the right products or learned how to apply it to your face. There is an art to applying makeup so that you look natural. A good makeup artist can teach you how to properly apply makeup, and many of the consultants working behind cosmetic counters are trained to help you. To achieve the best look from makeup, the right color should be used sparingly, be well blended, and be appropriately applied. Mascara will lengthen your lashes and open your eyes, and a little blush and lipstick will brighten your face. When you wear neutral colors, you will not feel "made up." When you wear makeup, you add a touch of polish and a sense of completion to your overall look. Makeup should never be a distraction.

Women who don't wear makeup don't like to be told they should, just as men who wear full beards don't like to hear their beard could cause people to mistrust or misread them. Some men grow a beard each winter and shave each summer, but most men with facial hair have had their beards or mustaches for years.

When I present a workshop, I always ask the men in the room with facial hair how long they've had it. It never fails: I rarely hear, "Oh, I grew it last week." Instead, I hear five years, 10 years, or more. Others have never seen some of these men looking any other way.

I always challenge these men to consider shaving to see what lies beneath the hair on their faces. Many resist, but quite a few have accepted my challenge. I didn't realize how significant the change could be until I ran into a client, Greg, one day. After talking to him for several minutes, I finally said, "Greg, there's something different about you. Are you happier or something? You seem to be smiling more." Greg replied, "No, I shaved my mustache." I hadn't noticed that about him, but I did notice a difference. I realized I'd never been able to see his mouth before—or his expression. He looked happier because I could see his smile, which I'd never seen before!

When a mustache or beard obscures a man's facial muscles, others often have a hard time reading him. Some people actually interpret facial hair as rebellious or indicative of a need to hide something. Facial hair hides the facial muscles and facial expressions, which you now know are very important! Imagine what happens when people can't see any expression at all!

Facial hair is not always bad, however. In fact, for many men it enhances their looks or features. Facial hair can make a youthful, baby-faced man look more mature. Someone losing hair on his head may balance his look by having hair on his face. Some men want to cover their mouth, their complexion, or their double chin.

The safest, most professional, and acceptable look in business, however, is a clean-shaven face. This leaves nothing to be misunderstood. Many industries have become relaxed enough so that a mustache poses no problem as long as it is neatly trimmed and not a handlebar mustache. As long as you keep yours neatly trimmed and free of food or crumbs, you should be fine. Use a little more caution with beards. Judge whether a beard is appropriate based on your particular industry as well as your own preferences. However, if you have worn your mustache or beard for years and would never consider shaving, reconsider. Any time we resist change, we might want to look at our reasons for doing so.

If you refuse to wear makeup or refuse to shave, look at the reasons why. You may not see the need, but the people looking at you may see something you don't see.

LET YOUR HANDS DO THE TALKING

Everyone notices hands and nails. If you make presentations or speeches, conduct meetings or seminars, or just shuffle papers during the day, your hands *will* be seen. Dry, chapped hands, ragged or bitten nails, hang nails, and unclean fingernails will be noticed. Clean, well-manicured hands show you pay attention to detail.

Make sure your nails aren't too long. Many women enjoy acrylic nails, and all of the jewelry art available for nails today. However, in business, extremely long nails or missing nails are a distraction. Because brighter colors are more visible, wearing bright colors draws attention to your nails. Colored nail polish is fine, but avoid shocking fluorescent colors and dark browns, purples, or black. Fill in the color when you have chipped polish, and repair broken nails. One of the least expensive luxuries around is a professional manicure, so treat yourself to one. Whether you're male or female, well-manicured hands are a plus.

ACCENT WITH ACCESSORIES

Accessorizing is one of the least costly and most effective ways for people to create their own sense of style. If you feel confined in a suit or too conventional in a jacket, don't despair—there are options for you. Choosing appropriate accessories can help coordinate your overall look and give you a sense of individuality.

Accessories include jewelry, belt, purse, wallet, briefcase, eyeglasses, and even the pen you use.

The general rule about jewelry: Less is more. Avoid extremely large or gaudy jewelry, long, dangly earrings, and ankle bracelets. Wear no more than one ring on any one finger (unless it's a wedding set), no more than one or two rings on each hand, no more than one pin, and keep the number of bracelets you wear to a minimum. Avoid noisy jewelry, metal chains, and any item too trendy or questionable. Buy the best quality watches and jewelry you can afford, and stay away from any jewelry that looks cheap.

Think twice before you show up for an interview or go to work with any part of your body or face pierced, other than your ear. When the area that is pierced is unique, such as the eyebrow, nose, lip, or tongue—or if you have multiple piercings—you've separated yourself from the mainstream. This isn't always bad to do, but if your goal is to fit in and be recognized for your ideas and contributions, not your look, it won't help you. It could even hurt your chances of a job offer or advancement opportunities. Some people view body piercing negatively; you risk being viewed as rebellious, unusual, or simply too young to work in a mature environment. As business owners try to create a certain image for their business, they may worry about the reaction customers will have to your piercing. Although it's your decision, it's important for you to understand how you could be perceived and the potential consequences of looking different.

Earrings for men should be avoided; although this look is gaining accept-ance, it isn't the norm in business yet. Women should avoid wearing too many earrings in each ear: One earring per ear is the most traditional and acceptable. Like ponytails on men, certain looks just don't fit with a business suit or other professional styles. If your earrings or other pieces of jewelry are symbolic and very important to you, know the risks you are taking. You risk being perceived negatively by people who oppose a unique look, but you're always safest when you fit into the norm.

TATTOOS ARE TABOO

If you're thinking of getting a tattoo, don't. If you've already got one, cover it up. Tattoos may be growing in popularity, but they remain unpopular among busi-ness establishments. Tattoos are highly individual and are sometimes contro-versial. They can be distracting, unattractive, and potentially offensive to others.

Increasing numbers of companies are restricting visible tattoos and includ-ing guidelines in their policy manuals. In some instances, exposed tattoos are strictly forbidden.

Monty related his experience to me during a discussion about tattoos. His arms were covered with tattoos. He never gave it a second thought until his company decided to prohibit visible tattoos; tattoos had to be covered at all times. Although he lived in a warm climate, he could no longer wear short-sleeved shirts to work. Even women with small ankle tattoos were required to wear opaque tights or slacks at all times.

The new rules took Monty by surprise, but don't let it surprise you. More and more companies are adding similar clauses to their policies. Even if your tattoo is in an inconspicuous place, such as the lower part of your back, beware. If your pants sit low on your waist and your shirt rides high when you sit or bend, your tattoo will be exposed.

Think twice before you get a tattoo, and if you already have one that is obtrusive, consider having it removed. When it comes to tattoos, consider them all taboo.

CARRY IT WITH YOU

Your purse, briefcase, planner, and anything else you carry with you is an extension of what you wear. These things are part of your total look and will be noticed. Always buy the best quality item you can afford, and keep it clean and in good condition.

Rather than carrying a purse, a planner, and a briefcase, find an item that will hold all of your things. You don't want to be bogged down with all you have to carry. Make sure you keep your things neatly organized. You will look sloppy and out of control if your briefcase or planner is bulging at the seams and you have a difficult time finding what you need.

Always carry your business cards and your calendar with you. Keep your business cards in good condition; a carrying case for your cards is an inexpensive way to protect them from becoming bent or frayed at the edges. Always have a pad of paper and a pen or pencil with you. It's important to be able to take notes, jot down important information, or sign a document. As a professional, you should always be prepared to tend to business. Buy and use a pen that is neither cheap nor overly expensive. A chewed up, cheap-looking pen isn't going to contribute well to your overall professional image. While you don't need to spend a lot of money on the pen or pencil you use, purchase an attractive, good-quality writing tool. When you have something of value, you are less likely to lose it. Your pen, like your watch and your rings, will be noticed.

EYE CAN SEE YOU

When was the last time you changed eyeglasses? If it has been more than a couple of years, think about shopping for new frames. Eyewear should be current, in style, and flattering to the shape of your face. Frames are available in many fashionable styles and colors. Some people choose to buy several pairs and use them as an accessory to change their look. Avoid any frame that is too big, too small, too decorated, or too distracting in any way. Make sure your eyes are visible through your glasses, and that nothing gets in the way of your ability to make eye contact and connect with others.

Avoid wearing sunglasses indoors and buying tinted glasses. Tints create odd skin coloration around the eyes and may block eye contact.

Before selecting new eyewear, think about the look you want to achieve. If you're young and wish to appear older or more knowledgeable, glasses can do the trick. The general perception is that glasses can serve to make you appear more mature, knowledgeable, or intellectual.

If glasses are not something you enjoy or choose to wear, consider contact lenses. Contacts can be a great alternative to glasses, giving you the corrective lens you need without the bother of getting accustomed to frames.

TAKE CARE OF YOUR TEETH

A good smile is an important business tool, and fresh, clean teeth are a must. Proper hygiene, including flossing, checking your teeth often after eating, and regular brushing are the minimum you need to do to take care of that smile. Visit your dentist for regular preventive maintenance checkups, and don't put off dental work suggested by your dentist.

Your smile is important in almost any situation, and if you're embarrassed by it, you won't use it. People have experienced personality changes as a result of cosmetic dentistry. If you are self-conscious about your teeth, consider a visit to your dentist. Many adults bleach their teeth, wear braces or retainers, and opt for a variety of other common procedures. As a result, they find themselves feeling more confident and pleased with their appearance.

Cosmetic dentistry works miracles! Teeth that are naturally yellow, crooked, chipped, or cracked can be changed or repaired by your dentist. Bleaching, bonding, or applying laminate veneers are procedures often done to front teeth to correct the most visible tooth problems. Cosmetic dentistry can also involve straightening teeth that aren't aligned properly; teeth with gaps, or those that overlap, can be corrected by an orthodontist. You can also do your own bleaching at home; many products on the market produce excellent results at a fraction of the cost. If you choose to have work done on your teeth, you'll have a more confident, healthy smile.

Another important reason for proper dental care is your breath. Even when you look great, bad breath will destroy your overall image. Good oral hygiene is the most important step to fresh breath. Keep mints or breath fresheners around for those moments when you experience a bad taste in your mouth. However, avoid anything with too strong a smell; others shouldn't have to inhale your mints too.

THE SMELL OF SUCCESS

The employees of a small bank had a customer they referred to as "Mr. Smells." It wasn't his real name, of course; he acquired it because of his smell. Every time he came in the bank, he brought in a smell that lingered long after he left. Other customers noticed it too, and the employees couldn't figure out how everyone *but* Mr. Smell could smell the odor.

The reason is fairly simple: people become accustomed to their own scent within 15 minutes.

When we smell something pleasant, we respond favorably. When we smell something negative, we respond negatively. Smell is individual; you may love a lavender scent, but others may not. People seem to understand the importance of a good scent and look for ways to smell good. However, too much of a scent, no matter how pleasant it is, can be too much of a good thing.

The use of cologne or perfume is acceptable, but only if used lightly. Perfume can trigger an allergic reaction in some people and result in sneezing, headaches, or asthma attacks. For highly sensitive individuals, even the smallest whiff of perfume can send them into an allergic reaction. Wearing too much of any scent can easily become overpowering for those around you.

We're used to seeing no smoking signs, but I was surprised the first time I saw a "No Fragrance" sign. They are popping up in different places. I've heard about schools and public buildings banning fragrance, and I once saw a sign on the office door of a business owner that said, "STOP! If you are wearing perfume or cologne, DO NOT ENTER." Imagine someone ignoring the sign, walking in the office and triggering an allergic reaction as a result. What if you had an appointment, but had to cancel because you realized you wore perfume that day? What if you wore a fragrance you loved and discovered it reminded the person you were with of someone else? What if the "someone else" was someone he or she didn't care for?

Our sense of smell is powerful, often reminding us of past experiences and events. You never know what memory, good or bad, you may trigger in someone.

If you smoke, beware of the smell of smoke that tends to follow you wherever you go. You won't be able to smell the smoke on your clothes, but other people will. Smoking may have been prestigious years ago, but today smokers are viewed differently. Some people view smoking as a weakness and draw negative conclusions about people who smoke. Tobacco smoke is not considered a pleasant smell, so if you smoke, you'll need to take extra precautions to get rid of the smell. There are products on the market designed to neutralize the smell of smoke. Use them.

Bad breath is another sensitive issue to address. Nothing is worse than talking with someone who reeks of garlic and onions. Think twice about the food you eat, especially if you will be working closely with others. Certain odors tend to linger, and no matter what you do to cover them, it's difficult to do. It's a good idea to keep breath mints with you; however, even mint can be an overpowering smell. Consistent bad breath can be a system of a health problem, so check with your doctor with any concerns.

The best and safest smell of success is no smell at all. Here are some tips for the smell of success:

- Shower and bathe every day

- Use deodorant daily

- Brush and floss your teeth after eating

- Avoid eating foods with long-lasting odors

- Carry breath mints with you, but then use sparingly

- Air out your clothes after being in a smoke-filled room or restaurant

- Wash and launder your clothes frequently and check for odor after wearing

- Use fragrance sparingly, if at all

- Avoid scented hand lotions and hair sprays

- Beware of coffee breath

- Watch for nonverbal reactions; people who back away from you may be trying to tell you something

READY, SET, *OH, NO!*

If something happens in spite of careful planning, always go forth with confidence and try not to focus on the problem. It's likely to be noticed, yes, but don't allow yourself to be irretrievably distracted or defeated by it. Keep your chin up and sell *yourself.*

In some cases, if the problem is an overwhelmingly obvious one (such as lunch spilled down your front) and is so noticeable that you would feel better drawing attention to it right away, then do. Your "audience" will notice it anyway, but don't dwell on it; explain, apologize, and *move on.*

Reduce your chances of surprises later by taking a little extra time before you face your day. Before you head out the door each morning, run through this checklist to make sure you've taken care of those final touches.

- Is clothing clean?

- Is clothing free of spots and stains?

- Is clothing lint-free?

- Does clothing fit properly?

- Are buttons buttoned and zippers zipped?

- Are garments well pressed?

- Are undergarments hidden?

- Are shoes and briefcase polished and in good condition?

- Is hair neat, clean, and styled?

- Is breath fresh?

- Are teeth cleaned, flossed, and free of food?

- Is makeup blended?

- Are hands well groomed?

Last, before going out the door, check yourself from all angles in a full-length mirror. When you're paying attention to detail, you're staying on top of the little things that could make a big difference.

POINTS TO REMEMBER

1. **Update your hairstyle.** You don't want to look like you did years ago; create a new look that represents who you are today. Change your hairstyle every few years, just as you change your style of clothes.

2. **Accessorize on the conservative side.** Limit your accessories and avoid wearing jewelry any place other than your ears, neck, wrists, and hands.

3. **Carry an emergency kit with you.** Be prepared for last-minute emergencies and always present yourself in the best manner possible.

4. **People notice hands.** Take care of your hands and keep them clean and well manicured.

5. **Smile!** Maintain your best professional tool—your smile! Pay attention to daily and preventive care, and do talk with your dentist about what you can do to improve your teeth and ultimately your smile!

6. **Be scent-free.** No smell is better than the wrong smell; go easy on perfumes, bathe daily, and keep your breath fresh.

7. **Maintain your clothing.** Dry clean, launder, and use fabric protector on clothing. Always make sure your clothing is clean, pressed, lint-free, and in good condition.

True or False?

1. The safest smell in business is no smell at all.

TRUE.

It's better to smell fresh and good than bad, but what smells good to one person may not smell so good to another. Play it safe and keep your smell from getting in your way. No smell is the safest smell of all.

2. A great way to camouflage a bald spot is to grow your hair long on one side and comb it over the area where hair is thinning.

FALSE.

Don't try to pretend you're not losing your hair by stretching the last few strands across your head. Let your hair follow its natural hairline. If you are too uncomfortable with your hair loss, consider a hair transplant or a good-quality hairpiece.

3. Glasses can make you appear more knowledgeable and mature.

TRUE.

Glasses in an up-to-date style that are flattering to your face can add a distinguished, sophisticated look. A younger person often looks older and wiser in glasses.

4. Don't spend a lot of money on a pen. It's a disposable item and is too easy to lose to justify a big investment.

FALSE.

Little things do make a difference. When you use a cheap pen, you simply don't project a professional image. Every detail of your look should be consistent with the image you want to project, even something as small and seemingly insignificant as a pen.

5. Tattoos are fine as long as they aren't too big or too visible.

FALSE.

Tattoos are taboo in many business environments, no matter how small. Some companies have policies banning tattoos. Keep your tattoos covered.

6. People become accustomed to their own smell very quickly.

TRUE.

We become accustomed to our own scent within 15 minutes. You will not be able to smell your cologne or body odor, but it doesn't mean others can't.

Chapter 9

Tune in to Technology

True or False?

1. You should use your first and last name when calling someone.

2. When you're participating in a teleconference and need to step away, mute the call.

3. It's poor business practice not to return calls.

4. Don't use smiley faces in business correspondence.

5. Ask permission before faxing a large document.

6. It is rude to answer your cell phone when you are in a meeting.

7. Don't use the return receipt feature when sending e-mail unless you must.

THE TROUBLE WITH TECHNOLOGY

Technology has changed the way we do business, interact with others, make purchases, and spend our free time. Have you ever wondered what it would be like without some of the technological conveniences you've become accustomed to? What if you didn't have access to voice mail, couldn't send e-mail, and didn't own a cell phone? Would it be a minor inconvenience or a dramatic shock to your system? What aspects (if any) would you enjoy, and what do you think you would miss or struggle with the most?

The following exercise will give you an opportunity to explore some of your attitudes and beliefs about technology's impact on you. Please read each statement and note whether you agree or disagree with each one.

Do you agree or disagree with the following statements?

1. If I have something difficult to say, I'd rather say it an e-mail than in person.

2. I've said things electronically that I would never say in person.

3. I use caller ID to screen my calls.

4. I'd rather leave a voice mail message than talk directly with someone.

5. Sometimes I wait to call someone until I am sure I will get a person's voice mail.

6. I would be lost without my cell phone.

7. I talk on my cell phone in public places.

8. I don't always proofread the e-mails I send.

9. I have relationships with people I never see or talk to; we only communicate electronically.

10. I talk on the phone and use my computer simultaneously.

Look over your responses, focusing on the statements you agree with. Think about the implications of each statement. As you read this chapter you will become more aware of your "electronic image." The tips and ideas you pick up will help you maximize your use of technology.

Technology has improved our lives over the years, and according to predictions, even bigger changes are yet to come. Most of us have become accustomed to working alone; we've forgotten that tasks once requiring the help of another person are now completed without communicating with anyone. It may be more efficient, but what is the cost? Are we paying a price for our lack of human interaction?

Many people have a love/hate attitude toward technology. You might love the convenience technology offers but hate the constant pressure to stay connected. You might love being accessible to your family or clients but hate the intrusion on your privacy. You might love the ability to work from home yet hate the added time you spend working. It's become almost impossible to "get away from it all." Being accessible 24 hours a day can be taxing, but so can the feeling that comes from being disconnected. If you've ever had a computer or other important device malfunction, you know how paralyzing the experience can be. The trouble with technology isn't that we can't live without it; it's that we haven't figured out how we're supposed to live *with it*.

THE 411 ON THE TELEPHONE

In telephone and voice mail interactions, your voice says it all. Face-to-face, you have the added benefit of your gestures, eye contact, posture, facial expressions, stance, and body movements. These nonverbal cues influence what the listener hears and the meaning he or she ascribes to what you say. Phone and voice mail exchanges eliminate these nonverbal cues, forcing the listener to focus solely on your words and tone. *Remember, how you say it and your tone of voice are more important than what you say.*

Voice mail can save you time and trouble. Although you are better off talking with someone directly, when you aren't able to reach someone, use voice mail to your advantage. I've set up appointments, meetings, and lunch dates through voice mail without ever directly talking to the people involved. If you're friendly and efficient, you can make a great impression by using voice mail savvy! You can encourage people to make decisions and get answers to your questions. I've left stern, firm, direct, and urgent sounding messages on voice mail, often in frustration after repeated calls have been left unanswered. With the right tone and message, people will respond!

I once consulted with the ticket department of a national football team. The salespeople, who sold season tickets over the phone, had to deal with both happy and unhappy fans. I was hired to help improve their customer service and overall professionalism. One of the first things I noticed was that there were no standard telephone procedures. Each person answered the phone differently; there was no continuity. One of the first things we did was implement a uniform greeting and closing. Everyone agreed this would make a big difference both for the salespeople and the customers. No longer did the mood or stress level of a salesperson determine their greeting; the positive attitude conveyed when answering the phone set the tone of the conversation and influenced customers' impressions of the entire ticket office.

How do you answer *your* phone? Does your greeting convey warmth and friendliness? Do you sound rushed or hassled? Think about the impression you *want* to make and *plan* a greeting accordingly.

In all of your telephone conversations, you are judged by the emotional quality in your voice. That emotional quality is affected by whether you're stressed, tired, or impatient. If you're speaking fast or slow, loud or soft, or in a monotone without expression, you're sending some unintended messages.

Did you know that your mental and emotional state of mind can cause physiological changes in your body that affect your voice? For example, if you're stressed, the tension in your body constricts muscles, including those in your face and around your mouth and throat. Tighter muscles in these areas change the quality of your voice. Before getting on the phone, get into the habit of taking a few deep breaths to help you relax. This will improve the tonal quality of your voice, as well as the pace of your message. Clear your throat *before* you pick up the phone. Keep water nearby and drink plenty of it if you use your voice frequently. Record a few voice mail messages and play them back. Rerecord until you're satisfied with how you sound.

Many people change their messages daily, stating the date, their where-abouts, and their availability. When you find the right words, practice how you say them. And watch out for the deadly monotone that creeps into many of our recorded messages! Most important, if you plan on changing your message each day, *remember to change it each day.* It is irritating to callers to listen to the recitation of your schedule from a day, a week, or a month ago. No matter how friendly you sound, this lack of attention to detail will be distracting.

Don't say you'll return a call if you're not going to. Most of us leave a standard message, "I can't take your call right now. Leave a message and I'll get back to you as soon as I can." Yet most of us lie! Many never intend to return calls at all yet leave a message that says they will. If you know you will not return calls, do not say that you will! If you receive so many calls that you cannot possibly return them all, then either have someone else return them for you or state on your message that you cannot return all calls. Suggest they send you something in writing, but do not make promises you will not keep.

Start paying attention to all the excuses people give you for failing to return a phone call. "I've been so busy." "We've been bogged down." "The work load is incredible." "I've been out all week." What all of this really says is, "I'm too busy to call you—you're not that important."

If the president of a company or an important client left you a message, you *would* find the time to call him or her back. The fact is, we're all guilty of mak-ing judgments and assumptions about the intentions of others. Although it might be a perfectly natural reaction to be put off by calls from those you don't know, especially when they might be trying to sell you something, you never know what opportunity that call might present.

I've dealt with company presidents who I would never have expected to return my calls, yet they did. And I've worked with other people who *never* returned my calls, even after we'd met and they'd promised a return call. Returning calls promptly says something about you and your professionalism. What kind of reputation do you want to have?

It's easy to present a polished professional image over the phone.

- Answer as many calls as you can in person.

- Always answer your phone by the third ring. If you can't answer your phone quickly, then have someone else do it or switch on your voice mail.

- If you can't return a call, leave a message that states you cannot return all calls. Suggest the caller mail or e-mail his or her request or information to you.

- Leave a warm and welcoming message that conveys as closely as possible when you'll be able to return calls.

- Always identify yourself by your first and last name when calling someone and give your company name as well. Except for close business associates with whom you talk frequently, do not assume the person you're calling will know who you are without identification.

- Return calls promptly within one business day.

- Return *all* calls; even unknown callers might represent potential opportunities.

- If you can't return your calls personally, have someone else get back to the callers on your behalf.

- Don't wait until after business hours to return calls. Many people do this solely because they can leave voice mail messages, effectively shortening the total time it takes to return calls. All you gain is time. You lose your edge in being able to control your image, message, and sense that you're ready to take on whatever the challenge is and find solutions—now.

- Don't put anyone on hold for more than 30 seconds without checking back and giving the caller the option to continue holding, leave a message, or call back.

- Try not to make it a habit of passing messages to others to handle. Doing so sends a message to callers that they are not important enough for you to personally respond. Return your own calls so you're in a key position both to know what's going on and to offer your skill or expertise to the situation at hand.

- Coach secretaries or receptionists to screen calls in a way that is not obvious to the caller. Saying, "I'll see if he's available. May I tell him who's calling?" is a polite way to learn the caller's identity and allow you to determine whether you want to take the call at that moment. But again, take as many calls as you can. Messages just pile up for later, and you sacrifice that sense of immediacy, readiness, and availability that can be very important in relations with clients, customers, and coworkers.

- Keep messages you leave on others' voice mail short and to the point. State your name and number clearly.

- Remember to speak *slowly* when leaving a telephone number or address. The person on the other end will need to write it down.

- Always repeat your name and telephone number at the end of your message.

TELEPHONE TACTICS

If you are with someone and the phone rings, think twice before answering it. Not answering the phone or letting it go to voice mail is a compliment to the person you are with because it shows respect for his or her time. However, when you know you will need to take a call during a meeting, inform your visitor at the beginning of the meeting. When you take the call, make it brief. Any time you take a call when you are with someone else, you are clearly communicating that the *caller* is more important than the person you are with.

When you are with someone who takes a call that lasts more than a few minutes, you can choose to leave. You may decide the meeting is over or simply take a brief break. By doing so, you are not only giving the person some privacy to continue the conversation, but making better use of your own time as well. You can indicate that you will be back in a few minutes or inform the person that you will be in your office if he or she would like to continue the meeting once he or she is off the phone.

When you are trying to reach someone and have left several messages without getting a response, get creative. Try talking to the receptionist to find out the best time to reach someone. Vary the times of your calls to increase your chance of connecting. Call before nine o'clock in the morning or after five o'clock in the afternoon and you just may reach the person before or after normal work-day hours. If you've tried everything and you still can't get people to return your calls, consider that they might be sending you a message. *The lack of a response is a response.* It may not be the response you wanted, but you need to pay attention to and understand the silent message you are receiving.

Too often we dismiss calls from unfamiliar names and voices, but sometimes opportunities await us. This is why it is important not to jump to conclusions before understanding the reason someone is calling. Some people screen their calls, and if the name that comes up on the caller ID is unfamiliar, they won't answer it. Doing so is a short-term convenience that could cost you in the long run.

A seminar participant, Leslie, once shared a great story about not returning phone calls. Once, when she needed some legal advice, Leslie called and left a message with an attorney in another town who had been highly recommended to her. He didn't call her back, so after a week or so she hired another attorney. *Two months later* Leslie received a collect call from the first attorney. Obviously Leslie had no business to give him and, put out by the collect call, told him so.

At a meeting some six months later, Leslie was introduced to this same attorney. He said, "Your name is so familiar—do I know you?" Leslie replied, "Well, I called you about six months ago. It took you two months to return the call and then you called collect—but no, we've never met!" Embarrassed, the attorney replied, "Gee, I'm sorry. I didn't realize you were a client of mine." "I'm not," Leslie answered, "But I *could* have been had you returned my call!"

Early in my business career, I approached the president of a major retail chain as a potential client. Not only did I get through to him personally, but he gave me an appointment for the next day. He didn't know me, and was a busy man. He was willing to reach out rather than use his assistant to fend off callers. His business is thriving. His accessibility to a perfect stranger reflects his openness to the people who work for him as well. What an impression he made on me and how rare to find that kind of accessibility in a busy chief executive!

Failing to return or accept calls limits you. You convey a nonverbal message to those you avoid: "I'm not interested in you; I'm too busy." *Being accessible will improve your image and potential for success.*

Don't ever assume anything! I receive many calls soliciting *my* business, and I try to practice what I preach by returning every call I receive. On one occasion, I had recently been featured on the news and was receiving many calls. One was from a printer, and the message was simply to call Rhoda at XYZ Printers. I called back to see what she wanted, but she was unavailable. I assumed she wanted to try to solicit my business for printing, so I said "Tell her Sue Morem called. I am returning her call, and you can tell her I'm not interested in any printing. I am very happy with the printer I am using." Well, Rhoda called me back and let me know that she was *not* trying to sell me printing. She actually had a business opportunity for me—she was looking for a speaker for an annual meeting. I was embarrassed and apologized, but knew I had blown it; I did not make a great first impression.

Do you think I got the job? No, I did not, and I can honestly say I didn't expect to. My attempt at efficiency backfired. I inaccurately assumed I knew the reason for the call. The "clues" we get aren't always enough to solve the message puzzle. Don't jump to conclusions, and always leave a bit of information as to what you're calling about when you leave a message to help others avoid the same kind of mistake I made.

When you make outgoing calls, basic rules of etiquette are important. Recall the habits and mannerisms that irritate you when you take calls from others and avoid doing those things yourself. Practice your opening words so you always sound confident and friendly in those crucial first few seconds. Remember, first impressions happen whether the contact is made in person or by phone. Your opening words, your tone, your pitch, and the warmth of your voice will make a lasting impression.

Avoid using a speakerphone unless you need to take notes or are including other people in the conversation. Sound is amplified through a speakerphone, and you risk your conversations being heard by everyone within listening distance. Always inform someone when you are on a speakerphone; unless you do, the person on the other end could say something unintended for others who may overhear. If you like the convenience of having your hands free, invest in a headset instead. When several people are using a speakerphone from the same location, start the conversation by identifying each person who is in the room. Each time someone speaks, he or she should identify him or herself before talking.

Read through the following list of good telephone protocol. When these rules are violated, we often feel put off, even angry. Note the rules you personally *most* dislike to have violated. Then hold that thought— you'll remember to be sure not to do those things to others when phoning and leaving messages. Add a check mark to those you know you need to work on.

- Good telephone etiquette requires that all phone calls be returned within one business day.

- Make sure you have a purpose for your call, because a call interrupts someone and takes time away from doing something else.

- Get to the point; avoid lengthy small talk.

- Give oral feedback; don't let your listener hang on in silence.

- Don't eat, smoke, or chew gum while on the phone, and if you have to sneeze, cough, or blow your nose, cover the mouthpiece or place the person on hold.

- Don't use speakerphone without permission.

- If you reach a wrong number, apologize.

- If a caller dials your number by mistake, graciously tell him or her that he or she reached a wrong number.

- Avoid calling anyone at home before 8 A.M. and after 10 P.M.

- Give full attention to the person on the telephone; don't try to multitask.

- If disconnected, the person who placed the call should reestablish the call.

- Answer the telephone by the third ring.

- Don't take calls when someone is in your office.

- If a call comes when you're in someone's office and he or she needs to take the call, offer to step outside.

- Identify yourself and your company when making a call.

- Smile while on the phone and you will sound friendlier.

- Stand up when on the phone and you will sound more energized.

- Don't say you will return a call unless you know you will.

PUT AWAY THE CELL PHONE

If there's one thing that gets people talking, it's cell phones. People are talking *on* them and talking *about* them. Many people agree that cell phone use has spun out of control. Just because you *can* be accessible 24 hours a day doesn't mean you *should* be. Asserting your right to talk to whom you want whenever you want to infringes on the rights of others; no one wants to be forced to listen to the details of your personal problems or medical conditions.

Cell phones ring and distract people *everywhere*. It's disturbing to hear a ringing phone when you are intently listening to a speaker, attending a concert, or watching a play. It's even worse when a phone rings during a funeral, a wedding, or any other sacred event. Embarrassed cell phone owners shrug their shoulders and apologize but often fail to do the responsible thing and *turn off the phone*. Instead, they answer it, then look for a place to take their call. Be a responsible cell phone user:

- Never use your cell phone for business calls unless you must. The quality of the connection is too unreliable.

- Don't yell or shout when on the phone. Most people talk louder on a cell phone, so keep it down.

- Turn your phone *off* when you are in a meeting, listening to a speaker, attending a performance or a ceremony, or are in a medical facility, theatre, library, classroom, or on the golf course.

- Turn your phone *off* when you are with someone else.

- If you are expecting a call you must accept, inform those you are with ahead of time.

- If you must take a call when in a meeting, at a restaurant, or with others, step outside.

- Honor environments that are phone-free and follow all requests to turn your phone off.

- Use the vibrate feature when you must keep your phone turned on when with someone or in a public place.

- Keep your ringer volume turned down.

- Keep your eyes on the road, whether you are walking or driving. In some states it is against the law to talk on a handheld cell phone and drive. Use an earpiece and pay attention. Better yet, don't talk on the phone!

- Find a private place to have your conversation. Avoid talking on your phone when you are in close quarters with others or in a public place.

Common sense and common courtesy are the basics of good cell phone manners. The easiest way to minimize your risk of offending someone is by putting away your phone. The less you use it, the less offensive you will be. And always remember to *think before you speak*.

You never know who might be listening.

GET THE MOST OUT OF VIRTUAL MEETINGS

Nothing is quite like a face-to-face meeting; always make it your first choice. However, when distance and time make it difficult or impossible, you do have other options. You can set up a conference call or hold a teleconference, a videoconference, or a web conference. There are growing numbers of ways to hold virtual meetings, which are increasingly replacing standard business meetings. Although some protocol is specific to conference calls, the courtesies common to any type of meeting will be expected.

1. Schedule the meeting; set the date and determine the time it will begin and end. Notify all participants and distribute an agenda in advance, including the purpose and objective of the meeting.

2. Begin and end *on time.* If you are dialing in to join a larger conference call, dial in a few minutes early so the meeting can begin on time.

3. Participate from a quiet location; shut your door and shut out background noises. Turn off the radio, the television, and silence the ringer on your phone. The sound of you eating, shuffling papers, or typing on your computer will be heard over the phone and be disruptive to the call.

4. Announce your arrival and introduce yourself. State your name each time you begin to speak.

5. If you are leading the meeting, make it as interactive as possible. If you are participating, *participate,* but don't monopolize the conversation or interrupt.

6. If you are listening to a speaker and are not participating or need to leave momentarily, mute your phone. Don't use the hold button unless you are certain no music will play when you do.

7. If you are participating in a videoconference, dress professionally and in neutral colors. Look at both the camera and other participants in the room when speaking, speak loudly and clearly, listen carefully, and don't carry on side conversations. Most important, show some personality; smile, nod your head, raise your eyebrows, and look interested.

8. If you run out of time, either ask permission to continue the call or decide to schedule another meeting.

9. Conclude the meeting and bring it to a formal close.

PUT IT IN WRITING

Memos are a primary form of internal business correspondence, ranging in use from "Meet me for lunch at Tony's" to "Bring your full report to the investor's meeting and be prepared to present it." Whether you use e-mail or handwrite a memo, how you look on paper (or a computer screen) has its first and lasting impression too. If you make a mistake, it will be remembered for a long time.

Do you ever get memos with your name misspelled? Or ones with a typo? How about a memo with incorrect information or the wrong meeting time or place that has to be followed up with a memo correcting the first memo? Any one of these things has a tendency to be remembered. Two or more of these kinds of correspondence errors *really* stick to you.

All memos and other written correspondence should be carefully prepared. Use the same process as you would to prepare a speech or other verbal presentation. Written messages or information can convey several different meanings, depending upon word choice, content, etc. The overall impression a written document makes depends on grammar, punctuation, spelling, accuracy of content, and neatness of format.

To make a positive impression, follow these tips:

- If your signature is being used, read the document personally before sending it. Don't depend on anyone else for final proofreading.

- If your signature is required, sign it yourself. Don't allow someone else to sign your name.

- Proofread all correspondence. Check for grammar, punctuation, and spelling.

- Make sure all written documents are clearly and neatly formatted so they're easy to read and look professional.

- Print all written correspondence or other reports or documents on good-quality paper using a high-resolution printer.

- Check and double check the content for accuracy. If the meeting is going to be in the A conference room at the Savannah Hotel at noon, double check all the details with the hotel before the memo goes out.

- If you have to send a memo out to correct a problem of some kind, don't blame anyone. Simply state the correction and apologize briefly for any inconvenience caused.

- Handwritten notes are acceptable, but they must be legible. They show a personal touch and sincerity, especially in thank-you notes.

I once worked with a man named Kim. When I was out of the office, I had my assistant draft a memo to Kim to get out that day. When I returned to the office, I found to my horror that the memo was addressed to Ms. Kim Smith—and I'd had my secretary sign my name to the memo as well! I was very embarrassed and made an apology. I had met with Kim face-to-face so, of course, I knew he was a man. I learned never to let anything with my name on it go out unless I've read it. I now sign all of my own correspondence.

Another time I had a proposal go out without seeing it first. Only after it was too late, I noticed spelling and other errors. It was a hard way to learn an important lesson. I've learned never to assume anything and to be very specific with every detail when turning things over to someone else. After all, the final responsibility lies with the one who signs the document.

FAX FACTS

When fax is your preferred use of communication, follow a few basic guidelines:

- Call to notify the person you're faxing to expect the fax, including the number of pages.

- Mail a hard copy when the document should be retained in files for future reference.

- Don't fax thank-you notes.

- Number each page and note the total number of pages you are sending.

- Avoid sending or asking for very large documents to be faxed unless necessary.

- Make sure you write the name of the person the fax is intended for on the cover page.

- Make sure *your* name, fax number, and phone number are on the cover page.

YOUR ELECTRONIC IMAGE

E-mail has become the preferred choice of correspondence for most people. It's easy to send and receive and saves both money and time. Some people believe e-mail correspondence is meant to be casual, while others perceive the only difference between e-mail and standard mail is the speed with which it is delivered. Both points of view are valid, but neither one is completely accurate. The medium you choose to send your mail shouldn't be the determining factor; you must consider the type of document you're sending, whom you're sending it to, your objectives, and the kind of impression you want to make.

If you want to play it safe, treat e-mail the same way you would treat any other type of mail; by following the basic standard letter-writing procedures. Every e-mail you send should be a positive reflection of both you and your organization. Once a document is sent to someone else, you have no control over who sees it or what happens to it. Your document can be deleted, printed, filed, distributed, or forwarded to one or 1,000 people. *Anything* you put into writing has the potential to be used against you. Think twice about *everything* you put into writing.

Always strive to present a professional image, whether you are communicating in person, on the phone, or in writing. As communication becomes more frequent with someone, you'll have more latitude in deciding how casual or formal you need to be, but don't make preemptive assumptions about anyone. The way you present yourself through e-mail should be consistent with *every* aspect of your professional image.

Many organizations monitor employee Internet use. Familiarize yourself with the policies of your company, and *always* follow proper procedures. E-mail is so easy to use, we often forget there are rules we should follow. Follow the rules of e-mail etiquette—often referred to as "Netiquette"—and use e-mail to your advantage. Some Netiquette fundamentals are:

- **Be responsive.** Respond to e-mail promptly, preferably within one business day. When you are unavailable, inform others by using the auto-response feature.

- **Be concise and to the point.** Increase the chances of your e-mail being read by being brief.

- **Maximize your subject line.** The more informative the subject line, the more likely your e-mail will be read.

- **Be bland.** Adding stationary, fancy fonts, or bright colors to your e-mail makes it more difficult to read.

- **Cut out the cute stuff.** Forgo using smiley faces :), frowns :(, or any other emoticons.

- **Write out words.** Avoid using abbreviations or Internet slang.

- **Proofread.** Never send e-mail without proofreading it first. Check for grammatical and spelling errors, flow, and intent.

- **Sign your e-mail.** Include a signature with your name and contact information.

- **Ask before sending.** Don't assume its OK to send attachments; company policy may prohibit opening them.

- **Don't SHOUT.** Using capital letters is the equivalent of shouting at someone.

- **Rethink the return receipt option.** This option is a benefit to *you,* not the recipient. If you wouldn't send it certified mail, then don't request a return receipt.

- **Use complete sentences.** Sending an e-mail that says "yes" or "sounds good" is insufficient information. The recipient of such e-mail will not know what you are responding to. Take the time to write out what you need to say.

- **Know your priorities.** Few messages are truly urgent. Don't overuse the high priority feature; save it for a really important and urgent e-mail.

- **Forgo forwarding.** Do not forward chain letters, jokes, stories, warnings, or any other unimportant information to anyone unless they've asked you to.

- **Sit on it.** Never send an e-mail you've written while upset or angry. Save it, leave it, and come back to it once you've had a chance to cool down.

DO YOU HIDE BEHIND TECHNOLOGY?

Use technology to your advantage, but don't depend on it or use e-mail as your only form of communication. Sending e-mail or leaving a message on voice mail is convenient and takes less time than meeting with someone in person. However, both lack interaction, and neither is completely reliable. There is no guarantee your message will arrive or that your intentions will be understood.

It is difficult to *feel* compassion without *hearing* the gentle tone in someone's voice and *seeing* the tender expression on someone's face. *Reading* the words "I'm sorry" is not equivalent to *hearing* them.

If you want to have strong relationships, you need to make time to nurture them. Good relationships require time and effort. Don't rely on e-mail; get into the habit of picking up the phone to say "hello" and schedule time together with people who are important to you.

Technical interaction will never replace human interaction. It might be *easier* to send an e-mail or leave a voice mail message, but the easy route is rarely the most effective one. Don't hide behind e-mail or any other type of technology.

If you have something important to say, **say it.** *Better yet,* **say it in person.**

POINTS TO REMEMBER:

1. **Smile when you are on the phone.** Put a smile in your voice; the person on the other end can't see you, but he or she can hear your interest or lack of it.

2. **Return all phone calls within one business day.** The faster you return a call, the clearer you communicate your interest and professionalism. If you know you won't be able to return calls, don't say you will.

3. **Be a responsible cell phone owner.** Your cell phone is your responsibility; keep it on vibrate, or better yet, turn it *off.* Give priority to the people you are with, not your phone.

4. **Proofread every document you write or send.** Catch mistakes before they catch you off guard; it's easier to correct a problem *before* it becomes one.

5. **Be polite.** Whether you are on the phone, leaving a message, sending an e-mail, or are in a virtual meeting, be just as polite and resourceful as you would be during in-person interactions.

6. **Don't hide behind technology.** Don't take the easy way out or shy away from people. Keep up your interpersonal skills; if you have something important to say, use your voice to say it—*in person.*

True or False?

1. You should use your first and last name when calling someone.
TRUE.
Never assume someone knows you well enough to recognize your voice. The person you are calling probably receives many calls and may be unable to place every Chris or Kelly without additional information.

2. When you are participating in a teleconference and need to step away, mute the call.

TRUE.

It is the only way to be certain you won't disrupt the meeting.

3. It's poor business practice not to return calls.

TRUE.

You might be busy or have an important position, but it's no excuse for failing to return calls.

4. Don't use smiley faces in business correspondence.

TRUE.

If you wouldn't put a smiley sticker on your business letterhead or draw faces on a proposal, then don't include them in your e-mail. Smiles and other emoticons are too cutesy for some and are downright offensive to others.

5. Ask permission before faxing a large document.

TRUE.

A large fax will tie up the fax machine, making it inaccessible to others, which can be a problem in some offices. When you have a large document to send, check before you fax and make sure it is the preferred method of sending it.

6. It is rude to answer your cell phone when you are in a meeting.

TRUE.

If your phone rings because you forgot to turn it off or place it on vibrate, apologize. Turn the ringer off, but don't answer it unless you must. It is rude to take a call when you are in a meeting with one or 100 people.

7. Don't use the return receipt feature when sending e-mail unless you must.

TRUE.

The return receipt feature should be saved for the times you must be certain your e-mail arrived, not to satisfy your curiosity.

Chapter 10

Social Graces in Business Places

True or False?

1. Good manners can be cost-effective.

2. Profanity can add impact if used sparingly.

3. You should always plan to arrive at business events "fashionably late," which means about five to 10 minutes late.

4. Where you sit can influence the outcome of an interaction.

5. Working at home is easier than working in an office.

6. The decision to date a coworker is no one's business but your own.

7. Men should show their respect for women by opening doors, pulling out chairs, and helping them put on their coats.

8. Attendance at the company holiday party is optional.

KNOW THE UNWRITTEN RULES

Your social skills and understanding of business etiquette are crucial to your professional success. Appropriate behavior and manners are just as important in the office as they are at a business lunch, a formal black-tie affair, or a social function related to business. Understanding and following the basic rules of business etiquette will give you an advantage. It's simply a matter of knowing what to do, and how and when to do it.

Every office, every business, and every industry has its own unwritten (and often unspoken) code of behavior and rules. You can learn much of what you need to know about etiquette in your workplace simply by watching those around you. You might be fortunate enough to have a mentor who is willing to teach you the rules, including that "silent code." But if you don't have such a person or network in your life, observe people you admire or those who hold positions you strive to obtain. Watch for quiet clues: notice how they look, act, and present themselves. Your goal is to look and act like someone who is already where you want to be.

Although there are exceptions to every rule, most professional people know not to swear, spit, touch, holler, or belittle anyone. It is not always easy to maintain a professional demeanor and can take a tremendous amount of self-control in certain situations. The most professional and respected people are those who exhibit restraint and self-control, are aware of themselves and others, and strive to be a positive influence on those around them.

View etiquette as a powerful tool to enhance your image. Look at etiquette as an absolute, must-learn skill. Without this tool, you simply can't move ahead. If you want to be taken seriously and earn the respect and trust of others, you don't need be uptight, but you do need to be in control! Etiquette finishes off an image that tells others you're savvy and in command of any situation.

OFFICE AND CUBE ETIQUETTE

If you have a private office, consider yourself fortunate; most people work without such luxuries. Millions of people work in a cubicle or "cube" and have little space to call their own. Working in an open office environment can be challenging. Working in tight quarters can either cultivate camaraderie with coworkers or be a source of irritation and hostility between them. Anything and everything you do to foster good working relationships will make your life much easier. It is important to respect the privacy of others, even when it appears there is little or no privacy to respect. It doesn't matter if you like your coworkers or simply tolerate them, your days will run smoother and be more productive if you can get along with the people you see and work with every day.

Start by acknowledging and getting acquainted with the people you work with; not just the ones you deal with day to day, but also others who you see infrequently. Don't be so preoccupied that you fail to acknowledge the people you pass by every day. Greeting people you work with sets a positive tone. Just because you talked with someone the previous day doesn't mean you shouldn't say hello the following day.

Our coworkers often mean more to us than we realize on a day-to-day basis. I remember how moved I was as I watched a woman being interviewed on a television news program on September 18, 2001, just one week after the attack on the World Trade Center. She spoke about how much that experience changed her perspective on many things, including her colleagues. She couldn't believe how much she missed them, and how anxious she was to see them all again. When they showed the tearful reunion of these coworkers meeting one another for the first time since the day of the attack, I realized that up until that moment, they didn't know if they'd ever see each other again.

Tragedy and loss have a way of forcing us to put things in perspective, but it shouldn't take such unhappy events to make us take a good look at the people who surround us. Have you taken the time to get to know the people you work with? It's easy to get so caught up in our day-to-day activities that we lose perspective. It's not just the work we do that's important; the people we work with are important too. Over your lifetime, you probably will spend more time with the people you work with than you will with some of your closest friends and family. You may as well get to know these people.

While you will probably develop closer relationships with some of your cohorts more than others, it is important to show respect for *everyone,* including each person's personal workspace, no matter how minimal it may be.

COURTESY COUNTS

I'm not surprised when people tell me that some of my advice is common sense. It is. When it comes to treating people well, there isn't a lot of new information available. The rules haven't changed much over the years. You either treat people well or you don't. You're either courteous or you're not. It's that simple.

You probably already know the basics of common courtesy, but do you tap into that knowledge? Do you consistently treat people courteously, or do you dismiss what you know about being courteous because you assume it's old-fashioned?

Think about *your* social graces outside the office. Then think about a typical day and picture yourself going about your daily activities in the office. Are you as aware of your behavior *in* the office as you are outside of it? Are you a pleasure to be around or a source of irritation to your coworkers?

Every phone call you make, e-mail you send, conversation you start, and question you ask creates work for someone else. The time it takes to deal with and respond to you takes time *away* from something or someone else.

When you have a question, do you attempt to find the answer or do you take the easy route and ask someone else to answer it instead? Do you avoid interrupting someone when you see he or she is busy working, or are you so focused on what *you* want and need that you don't even notice? Think twice before you impose your wants and needs on someone else.

When you enter someone else's office, you are technically an intruder. Unless you've been asked to come by, you may not be welcome. You wouldn't make a habit of popping by, unannounced, to someone's home; don't make a habit of popping into someone's office or cubicle too often either. Think twice before barging into someone's personal office space. Always knock before entering, and if there is no door, stand in the entrance and ask permission to enter before going in. Once you are in someone's space, don't get too comfy too soon; before you plop yourself down in a chair, ask if it's a good time to talk with them. The time may be perfect for *you,* and *you* may have an important question you want answered, but it may be a bad time for the person you are interrupting. When you initiate an unsolicited visit, you *are* interrupting someone.

When someone enters *your* office, stop for a moment and look up to acknowledge him or her. If you are expecting the person, stand up, greet them warmly, shake hands, and indicate with a hand gesture where to sit. Wait for your guest to be seated before you sit down and wait to be seated until invited to do so when you are in someone else's office.

Whether you like your coworkers or simply tolerate them, it is important to act professionally and treat everyone with courtesy and respect. Treat people as you would like to be treated, and do so in all situations. Working in tight quarters can put your patience and tolerance level to the test; your coworkers will appreciate your attention to the following:

- Keep sound levels low. Turn down the volume on your computer, phone, and radio, and talk quietly when you are talking with someone, whether it is on the phone or in person. Never use a speakerphone, as sound is amplified on a speakerphone and your conversation will echo throughout the entire office.

- Keep aromas and scents to a minimum. Avoid eating strong-smelling foods or wearing strong colognes or perfumes. Think twice before removing your shoes. Save the room freshener and potpourri for your home; the best smelling office has a neutral smell or no smell at all.

- Keep your decor simple. Remember, this is your *office,* not a dorm room or private home. Don't overdo it with photos or posters, and make sure anything you display is in good taste and appropriate for an office environment.

- Keep your personal office area neat and clean. It may be your desk and your work area, but others have to walk by and see it. Take time each day to get rid of old food bags, empty soda cans, and other junk lying around. Limit the number of piles you have, and if you see your desktop, file cabinets, or computer could use a dusting, dust it.

- Keep out of other people's cubicles or offices unless you have been asked to step in. Ask before borrowing or taking anything from someone's desk. And when you are in someone's office, whatever you do, do not snoop.

- Keep your questions, conversations, and idle chitchat brief; remember you (and everyone else) have work to do—that is why you are there, so get back to work.

- Keep confidential conversations confidential; anything you talk about can, and likely will, be heard by others. There is little if any privacy in most offices. Take private calls or conversations into a conference room or someplace else.

- Keep your complaints, anger, foul language, and frustrations to yourself, and don't bad-mouth or gossip about others.

- Keep what you overhear to yourself; you might get more than an earful of juicy information just by sitting at your desk. When your neighbor is on the phone, there will be times you can't help but hear what is being said. Resist the urge to comment or gossip about what you overheard. Remember that you weren't meant to be a part of the conversation.

- Keep your awareness level high; you may not be aware of the sounds you make when you chew gum, and you may not hear the creaking sound others do every time you move in your chair. Watch (and listen) for what can be irritating to others—tapping your pencil, humming or singing, clearing your throat or sniffing excessively, belching, passing gas, and anything else that has the potential to annoy your neighbors.

- Keep fund-raising requests to a minimum. I know how important it is for you to help your children with their fund-raising efforts, but continuously asking for donations from your coworkers is not the way to do it. In may not be allowed either; always get permission from management before you solicit anyone for anything.

- Keep up with your share of the work. If you share a kitchen area in the office, always clean up after using it. If you use the company fax machine, printer, or copier, make sure it is in working condition for the person who uses it after you. If the paper jams, take care of it before you walk away. If you use the last piece of paper, refill it. You expect the equipment you use to work, and so do others. Courtesy counts!

HOME SWEET HOME: WHEN HOME IS YOUR OFFICE

Having your office in your home has its advantages and disadvantages. As much as you might loathe the long commute, the annoying coworkers, and all of the other stresses that accompany a job, you might find you miss these things when you are away. If you're used to interacting with people every day, you might feel cut off from the rest of the world on the days you are at home. When you work at home, it is important to maintain outside relationships and stay involved in work-related activities. Becoming an active member of an association and setting regular breakfast or lunch meetings with business acquaintances will benefit you.

Technology makes it easy to work from most any location. If you are considering working from home full-time or just one or two days a week, know what you are getting into. Working at home is not ideal for everyone; evaluate the pros and cons to help you determine if working at home will work for you.

Characteristics you need to succeed when working from home

Self-disciplined: You will face many distractions when you work at home, and there will be times you will be tempted to skip the work you're supposed to do in order to do other, more interesting things. Do you have enough self-discipline to set and stick to a work schedule? Will you be able to resist doing other, non–work related tasks and get your work done during work hours? If you know you can resist the temptation to leave your work until later, you should have no problem working at home.

Self-motivated: What motivates you? When you have no time clock to punch and no one to reprimand you if you don't start your work on time, will you be motivated to get up and get to work? Will you stay motivated? As long as you are self-motivated and can *stay* motivated, you should have no problem working from home.

Self-starting: Do you need someone to push you, cheer for you, or help you? Do you need permission to try a new way of doing something, or are you willing to take risks? If you are afraid of making mistakes or find yourself wondering what to do when no one is around to guide you, then working at home may not be for you.

Self-confident: Do you believe in yourself? Do you *know* without a doubt that you can do whatever you set your mind to? When people question you because they don't understand why you can't talk on the phone or stop working for awhile, will you be able to stand up to them and stand up for yourself? Do you have enough confidence to feel good about what you are doing no matter what other people think? If so, you will do just fine, but be prepared—not everyone will take your job as seriously as you do.

Self-reliant: Do you typically end up doing things yourself because you'd rather not depend on others to do things for you? If you enjoy time alone and work best when you don't have to worry about others, you will enjoy the benefits of working at home.

Self-serving: Do you feel guilty when you say no to others, or do you know the importance of taking care of your needs first? If you have family at home, they may have a difficult time leaving you alone. Will you be able to establish and reinforce your expectations and boundaries? If you are the type of person who will feel guilty every time you have to turn away a family member or friend because you have work to do, you may face difficulties in taking the time you need to do your work.

How to create a professional home office

- Establish a "work only" work area. A room with a door you can close is ideal, but if it isn't possible, designate a work area that is off-limits to everyone else.

- Install a phone line designated as your business line. You are the *only* one who should answer this phone.

- Set your voice mail to pick up all calls by the third ring.

- Create a separate e-mail address that no one but you can access.

- Get up at the same time each day.

- Establish regular work hours and breaks; begin and end your day on time and try not to work during nonworking hours.

- Keep your work area clean and tidy.

- Shower, shave, do your hair, and get dressed for work each day. Not only will you be prepared if you need to run out to deliver something or attend an impromptu meeting, but you will feel more professional when you're out of your pajamas and in regular clothes.

- Minimize background noise (washing machine running, kids playing, dogs barking, etc.) when you are on the phone.

- Hold meetings away from your home when possible.

MEETINGS MATTER

Who sits first? Who sits where? Who should be the first to signal an end to a meeting or business interaction? Whether you are meeting with one, two, 20 or more people, you want any meeting you are a part of to run smoothly. Your ability to react and respond effectively will convey your sense of presence and poise, and likely will be noticed by others.

Where you sit in a meeting *does* make a difference. The most powerful position is at the head of the table, facing the door. This allows the person in charge to see who is coming and going. In meetings, allow others on a higher level to sit first. Select a seat in which you will feel comfortable, but do it discreetly, quietly, and graciously, without clumsily jockeying for a position. Sitting directly across from someone tends to be less cordial, and potentially more threatening, than if you are on the same side of a table or a desk, because furniture creates a barrier. If you have difficulty working with someone, try switching positions. People tend to be more cooperative and friendly when working together on the same side of a table or desk.

When you bring documents to the office of someone sitting behind a desk, ask permission to come around to where he or she is sitting so you both can see the documents better. Or suggest that the other person come around and join *you*. If you're the one behind the desk, greet your visitor, seat him or her in a setting with two chairs situated side by side, and then sit down in the other chair.

Meetings come in many forms and can be formal, informal, long, short, effective or ineffective. There are guidelines for effective meetings and a code of conduct to follow; however, these are often implied, not clearly communicated. Basic etiquette guidelines apply to all interactions you have, including meetings. Whether you are in charge of a meeting or are merely participating, your role is important to the overall success of the meeting.

When you are in charge of a meeting

- Determine the reason for the meeting. If there isn't a specific reason or purpose for the meeting, don't hold one. People are too busy to waste their time attending a meeting with no value.

- Prepare an agenda and send it out to all participants *prior* to the meeting.

- Always begin *on time*.

- Make people feel welcome and comfortable; greet people as they arrive and, whenever possible, take time to make brief introductions.

- If possible, serve refreshments.

- Take a few moments at the start to restate your reason for holding the meeting, and briefly review the agenda. Let people know when to expect breaks.

- If you prefer people hold questions and comments until the end of your presentation, say so at the start of the meeting.

- Follow and stick to the agenda, and keep the meeting moving along.

- End a few minutes early if possible, but *always* end on time. The person leading the meeting is responsible for ending it.

When you are attending a meeting

- Arrive a few minutes early.

- *Turn off* your cell phone. If you forget, and it rings, *do not answer it during the meeting*. If you must take the call, step outside.

- Do not bring your computer with you unless you will need it. Whatever you do, do not play games, write or read e-mail, or surf the net when you should be paying attention.

- Be prepared; bring a pad of paper, a pen or a pencil, and any other pertinent supplies.

- Pay attention to the person who is speaking; avoid side conversations.

- Sit up straight and maintain good posture throughout the meeting.

- Listen when others are talking; don't interrupt, make comments, or dominate the discussion.

- Be respectful. You don't have to agree with all points of view, but don't be argumentative. If you have an issue with someone, address it after the meeting.

- If you must leave early, inform the presenter at the beginning of the meeting. It is rude and disruptive to walk out during a meeting for any reason.

COMPANY GATHERINGS AND HOLIDAY PARTIES

For some reason, the good etiquette displayed at work tends to disappear at company social events. The annual holiday party, in particular, is a breeding ground for obnoxious and career-busting behavior. Although office parties and celebrations are intended as social events, they are business events. Just when I thought I'd heard it all, I'll hear about some employee who did a striptease number while dancing on the dinner table or about another who pulled off the boss's toupee. Let me assure you, this kind of behavior is never forgotten, and it has sabotaged careers.

Some people hear the word *party* and see an opportunity to let loose and show their wild side. Too many people view the office party as a setting in which anything goes and a time to wear the sequined minidress, sit all night on Santa's lap, or make a pass at the new intern. The nuances that differentiate a consummate professional from a befuddled slouch are seldom taught and, unfortunately, are often learned only from embarrassing mistakes. The best thing you can do is to learn from the mistakes *others* have made, and *avoid* the disastrous behavior of years past.

Ironically, those who decide to let their hair down at company events rarely feel responsible for their actions and frequently tend to minimize the long-term effect. Alcohol is the biggest contributor to inappropriate and regrettable behavior. If you choose to drink, drink responsibly. If you can't control your drinking, you shouldn't be drinking. Don't ever feel you must drink just because alcohol is available.

Company gatherings of any kind are inevitable. Unless you have a legitimate reason for not attending, your absence will be noticed—and noted. By attending, you show your support for your company and team members; when you don't attend, the negative message you send through your absence could hurt your advancement opportunities. Attend company gatherings and show your support for others. Most important, be on your *best* behavior; you may not think anyone is paying attention, but act as if your behavior is being observed every minute, because it is! The following tips will help you behave well, whether at the holiday party, during happy hour, or at any other event:

1. Think "business hours," not "party time."

2. Limit your alcohol consumption. Drink if alcohol is served, but don't drink to get drunk.

3. Dress for the occasion, which is *business*. Don't try to be sexy, sultry, trendy, or macho.

4. Be the first to arrive but not the last to leave. Don't arrive late or stay just a few minutes. A lot of time and money has gone into the planning of the event; stay around and enjoy it.

5. Be generous with praise for others but stingy with praise for yourself. This isn't the time to brownnose, ask for a raise, or brag about your accomplishments.

6. Take an interest in others, but don't assume anyone is too interested in you. In other words, be a good listener, not a compulsive talker.

7. Be friendly, but don't be a flirt; stay off of Santa's, or *anyone's*, lap, and keep your hands to yourself.

8. If you are involved in a gift exchange, use good taste. A gift to a charity in someone's name; a gift certificate to a restaurant, bookstore, or coffee shop; or a useful office item are neutral and safe gifts to give.

9. Greet and speak to people outside of your core group of coworkers and friends. Keep the conversation light; avoid telling off-color jokes and don't discuss other people, religion, sex, or politics.

10. Be a gracious host; if you bring someone with you, stay with him or her. Think twice before bringing a casual date. Someone you barely know may not fit in or, worse yet, end up embarrassing you with his or her inappropriate behavior.

11. Be an appreciative guest; greet your boss when you arrive and say thank you when you leave.

12. Eat something before you go; this way you won't be drinking on an empty stomach, nor will you devour the food.

THE LOVE CONNECTION

If you are single and interested in meeting people, you may not have to look too far. You are in one of the easiest and most common places singles meet: the workplace. The makings of a love connection are in place; you are in a safe environment, already have at least one thing in common (working at the same place), and can get to know someone without ever going on an actual date. That's the good news. The bad news is that finding love and maintaining a love relationship at work does have drawbacks.

While growing numbers of companies realize love will bloom at work, before you look for a date (or mate) at work, you'd better find out how your company will feel about it if you succeed. Most companies discourage supervisors from dating or becoming romantically involved with subordinates. The potential for complaints of harassment and unfair treatment is too great.

When you meet and fall in love with someone at work, going to work each day becomes more enjoyable. However, if the relationship sours, it can be difficult to end a relationship and move on when you continue to see the person every day.

If you do find love at work, be *discreet*. Think twice before telling others, and don't rush to announce your relationship or discuss the details of every date you have. Your focus at work should be work. It may be tempting to change your routine in order to be with your new love during your breaks, but resist the temptation. It's important for you to preserve your other friends and relationships at work. Above all, *restrain yourself*. You will draw attention to yourself and make others uncomfortable if you are overly demonstrative. Save the kissing, hugging, hand-holding, baby talk, and goo-goo eyes for after hours and away from coworkers. Go ahead and let yourself fall in love, but if it's with someone you meet at work, be very, very careful.

IT ISN'T ABOUT THE SEX

Both men and women have had to work hard to deal with the role changes that have taken place in business over the years. There are advantages (and disadvantages) for either sex. Gender issues don't have to be difficult. If you operate by one simple rule, you'll probably never find yourself wondering how to handle potential gender issues. The rule: *Treat men and women equally.*

When I first began writing my newspaper column, I received a question from a man who said he was avoiding women at work because he was afraid of offending them and getting into trouble. He wondered how women wanted to be treated. I responded by saying he should simply treat women the same way he would treat a man, stressing that gender should not make a difference; treat *everyone* respectfully, regardless of gender.

I received a huge response to that column. The women who responded agreed with my advice, but the men who wrote to me were outraged. As one man said, "Women are so sensitive that we have to walk on eggshells around them; we're afraid to open our mouths for fear of being sued."

Although the battle of the sexes continues, treating all people with professional respect, regardless of gender, status, or any other difference, is just common sense. I'm talking about the basics here, just a few simple courtesies that help establish boundaries and expectations. Among the greatest concerns for businesses is the issue of sexual harassment. Managers and staff are expected to treat everyone equally, professionally, and respectfully at all times.

When you observe a few formal rules of etiquette and conduct yourself professionally, you prevent misunderstandings that could lead to bigger problems. Dressing, acting, and carrying yourself professionally, and sticking to business topics in conversation will help everyone feel more comfortable and eliminate misinterpretation and misunderstanding. Your business transactions won't be clouded with distracting questions such as, "What did that remark mean? Is he or she ignoring me because of my gender?"

Treating everyone with respect is simple, easy to remember, and easy to interpret in all circumstances. Remember to apply the same etiquette and fairness rules in social situations that overlap with work. Office parties, business lunches, or out-of-town travel shouldn't create a question in your mind about how to behave; the same rules of day-to-day office and business etiquette apply.

Many people have made the mistake of stepping over that professional boundary outside the office; don't make that same mistake. Social work functions can tempt you into indiscreet behavior or remarks you might later regret. Think about the things you say and do, and always present yourself in the best possible manner.

Men: Don't go out of your way to run to the door first to open it or block an elevator entrance when you're in front just to let a woman out first. Whoever is at the door first should open it, and whoever is in the front of the elevator should exit first. If you see someone struggling and in need of some help getting a coat on, by all means, help him or her. While there's no need to jump up to pull out a chair, rising is always a nice gesture when you greet someone, whether male or female. Consider business etiquette in all areas one of the most important skills you can develop to help you meet your career goals. When you act properly, you earn a good reputation and avoid many misunderstandings and problems. Failing to act appropriately and displaying poor manners shows ignorance. Your lack of knowledge and awareness may be interpreted as shallow or uncaring.

Good manners can be cost-effective. Acting properly and treating people well makes good business sense. Negative behavior can cost you a promotion, a job, a customer or a client, and even result in decreased productivity and profit. Don't risk being perceived as aloof; you know what's expected—all you have to do is act accordingly and use that knowledge.

POINTS TO REMEMBER

1. **Consider business etiquette vital to your success.** Mastering the trends in business etiquette is one of the most important skills you can develop to help you meet your career goals.

2. **Respect all coworkers' personal office space.** Even in an open office setting, each person's personal work area should be theirs to call their own. Don't take anything without asking, and always wait to be invited before walking into someone's office space or behind their desk.

3. **Keep your awareness level high.** Be aware of the sounds that come out of your office, and turn down the volume on your computer, radio, telephone, or anything else that might be disruptive. Watch what you say, watch what you eat, and watch for the reaction of the people around you; if you sense you are irritating someone, find out what you can do differently.

4. **Make your meetings worthwhile.** Whether you are leading a meeting or just attending, come prepared. Bring any pertinent information

you need, and always carry a pen and paper. Do what you can to make any meeting you are a part of a success. Be an active participant, pay attention, and keep things moving; people are too busy to waste their time in an unproductive meeting.

5. **Treat everyone with courtesy and respect.** Forget about rank and sex; treat *everyone* well, and *you* will do well.

6. **Think "business event," not "party time."** Jump at opportunities to socialize with coworkers and business acquaintances, but never forget you are at a business event; be sure you behave in a way that will make you and your company proud.

7. **Learn the unwritten codes of expected behavior.** Every office, every business, and every industry has its own unwritten code of behavior and rules. Be an astute observer of others, and know what is expected. It is up to you to know and understand this code.

8. **Make your home office a *professional* office.** Separate your personal and professional life. Create a space for your work, set a schedule and stick to it, and stay connected with others.

True or False?

1. Good manners can be cost-effective.
TRUE.

Good manners are essential. Acting properly and treating people well makes good business sense. Negative behavior can cost you a promotion, a job, a customer or a client, and even result in decreased productivity and profit.

2. Profanity can add impact if used sparingly.
FALSE.

*Swearing is never impressive, and the only impact it can have is negative. You actually diminish your credibility when you use profanity because you appear out of control. Profanity is **never** acceptable in a business environment.*

3. You should always plan to arrive at business events "fashionably late," which means about five to 10 minutes late.
FALSE.

There is no such thing as fashionably late. Late is late, and is inconsiderate whether it's five, 10, or 30 minutes. Always plan to arrive five to 10 minutes early so you won't hold things up and will be ready to start on time.

4. Where you sit can influence the outcome of an interaction.
TRUE.
Anytime you are seated across from someone, especially if there is a barrier, such as a table or desk, you are in what sociologists call the "conflict position." Removing the barrier and sitting on the same side of a table or desk will help create a feeling of camaraderie and is referred to as the "cooperation position."

5. Working at home is easier than working in an office.
FALSE.
Working at home requires hard work and self-discipline, among other things. If you are the type of person who thrives on the hustle and bustle of an active environment or needs direction and reassurance, the solitude may be unbearable. However, if you are a self-motivated, self-starter, you can do very well working from home.

6. The decision to date a coworker is no one's business but your own.
FALSE.
Depending on your position and the company you work for, if you date or become romantically involved with someone at work, you could be risking your job. In addition, no matter how secretive you try to be, others are bound to find out about your relationship. What you do is your business, but when it involves someone at work, it becomes company business too. Know your company's policy.

7. Men can show their respect for women by opening doors, pulling out chairs, and helping them put on their coats.
FALSE.
If you happen to be at the door first and can hold it open, by all means do it. If you see someone struggling to put on a coat, offer your help to anyone who needs it, regardless of gender. You don't need to give preferential treatment to women to show your respect. Treat everyone you encounter with courtesy and respect.

8. Attendance at the company holiday party is optional.
FALSE.
You won't lose pay, and technically, no one can force you to attend, but failing to attend sends a negative message to others and reflects poorly on you. Your lack of attendance separates you from your colleagues and shows a lack of team spirit and commitment to your job and company. You must have a really good and valid reason to miss such an event, and there are very few acceptable excuses.

Chapter 11

Business, Pleasure, and Hunger— A Dangerous Mix

True or False?

1. If you drop a piece of silverware on the floor, leave it there.

2. When you leave the table during a meal, place your napkin on your chair.

3. Always eat French fries with your fingers.

4. If you have something stuck in your tooth, using a toothpick is acceptable and not likely to offend anyone.

5. Wait until you've finished eating to bring out business papers.

6. When you are asked to pass the salt, pass the pepper also.

7. When dining with coworkers or clients, you will be better off not drinking, even if others are.

HAPPY HOUR TURNED SAD

Joe was asked to join the other team members for happy hour following his third interview for a prestigious position. He accepted, and when happy hour evolved into dinner, he was certain it wouldn't be long before he was offered the job. But the offer never came.

As he struggled to figure out what went wrong, he wondered if joining the group was a mistake. After talking it over with several people, he decided his biggest mistake that evening was that he drank. Everyone was drinking, so he assumed he should too. Although he was certain he wasn't drunk, he wasn't sure how much alcohol he had consumed. He was having so much fun that he forgot to focus on the main reason he was there, which was to demonstrate he was the right person for the job.

Whether you are interviewing for a job or dining with customers or business acquaintances, the people you are with can't help but notice your drinking and dining habits. If you drink, smoke, or eat too much, you demonstrate little restraint. If you talk with food in your mouth, pick your teeth, or drink out of someone else's glass, you might offend the people you are with. Everything you do will be noticed. When you interact with other business people, you are expected to know how to conduct yourself, whether it's in the company cafeteria or at an upscale restaurant. When you don't act as expected, others will notice and rightfully assume you are inexperienced, naive, or simply ignorant. Although the consequences of these assumptions are not always immediate, you likely *will* pay a price for your unrefined behavior. If you don't think your manners (or lack of them) influences the way people feel about you, think again.

MANNERS *DO* MATTER

Bill was well liked by everyone, and he had a promising future in sales. He was a good salesman, but he had a problem with his professional conduct. As you read the following story, see if you can uncover some of the reasons Bill ought to brush up on his etiquette.

Bill had invited an important client and his wife to dinner. He scheduled it for 7:30 P.M. at an Italian restaurant, but he didn't arrive until 7:45, 15 minutes late. His client, who had arrived a few minutes early, had been waiting for some time, but couldn't be seated because Bill had forgotten to make a reservation. The only available table was in the smoking section, and without asking his client, Bill accepted it. He didn't realize until later on in the evening that his client's wife was allergic to smoke. When he did find out, he didn't offer to switch tables; after all, he already knew another one wouldn't be available for some time.

Bill forgot to tell his client this was a casual restaurant, and although Bill had gone to his hotel to change into something more comfortable, his client got dressed up. Bill ordered wine for the table, but found out his client doesn't drink and ended up drinking most of it himself. Bill thought all seemed to be going well, but when the check came, it was quite a bit higher than Bill was expecting and he voiced his concern about his expense account, making his client most uncomfortable. The evening was one disaster after another, and although Bill had hoped it would help strengthen his relationship with his client, it weakened it.

What people like Bill don't realize is that they create obstacles for themselves because they remain oblivious to the norms and standards other people follow. It is true that some people, like Bill, are unskilled yet successful in spite of themselves, but it's much easier to do things the *right* way than to do *anything* that might cause others to question your competency.

So, what did Bill do wrong? First, Bill shouldn't have been the one to select the restaurant; he should have given his client a few choices and let *his client* choose where to eat. Once a reservation is confirmed, he can let his client know the time, place, and appropriate attire. He took a big risk choosing an Italian restaurant. What if his client didn't like Italian food or was allergic to tomatoes or cheese?

Second, Bill was late. As the host, he should have arrived *before* his client in order to be there to welcome and greet him. Third, he forgot to ask his guests if sitting in the smoking section was OK. Some people, such as the client's wife, are highly sensitive or even allergic to smoke. Always ask whether the person you are with prefers smoking or nonsmoking. Fourth, since Bill's client wasn't drinking, he should have abstained too. Always observe what other people are doing. Finally, Bill should have arranged payment in advance to avoid creating an awkward situation when the bill was presented. There was no reason for him to make comments about the amount. Always strive to make the people you are with feel comfortable.

Business is mixed with hunger and pleasure all the time. Although your hunger pains may demand your attention, you will serve yourself well if you stay focused on the people you are with. Sharing a meal with someone can provide an opportunity to build a stronger relationship. Place your emphasis on the person or people you are with; do everything you can to put others at ease. Awkward moments make everyone uneasy. Although you may not think twice about the way you hold your fork, lick your fingers, or chomp your food, other people do. As you've learned in previous chapters, it's often the little things that can get in the way of your image and, ultimately, your success.

WINING AND DINING

Whether you are eating lunch at your desk, on the go, in a fast food restaurant, or at a fine dining establishment, your manners show. The more prepared you are, the easier it will be to handle any situation.

When you are dining with business acquaintances

- Focus on the people, not the food.

- Maintain good posture; sit up straight and keep your arms close to your body.

- Be a good conversationalist; spend some time getting to know the people you are with; talk about things other than business.

- Eat and drink in moderation.

- Eat *slowly*.

- Do not smoke if you are with people who do not smoke—even if you are in the smoking section.

When you are the guest

- Stay within a moderate price range; don't order the most expensive thing on the menu.

- Keep your comments positive; comment on the delicious food and the attractive decor, but don't complain about the restaurant, the service, or the food.

- If you are a finicky eater, eat what you can without making a scene.

- If you don't finish your meal and your host suggests you take the food home, you can accept, but don't be the one to ask for a doggie bag.

- Follow your host; let him or her decide when to order and when to leave.

- Be a gracious guest; the person who invites is the one who pays; don't fight over the bill.

- Show your appreciation; thank your host for inviting you in person and again with a handwritten thank-you note.

When you are the host

- Ask your guest what type of food or restaurant he or she prefers, and offer a few choices to indicate the type of restaurant you are considering.

- Check with your guests in advance about any dietary needs or preferences.

- Arrive a few minutes *before* your reservation time.

- Make appropriate introductions and include everyone in the conversation.

- Allow your guest to order and begin eating their meal before you do yours.

- Check to make sure your guest has everything he or she needs when the food arrives.

- If service is slow or poor, the wrong item is served, or the food is not prepared as ordered, be assertive, but be discreet. You shouldn't make a scene in a restaurant or embarrass a server in front of your guests, no matter how much it might be deserved.

- Be respectful of time; don't rush through the meal, but don't linger too long either.

I'LL HAVE WHAT HE'S HAVING: ORDERING AND PAYING THE TAB

Once you are seated and have decided what you will order, close your menu to show you are ready. Deciding what to order is not always easy, but avoid being indecisive. Force yourself to make a decision to avoid holding up others. Some menus are easy to scan while others are much more complicated. It can be especially difficult to make a selection when you are the guest. You might not be sure in which price range to order, have difficulty pronouncing something on the menu, or simply be unfamiliar with the type of food that is offered. Whenever you are unsure about something, ask your host or server for recommendations. If you are in doubt, order what the others are having.

When you are the host, make it easy for your guests; offer suggestions and tell your guests what you will be eating. It's best to avoid difficult-to-eat or messy foods, such as spaghetti; large, stuffed sandwiches; or barbeque ribs. However, this isn't the time for you to order only the soup or the diet plate. Don't draw unnecessary attention to yourself or make others self-conscious about the amount of food they are eating.

Business talk can begin immediately after ordering, when the menus are put away. However, don't miss the special opportunity that sharing a meal gives you to build rapport with business clients and colleagues. Don't rush into business talk unless you must. Always start with some small talk and, depending on the amount of time you have, gradually build to the business discussion. If you have papers to bring out, wait until you have finished eating and the dishes have been cleared.

If you're picking up the tab and want to make sure you get the bill, make arrangements in advance by giving the waiter your credit card or telling him or her to give the bill to you. You can tell your server or the maitre d' to add a 15 or 20 percent gratuity and then sign the receipt in advance so the server never has to present a bill.

If the bill is presented at the table, it's appropriate for you to check it for accuracy, but do it briefly and without drawing attention to it. Mentally calculate approximately what the bill will be as each person orders so you can spot a large discrepancy without hauling out your calculator. If you do suspect an error, take the bill to your server (away from the table) to review it. Don't make a scene in front of your guests.

DINING DILEMMAS

If you've attended a formal function, you've seen how complicated and intimidating some table settings can be. If you ever find yourself seated in front of a foreign-looking place setting, do not fret. It is easier than you think to figure out which fork, knife, or spoon to use.

A place setting can be informal (a standard fork, knife, and spoon) or formal (including eight or nine pieces of silverware). The best rule to remember is to work from the outside in. Generally, the silverware is placed according to the courses, or what is going to be served first, second, third, and so on. If you are in doubt about which piece of silver to use, watch what others are doing and do the same.

Always put your napkin on your lap, with the crease toward you, as soon as you're seated. This way, you won't forget to do it when the food is served. Use your napkin to blot or dab your face, not wipe it. Your napkin should stay on your lap the entire time until you leave, and only then should you put it back on the table. If you leave during the meal, it isn't necessary to explain where you're going or to announce that you are leaving. A simple "Excuse me" will do. Set your napkin on your chair if you leave but will return during the meal. Others should not have to look at your dirty napkin during your absence.

If you find yourself wondering what foods you can eat with your hands and which ones require a fork, it often depends on what foods you are eating. When you order or are served finger foods, such as French fries, chicken wings, or sandwiches, you can and should eat them. However, if French fries are served with a breast of chicken or other foods that require a fork, then you should eat the French fries with a fork too.

If you're struggling to chew a piece of gristle or need to remove a bone, olive pit, or anything else from your mouth, the correct way is to remove it the same way it went in. If you put the food in with a fork, remove it with a fork; if you put it in with your fingers, remove it with your fingers. Try not to draw attention to your action. Place the object on your plate, and do your best to cover it up.

Keep your elbows off the table when you eat, but go ahead and rest them on the table to lean toward the conversation when you are not eating. Hold your utensils properly (don't grab them, hold them like a shovel, or clutch them), and chew small bites of food at a time. Never rush through a meal or shovel food into your mouth. When you've finished eating, wait for your server to remove your plate; don't push it away from you and into the center of the table.

Avert potentially embarrassing problems while dining by reacting quickly and discreetly. For example, if someone you're dining with has food on his or her face or teeth, you can subtly motion to the person to wipe it away or kindly tell him or her.

If you find something unpleasant on your plate, such as a hair or a bug, tell your waiter without interrupting the flow of conversation at the table or drawing attention to yourself. As shocking as discovering a foreign object in your food can be, try not to overreact. There is no point in disrupting everyone else or making a scene.

When you are finished eating, place your fork and your knife on the side of your plate in the four o'clock position to signal the server that you are finished and your plate can be removed.

FOOD FOR THOUGHT

Dining out can and should be a pleasant experience. The more comfortable you are, the smoother your dining experiences will be. No one expects you to be perfect. You will find that no matter how well mannered you try to be, there will be times you will encounter awkward moments. The more prepared you are, the better able you will be to handle *any* situation you encounter. Keep in mind the following tips:

- Don't talk with food in your mouth.

- Take small bites, and cut only the piece you are about to put in your mouth.

- Eat from *your* plate and drink from *your* glass; your bread plate will be to your left, beverages to your right.

- Pass the bread, butter, and anything else that needs passing; don't allow food to pile up in front of you.

- If other people at your table are served but you are not, and you see that people are waiting for you to be served before they start to eat, encourage them to begin eating.

- If you order a drink that comes in a bottle or a can, request a glass.

- Break off, butter, and eat small portions of bread or rolls, rather than preparing the whole roll at once and bringing it to your mouth to eat.

- If you have something stuck in your teeth, don't attempt to remove it at the table; excuse yourself and take care of it in the rest room.

- Unless you are expecting a very important call, do not turn on your cell phone at a restaurant. If it were to ring in the middle of a conversation, it would be disturbing and awkward for the person with you.

- If you plan to share an entree, ask the server to have it split in the kitchen and served on two plates.

- If something is wrong with your meal, discreetly notify your server without causing a scene and making others uncomfortable.

- To signal that you are finished eating and wish to have your plate removed, place your fork and knife crisscrossed on your plate in the four o'clock position.

- Keep your eyes from roving around the room; stay focused on the people at your table.

- Keep your briefcase, purse, cell phone, and all personal items *off* the table.

- If you are wearing a hat or a cap, remove it during a meal.

- If you drop a piece of silverware on the floor, leave it there and tell your server.

- Never belch.

- If you feel a sneeze coming on, turn away from the table and sneeze into a napkin or tissue. Don't blow your nose at the table; it's very unappetizing for those around you.

There's no need to save your table manners for special occasions. Practice using good manners *every day* and *every time* you eat, no matter where you are or whom you are with. Before you know it, your understanding of dining etiquette and your comfort level with doing the right thing will be second nature.

You won't have to worry or wonder about how you come across to others, because you will *know* you're doing just fine.

TO DRINK OR NOT TO DRINK?

Nothing is quite as tricky as deciding whether you should drink alcohol at a business event or with business acquaintances. If everyone else is drinking, you may be tempted to join the crowd, but if you do, be *careful*. The manner in which you handle your drinking conveys impressions you sometimes can't control. Nothing will sour your reputation faster than when others hear you slurring your words or witness you in a drunken stupor.

Even if you've never had a problem with drinking before, it is no guarantee you won't have one in the future. You never know for sure how you will respond to alcohol. Your responses can vary and will depend on the alcoholic content of the drink, how much sleep you've had, what foods you've eaten, and be affected by any medication (even over-the-counter medicines) you may be taking.

A single glass of wine or one drink might be acceptable, but you can never assume even one drink will have no effect on you. If no one else is drinking, *don't drink*. If you need to drive yourself home, *don't drink*. In fact, it is best (and safest) in *all* business situations to avoid drinking altogether. If you get drunk, *you* may forget the things you said or did, but others will not. Too often, even a small amount of alcohol can loosen your tongue. Alcohol use makes it easier to say, do, or even imply something that could cast a bad light on you. Why risk it? Even if others drink, moderately or heavily, watch *your* alcohol intake. *Self-control and restraint are characteristics of success*—in office politics, business negotiations, or personal conduct. Don't put your reputation on the line; always act (and drink) responsibly.

POINTS TO REMEMBER

1. **Improve your table manners.** Know, practice, and stay updated on all dining matters, including ordering, tipping, and picking up the tab.

2. **Demonstrate your sensitivity toward others.** Don't take or make phone calls, talk with food in your mouth, or smoke when dining with someone.

3. **Focus on building better relationships.** When you are dining with others, place your emphasis on the *people* you are with, not the food.

4. **Be a gracious guest and host.** Always strive to make others feel comfortable.

5. **Limit alcoholic beverages.** Curtail your drinking or simply forego alcohol altogether. How you handle drinking conveys impressions you sometimes can't control.

True or False?

1. If you drop a piece of silverware on the floor, leave it there.
TRUE.
If you drop it on the floor, it shouldn't go back on the table. Inform your server and allow him or her to pick it up and replace it for you.

2. When you leave the table during a meal, place your napkin on your chair.
TRUE.
If you are using your napkin throughout the meal, chances are it is stained. Placing a dirty napkin on the table is unappetizing to others.

3. Always eat French fries with your fingers.
FALSE.
When you eat French fries with a sandwich or other finger-type foods, it is fine to eat them with your hands, but if you are using a fork for everything else, use it for the French fries too.

4. If you have something stuck in your tooth, using a toothpick is acceptable and not likely to offend anyone.
FALSE.
Whether you use your finger or a toothpick, picking your teeth at the table is gauche. If you have something stuck and cannot wait to remove it, excuse yourself from the table and take care of it in the rest room.

5. Wait until you've finished eating to bring out business papers.
TRUE.
Typically, the time to bring out papers is after eating. This allows you to fully enjoy your meal and the company you are with.

6. When you are asked to pass the salt, pass the pepper also.

TRUE.

Think of the salt and pepper as a pair. One doesn't go anywhere without the other. When they become separated, if someone wants both, then two people have to pass instead of just one.

7. When dining with coworkers or clients, you will be better off not drinking, even if others are.

TRUE.

You never know how alcohol will affect you or how others will view your drinking. When you have the chance to dine and spend time with a valued business acquaintance, make the most of it; don't risk saying or doing something you might regret. The only way to stay in control is to be in control; when you drink, you leave everything up to chance.

Maximize Your Relationships

DON'T LET 'EM GET YOU DOWN

According to the lyrics of Barbra Streisand's hit song, people who need people are the luckiest people in the world. Based on the feedback I've received over the years, not everyone agrees. If we can't get along with someone, we often don't think we need them at all. Every person is unique, which can be wonderful because of the variety and frustrating because of the challenges we face in understanding one another. People get things done. People make businesses run. People make us laugh. And people can drive us crazy!

Typically, the majority of people who write to me with a question or concern don't feel lucky at all. Some of the letters I've received are heartrending. Working for a boss who is impossible to please or with a coworker who grates on your nerves can be a challenge for even the most tolerant individual. The following is an excerpt from a letter I received some time ago:

Dear Sue,

Six months ago, I got a new boss. This man has made my life a living hell. He dictates orders, questions my whereabouts, listens in on my conversations,

*and has taken all the joy out of the job I once enjoyed. I've lost weight, can't
sleep at night, and have recurring migraines. I can't quit because I need the
money, but it is getting more and more difficult to get up each day and go to
work. I've cried and I've prayed for an answer, but I don't know what to do.
Please help me.*

What advice would you give this person? You might suggest he or she quit,
confront the boss, or file a complaint, but that isn't always easy for someone to
do. "People" problems can become overwhelming and, if left unresolved, can
eventually overshadow every other aspect of a job. Problems with other people
contribute greatly to workplace stress and job dissatisfaction.

Unfortunately, there is no shortage of difficult people; they infiltrate every
office at every level and can be found in every occupation. It only takes one difficult person to disrupt an entire department. Difficult people make life difficult for everyone, including themselves. Meeting one is inevitable, but as long
as you learn how to deal with the difficult people in your life, you will be able
to resolve the problems you face and remain focused on the most important
aspects of your job.

The more time you spend fussing about someone else, the less time you
have to focus on yourself and your work. Get into the habit of addressing the
problems and concerns you have with others when they occur, and do everything in your power to resolve them before they escalate into bigger problems.
If you want to get along with people, you must be tolerant. Some people are
easier to work with than others. When you work with someone who is difficult, your patience will be put to the test.

Sometimes *you* may be the one who's hard to work with. It is much easier
to focus on the shortcomings of others than it is to focus on our own imperfections, so we often blame other people for our own frustration. "How could
he do that?" "I can't believe *she* said that." "No one can work with *her; she's*
impossible."

The next time you start blaming someone else for your problems, stop and
think about what you are doing and why. Is the problem you are having due to
something someone did or is the *real* problem the way in which *you* are
responding to what happened?

When you are upset with someone, it can be difficult to view what happened
objectively. Whoever upset you is likely to become the focus of your frustration. Before you start pointing fingers, remind yourself that no one can *make*
you react a certain way. Someone may push your buttons, but they are ones

you've created. *When you accept responsibility for all of your actions and reactions, the actions of others will have less impact on you.*

The next time you feel your blood boiling because of something someone said or did, instead of focusing on that person, ask yourself why *you* are responding so strongly. No matter how hard you try, you will never change someone else. The only person you have the power to change is *you.*

Try to view the difficult people in your life differently, and try to be grateful they are there. The challenges you face enable you to learn more about yourself and your own shortcomings. Instead of asking how someone can do something so irritating, try asking why you *allow yourself* to become irritated so easily. You can and must work on developing your people skills. When people like you, they are more apt to hire you, promote you, and buy from you. When you are skilled at dealing with people, even the difficult ones, you increase your overall value and effectiveness. People skills are every bit as important, and sometimes *more* important, than the skills you need to do your job. Streisand is correct. People *do* need other people. But until we learn to get along with people, we may never realize how lucky we really are to have others in our lives.

BUILD STRONG RELATIONSHIPS

The relationship aspect of your job is not optional. Good business is a result of good relationships. Strong relationships are the solid foundation on which businesses are built. You can have the best price and the best product, but if you don't have strong relationships, it won't make a difference. If people don't like you or trust you, they won't do business with you.

Throughout your career, you will have numerous opportunities to meet new people and make new business contacts. Make the most of every opportunity you have. If you treat people well and maximize your relationships, the rewards will be abundant. Remember, anyone can do what you do, but only *you* can offer your unique perspective; only you can be the best you. *Who you are* will make or break your career success. If your relationships aren't as good as they could be, work at improving them.

You've probably heard the saying, "It's not what you know; it's who you know." Your contacts are an asset. When you want to reach or meet someone you don't know, it will help if you have a personal connection. Unless you have a mutual acquaintance, you are a complete stranger to someone you might consider a potential prospect or future employer. You have an advantage when you know someone who is willing to introduce you, vouch for you, or help you in any other way. Sometimes a personal connection is the *only* way you will ever get through to someone. Most people are too busy to respond personally to every phone call or meeting request that they receive.

Solid, long-lasting relationships are built slowly. Every positive interaction you have with someone will strengthen your bond. There is a difference between collecting names and using people to help you get what you want and establishing a network of colleagues and friends. People will see right through you when your motives are self-serving or if you are looking to get more than you give. When you have authentic relationships, you will want to help others and they will want to help you.

Make an effort to expand your network each year. Be open to meeting new people, but never ignore those you already know; work hard at maintaining the business and personal relationships you already have as you develop new relationships over the years. People will appreciate your efforts, and you will enjoy the benefits that come from your connections with a variety of people. When it comes to networking, you can't do it alone.

GET A LITTLE RESPECT

Every interaction you have during the course of a day is important. The more respect you show others, the more respect you will earn in return. Don't put on airs or try to impress others in order to earn their respect. If you can be yourself and manage to do the following, you will have a much easier time achieving the respect you feel you deserve.

- **Respect time.** Be on time. Respect other people's schedules. Meet all deadlines on time and on budget.

- **Appreciate differences.** It is natural to gravitate toward people who share your interests and have similar lifestyles. We tend to prefer the predictable over the unpredictable. But if you never break out of your comfort zone, you are limiting yourself. Be careful not to overlook someone because of your differences or your fear of the unknown. Just because someone looks, acts, or speaks differently than you, don't assume you have nothing in common with him or her. You might have more in common than you think, but you will never know if you refuse to find out. The business world has become increasingly diverse. You have the opportunity to learn firsthand about different cultures. Why not take the time to get to know people who are different from you? Don't fear differences, appreciate them.

- **Notice people, not their disabilities.** Some disabilities are more visible than others, and more people than you realize have a disability. Treat everyone you meet or work with respectfully. When you are with someone who has a disability, act the same as you would toward anyone else. Don't focus on the disability—focus on the *person.* Your coworker might use a wheelchair to get around while you walk, but that may be the only difference between the two of you. Don't assume you need to talk louder, softer, or do *anything* differently when you are around someone who has a disability. Allow the person you are with to dictate his or her preferences before you assume you need to change your behavior. Get to know people before making judgments. *Look for the similarities, not the differences with everyone you meet.*

- **Be a problem solver.** When there is a problem, find a way to resolve it. Don't be afraid of conflict or jump to conclusions. Sometimes it's what *isn't said* that creates the biggest problem. Conflict isn't always bad and, once resolved, it often leads to stronger relationships. If you are having trouble getting along with someone it might seem easier to ignore him or her, but it won't make the problem go away. You must face your problems. Try viewing each obstacle you face as a challenge to be overcome. You will fare better by facing and solving your problems, and so will everyone else you deal with.

- **Be discreet.** Discretion is necessary at all times. Watch what you say and who you say it to. You never know who might overhear something you say, so don't say it if you don't want it overheard and repeated.

- **Value people, not their position.** Show respect for *all* people at *all* levels during *all* transactions, on and off the job. You will feel *so good* when you do, and you might be surprised at the number of people who will be proud to call you their friend.

- **Stay on task.** If it doesn't have to do with the business at hand or with the goals you need to accomplish, ignore it! That means avoiding gossip, toxic people, office politics, and other distractions in order to remain clearly focused on the task that are most important.

- **Be positive.** Offices are full of gripes, complaints, problems, and general morale issues. All companies function with ups and downs; don't criticize people or the company out loud. Acknowledge the reality of the situation and get on with it! And you can go one step further: Be a leader and encourage those around you to focus on the positive.

- **Think before you speak.** Play the devil's advocate with yourself and think through what you want people to know and what you want them to do. Anticipate the effect of what you're saying or proposing and, of course, never act or speak when you're angry.

- **Address problems immediately.** If you have an issue with someone or something in the office, be sure to talk to the appropriate person and do what you can to work it out. Don't bring the problem you have with one person to another who has nothing to do with it. Talk to the offending person directly and privately.

- **Control your emotions.** If you have a tendency to lose your temper, cry, or become emotionally volatile under stress, you risk alienating people. Raising your voice, swearing, crying, or pounding your fist does nothing to help an already tense situation. Learn techniques to control your emotions. Temperamental outbursts are unprofessional and do nothing for you or your relationships.

- **Show your appreciation.** You have to appreciate what you have before you can show your appreciation to others. Take time to notice all of the little things that add to your day in a positive manner. Pay attention to the people who support you. Notice and acknowledge the people who smile at you when your spirits need a lift. Take time to appreciate those who go out of their way for you and do nice things for you, and then show your appreciation. Everyone longs to feel valued and important; acknowledge people for who they are and what you appreciate about them. Send a card of thanks, write a personal note, take them to lunch, buy them a cup of coffee, or just say thanks. Whatever you do to show your appreciation will be appreciated by them.

BE A PEACEMAKER: WORK THROUGH PROBLEMS

Most of the people who write to me are experiencing people problems. When someone is dealing with a horrible boss, an irritating coworker, or a nosy officemate, the problem can overshadow every other aspect of what was once a great job.

There are times it may be preferable to let things slide, but if something or someone is becoming increasingly intolerable, you need to deal with it. Ignoring a problem will *not* resolve it or make it go away. *When you have a problem with someone, address it.* Difficult people can get by with their irritating behavior because too often we allow them to.

The behavior of an annoying coworker is far different from behavior that is malicious, insulting, or discriminating. If you are threatened, intimidated, bullied, harassed (sexually or other), or feel a superior is misusing his or her authority, take your complaint to a higher level. Talk with a supervisor, manager, or someone in the human resources or legal departments. If these resources are unavailable, you may have to seek outside council. You *do* have rights, and you *do not* have to tolerate such behavior—*ever.*

Learn to establish boundaries and reinforce them. People will test your limits, but don't allow your fear to get in the way. Bullies thrive on your fear and will continue to push you around as long as you allow them to. When you fear someone and therefore do nothing to stop his or her negative behavior, in a way you surrender to that person.

The next time you are facing a difficult situation, don't whine, complain or give up hope—take action! Don't spend all your time focusing on the *problem,* focus on the *solution!* Get into the habit of identifying and facing your problems, resolving them, and learning from them. Strive to resolve conflicts *peacefully.*

Confronting someone does not have to be confrontational. The following tips will help you gain insight into ways to address your problems effectively and *peacefully.* Take a positive approach toward resolution.

1. **Own the problem.** When you are upset with something someone did or said, it is natural to want to focus on the incident that happened or the person who upset you. When you become upset, even when it is because of the actions of someone else, *it is your problem* to deal with. *You* are the one who has a problem with what someone said or did; therefore *you* need to do something to resolve it. When you attempt to resolve a problem, *own the problem.*

2. **Speak in terms of "I," not "you."** When you have a problem with someone, it is your problem. You might be inclined to point fingers and cast blame, but it will only put the other person on the defensive and create more tension. Don't blame someone else for *your* problem; you will gain more cooperation when you speak for yourself and

about yourself. "I get upset when I don't receive credit for the project we both worked on" vs. "You make me so mad when you take credit for the project we both worked on" or "I have a difficult time concentrating on my work when I hear loud music playing" vs. "You play your music so loud that I can't get any work done."

3. **Don't react; *respond*.** A reaction is an immediate, instinctual, emotional response. Some reactions are more difficult to control than others. When someone comes up from behind and tries to scare you, you'll likely be startled and might jump or scream. Typically, you react so quickly you don't even think about what you are doing. Some reactions are physical while others are emotional. When we react to something, we are more likely to say or do things we might later regret. For example, what if the person who came up behind you to scare you is a practical joker who is always trying to catch you off guard? Once you calm down, you might think about the incident with regret, wishing you hadn't reacted at all. Changing your reaction, especially when you are caught off guard, is never an easy thing to do, although it can be done.

   A response differs from a reaction because a response is planned and well thought-out. You postpone making a comment in order to give yourself time to think about how you want to respond, rather than reacting impulsively to what happens.

   When you feel your emotions taking over, pay attention and do what you can to gain control. Take a deep breath, count to 10, request a time-out, or do whatever you must to clear your head, think things through, and then respond, rather than react, to what has happened.

4. **Think about it before you talk about it.** Give yourself time to collect your thoughts and think about what you want to say. When you approach someone you have a problem with, the more prepared you are, the clearer your communication will be.

5. **Identify your objectives.** What do you hope to accomplish? What changes do you want? If your purpose is simply to air your grievances, you might end up more frustrated than you were before. Focus on your desired outcome, but be open to *any* solution.

6. **Go directly to the source.** Telling Jane how upset you are with Jo will not do anything to help you resolve your problem with Jo. Always speak directly to the person you have the issue with.

7. **Change location.** Whenever possible, address your problems with someone in a private and neutral location. Taking the conversation into a private office or a conference room will work, and sometimes an entirely different environment can help diffuse a volatile situation. Sometimes a new atmosphere can help you view things differently.

8. **Focus on the *problem,* not the *person.*** The problem is not a person. Never attack a person's character or integrity. Focus on the problem you are trying to solve and the solution you want.

9. **Look for common ground.** You may differ in your opinions yet seek the same outcome. Try to find some common ground to stand on, no matter how small.

10. **Agree to disagree.** You might never see eye to eye with someone about an issue, but you don't have to. You can agree to disagree and still work peacefully and productively together. It is wise to try to understand another viewpoint, but when you cannot, resist the urge to argue; it will only make the other person feel defensive. Don't try to change your coworker; agree to disagree.

11. **Ask questions.** Rather than stating your position or making assumptions, ask questions. Get to know all you can about the other person's point of view. This will help to break down defenses and help you have a conversation instead of confrontation.

12. **Listen more, say less.** Listen to what is being said. Listen to the words and the intent. Avoid the temptation to interrupt or judge what you hear. When you speak, you reinforce your position; when you listen, you learn about someone else's.

LEARN TO LISTEN

Communication is essential to all good relationships. Good communication is more than good speaking skills; the best communicators are *good listeners.* Studies suggest most of us are *not* good listeners and that we miss much of what is communicated to us. Poor listening is at the root of many misunderstandings, hurt feelings, and, in some instances, costly mistakes.

Listening to someone is *not* the same as hearing what is being said. You *hear* sounds and noises all the time, but you may not *listen* to them. Have you *heard* a song on the radio without *listening* to the words? If you keep a radio on for background noise and you want to listen to a song that's playing, what do you do? You probably stop what you are doing, turn up the volume, and concentrate on what you hear; you *listen* to the words. That is quite different than simply hearing the song in the background.

Most people give themselves more credit than they deserve and consider themselves to be good listeners. The truth is that most of us are inefficient listeners, comprehending only 25 percent of what we hear. We can think we are listening even when we are not. Without even realizing what we are doing, we often engage in other activities when we should be focusing on the person who is speaking. You can talk to a friend as you check your e-mail or talk with your spouse as you read the paper, but you probably aren't communicating very well. In order to improve your listening skills, whenever you are in a conversation, you need to *stop* doing everything else and *focus* on what is being said—not always an easy thing to do. How well do you think *you* listen? Do you:

Look at the person talking to you (maintain eye contact)?   Yes/No

Avoid interrupting?   Yes/No

Clarify by asking questions?   Yes/No

Remain calm during disagreements?   Yes/No

Ignore distractions?   Yes/No

Avoid completing other people's sentences?   Yes/No

Avoid correcting other people's grammar or word choice?   Yes/No

Give feedback and response?   Yes/No

Eliminate distractions (e.g., looking through papers and watching other people)?   Yes/No

Wait to answer questions until the speaker is finished asking them?   Yes/No

Show interest in the conversation through verbal feedback?   Yes/No

Show interest through nonverbal feedback (nodding, positive facial expressions)?   Yes/No

Avoid changing the subject abruptly?   Yes/No

Now go back through your answers and count the number of "yes" responses. If you have answered yes to many or all of these questions, congratulations! You're a great listener. However, every "no" response deserves your attention and suggests you might need to polish up your listening skills a bit. Which skills do you need to work on? What actions will you take to improve your listening skills? Why not start working at being a better listener *today*?

THE FINE ART OF CONVERSATION

There really is a fine art involved in making conversation. Your ability to carry on a conversation is crucial in building relationships with others. The more natural a conversation is and the more comfortable people feel around you, the better. Conversation comes easily for some people, but for many it is a challenge. Developing this skill is worthwhile; the need for interesting conversation is *everywhere.*

You might be asking yourself, "What has this got to do with professionalism? Do I really have to spend time learning how to chitchat with people?" The answer is yes, absolutely! Conversation forms the foundation for business relationships. Your conversational skills can help you:

- Appear capable and friendly.
- Create strong relationships with clients, customers, and people in your organization.
- Set the background for business negotiations.
- Set the tone for important meetings.
- Identify potential clients or new business.
- Gather information about customers and clients.
- Stay up-to-date on industry trends.
- Establish yourself as a good listener and a sound resource.
- Break the ice at meetings and social gatherings.

You don't have to talk a lot to be a good conversationalist. A good conversation has nothing to do with impressive words or intelligent verbiage. The best conversations flow naturally and stem from a sincere desire to connect with people.

In his book, *How to Win Friends and Influence People,* Dale Carnegie says you can make more friends in two months by becoming interested in other people than you can in two years by trying to get other people interested in you. His best-selling book was written in 1936, yet his advice is as current today as it was all those years ago.

When the questions you ask are due to your authentic desire to learn, you will find that people open up to you. Anyone can ask questions, but if they are asked out of nosiness or feigned interest, it will feel like an interrogation. You either care or you don't. If you don't care, don't bother.

SAY IT IN A MINUTE

A good conversation has three distinct parts: The beginning (the introduction), the middle (content of conversation), and the end (wrap up and farewell). Every time you meet someone, you have an opportunity to establish a relationship. If you aren't able to quickly summarize your "story," which includes who you are and what you do, in under a minute, you might never get a second chance.

When people first meet you, they are not interested in hearing your life story, so don't bore people with insignificant details. Instead, try to generate interest and give others a reason to want to know more about you. A good introduction is brief and to the point.

In under a minute, and ideally within 30 seconds, you need to be able to tell the people you meet *who* you are, *what* you do, and *why* you are worth getting to know. The more interesting your introduction, and the more it is focused on the other person, the more effective it will be. In other words, telling others what *you* want or need is not likely to motivate anyone to talk with you. The more you can customize your introduction, the better, but if you plan on using a generic introduction, then make it unique. If you want to be remembered, you'd better say something memorable. I met a woman once who, when I asked what she did, told me, "I bring people home." I was curious by what she said and the way she said it, and wanted to know more. I've never forgotten her or the fact that she was a real estate agent. There are thousands of real estate agents, job seekers, and salespeople. Don't become one of the thousands—be the one in a million.

Your introduction will either open doors for you or close them. You will know if it is working by the response you receive. Take time to craft your introduction, and then practice it over and over until you are comfortable with it and can say it naturally and easily.

A good introduction will often lead to a good conversation. When you need to move on to mingle with others or want to end a conversation, do it tactfully, not abruptly. One of the best ways to end a conversation is to suggest continuing it at a later date. "I'd love to learn more about your mentoring program. May I call you next week to set a time to get together?" It's always good to end on a positive note ("I've enjoyed talking with you"), a plan for future contact ("I'll send you my brochure"), or a simple good-bye ("Enjoy the rest of the evening").

If you ever feel trapped or need an excuse to end a conversation, a simple "Excuse me" is all you need to say. You needn't provide a reason for leaving a conversation. Unless you are committed to being with someone for the evening, you are free to move around and shouldn't feel obligated to stick with any one person the entire time.

A conversation is meant to be a continuous exchange of ideas. When I am teaching people basic conversation skills, I try to get people to view it as a game and suggest envisioning an imaginary ball with every conversation. Whoever initiates the conversation has the ball, but the object of the game is to release the ball as soon as you can. The best way to release the ball is by asking someone a question. The person will have possession of the ball as long as he or she speaks. As soon as you begin to speak, the ball comes back to you. The object of the game is to keep the ball in the other person's court for as much time as possible. Always make an effort to release the ball within one minute of receiving it.

An ideal conversation is one in which the ball volleys. There is a rhythm to a good conversation, and as long as you keep the ball going back and forth, you maintain that rhythm. When someone holds onto the ball too long, the rhythm and flow of the conversation are disrupted.

CONVERSE WITH *ANYONE*

You can't ask intelligent questions if you don't know what's going on in the world. At a minimum, read newspaper headlines, watch the first five minutes of the television news, or check the Internet for the latest news. Take time to read as much as you can to have a current knowledge of a variety of topics to increase your chances for finding common interests. In-depth discussion of a few topics is less ideal than general knowledge of many things. For one thing, you won't intimidate those you're conversing with by delving too deeply into topics they might be unfamiliar with. The art of good conversation leaves your listeners with their egos intact!

- **Learn to remain quiet and listen.** Often, the art of really good conversation is not saying anything at all! Good listeners enjoy listening and sincerely believe that what the person is talking about is important. This skill translates to making the person feel interesting and important. Your good listening habits will prevent you from interrupting, overpowering conversations, or coming off in a pompous or overbearing manner.

I was at a convention when I struck up a conversation with Mary, the life of the party. Her stories had everyone around her listening, laughing, and asking for more. I sat next to her at dinner and I continued to ask her questions. She told me story after story. I learned a great deal that night and enjoyed listening to her. When it was time for me to leave, she told me how much she enjoyed talking with me. The truth was, I barely said a word, but she thought I was a great conversationalist! What I really was that night was a great audience! Any time we ask questions, we show we're interested in others and what they have to say. Asking questions to get others to talk is the best way to become a great conversationalist.

- **Learn graceful ways to change the subject.** When silences loom, interest in particular topics wanes, or a slightly embarrassing comment needs to be covered, learn how to control your conversations by deftly changing to another subject. Asking another question can help you change subjects: "What should we do if it rains on our golf outing tomorrow?" "What's the forecast for the rest of the week?"

- **Develop skill in drawing others into a conversation.** Quiet people or newcomers might need a bit of encouragement and help to enter a conversation successfully. You can help someone along by focusing your eyes on the person and finding a way to bring him or her in. "John, I heard you're quite a good golfer. How often do you play?"

If John appears a bit shy and gives you a simple answer such as, "I play whenever I can," don't give up on him just yet; continue to help him along. "Tell me more, John. Just how good a game do you play?" "How much would you *like* to play if you could?" "What courses do you prefer?" If you are sincere in your desire to get to know someone, and you ask relevant questions specific to the individual, you will find people opening up to you easily and quickly. If you encounter someone who is not responding after you have made an effort to connect, don't push too hard; wrap up the conversation and move on.

- **Use techniques to make people feel comfortable.** Show someone how much you care by facing them as you speak, maintaining eye contact, leaning forward, and giving both verbal and nonverbal feedback. Remember names and use them often, ask specific and tailored questions, and listen carefully to the responses you get. Look for commonalities. Whether you graduated the same year, grew up in a small town, frequent the same restaurant, enjoyed the same movie, or have children who are close in age, focus on the things that unite you. Discovering even the smallest connection with someone is a good start toward a real relationship.

- **Ask open-ended questions.** By asking questions, you indicate that you're listening and are interested in what others are saying. "How did you get into this line of work?" or "How did you get involved in the Chamber?" are good conversation openers and will get people talking. In contrast, "Do you like your job?" can be answered with one word—yes or no. Ask this and your conversation will be over in a minute.

Once you know someone, keep track of the things you learned, and each time you see that person draw upon something from a previous conversation to follow up on: "Tell me about your trip with your family to Disneyworld." or "How did the move go—I'd love to hear all about your new home!" are personalized and sure to make someone feel valued.

- **Avoid interrupting others.** Interruptions can take the form of correcting others, breaking eye contact by looking elsewhere, fidgeting, changing the subject, or speaking off topic. If you do any of these things, it is an indication that you weren't really listening to the exchange. Any of these actions leave others feeling slighted. They might even be a bit angry with you without your even being aware of it. The only time interrupting may be appropriate is when someone is monopolizing the conversation or meeting.

- **Don't say too much about yourself.** At some point in the conversation, the person you are with should show an interest in you. While you don't want to be too secretive or private, don't monopolize the conversation either. Respond, but don't become the focus.

- **Be upbeat and positive.** Share a positive outlook on the things you talk about and concentrate on generally positive, upbeat topics. Don't try to solve world problems over happy hour.

- **Stick with safe topics.** There's nothing worse than an animated conversation at a cocktail party about death, dying, cancer, and crime. General topics, such as sports, weather, hobbies, and work will keep you on firm ground, but don't get carried away bragging about your kids and grandkids.

- **Make good eye contact with others.** Look directly at people; engage them by linking eyes as well as hands through a handshake in greeting and parting. Then take time to listen. Show real interest in others. Ask questions, listen to responses so you can learn more about the other person, and perhaps even discover some real common ground or shared interest that sparks a genuine connection. Then you have a foundation for developing firm relationships that form solid groundwork for on-the-job allies, networking, mentoring, and/or good customer or client relations.

- **Avoid gossip.** Refrain from talking about others in a negative way. Those who talk *to you* about others will also *talk about* you to others.

- **Learn to give and receive compliments.** A modest smile, an appreciative nod, or even turning the compliment meant for you into an opportunity to acknowledge others will help you accept compliments without seeming either overbearing or passive. Look for opportunities to give sincere compliments. Giving a sincere compliment is a wonderful way to reach out to others. I'm not talking about buttering up someone, but noticing and recognizing the effort and work of others is valuable. If you make other people look good, you make yourself look good, too.

Receive compliments with similar sincerity and grace. Never disregard a compliment or suggest a person's opinion is wrong. For example: "Pat, you look great in that suit." If Pat replies, "Oh, this old thing? Are you kidding? I look awful today," how is the person giving the compliment going to feel? Probably put down and a little foolish. Why argue with someone's point of view, especially if it's a positive view of you?

- **Contribute to a conversation.** In order to allow a conversation to *evolve,* you have to *involve* yourself. Never allow yourself to become so mechanical that you distance yourself from connecting with people or allow your conversations to become interviews. While you don't want to monopolize the conversation, you don't want to withdraw from it either. Respond to what you hear and contribute to the conversation.

- **Be diplomatic.** Included in the art of making small talk and conversing with others is diplomacy. Frederick Sawyer once said a diplomat is ". . . a man who thinks twice and says nothing." That's a good reminder if you're wondering what's OK to say. Noncommittal, general conversation is always a good approach to take when you're unfamiliar with those around you and uncertain of the status of your relationships.

- **Be open-minded.** Become interested in learning more about another point of view instead of reinforcing your own. You know *your* point of view, but you don't always know how others see things. Make it a practice to learn what others think; be open-minded and willing to change your point of view.

- **Stick with safe topics.** When you are in the early stages of becoming acquainted with someone, certain subjects should remain off-limits. You don't know enough about someone to determine how he or she might react to your jokes, opinions, or personal preferences. Some topics are safer than others. Don't venture into dangerous territory.

Safe topics

Personal interests	Weather
Travel	Sports
Children and family	Work or business
Movies and entertainment	Books
Current events	Restaurants and food
Hobbies	Pets

Topics to avoid

Off-color racial, ethnic, or sexual jokes	Age
	Mental and physical health
Personal finances and income	Romance or personal relationships
Divorce or affairs	Religion
Weight	Politics

You can converse with anyone, regardless of status or position. Don't let fear get in your way. You never have to be intimidated by anyone; conversation will flow naturally when you focus on others and understand the importance of making them feel important. The one topic everyone can talk about, and almost always enjoys is talking about, himself or herself. When you can make people feel comfortable enough to open up to you, you will have mastered a skill most people lack. When you get others talking about themselves, not only will they enjoy the conversation, but you will be remembered as a great conversationalist even if you've barely said anything at all.

POINTS TO REMEMBER

1. **Develop conversation skills.** Don't just talk; become knowledgeable *and curious* about a variety of topics, and get people talking about themselves.

2. **People problems are inevitable.** Get into the habit of addressing the problems and concerns you have with others when they occur, and do everything in your power to resolve them before they escalate into bigger problems.

3. **People need people.** You can't network or have conversations alone; reach out to others and make it a point to meet new people, but keep in touch with your old acquaintances.

4. **Control your emotions.** Respond, don't react—or, worse yet, overreact—to what happens. If you are upset or concerned, your emotions might get in the way. Give yourself time to calm down and gather your thoughts before responding.

5. **Perfect your 30-second introduction.** Capture who you are and what you do, and be able to say it in under a minute. The more interesting, unique, and brief your introduction is, the better your results will be.

6. **Be a good listener.** Focus on the person speaking to you, ask questions for clarity, and avoid distractions.

7. **Learn to give and receive compliments.** Look for positive things to say and be generous with your praise. Never negate a compliment you receive; show your appreciation by saying thank you.

True or False?

1. If someone likes you, he or she is more apt to hire you, promote you, or do business with you.

TRUE.

The more likable you are, the more opportunities you will have. People like to be around people they enjoy. A good attitude and a pleasing personality are welcome attributes most anywhere.

2. Problems with other people are a leading cause of job dissatisfaction.

TRUE.

Problems with people tend to escalate when they're not dealt with and can become the focus of every work day. It is important to be tolerant of others and learn to deal with differences and irritations before they overshadow everything else about a job.

3. Good relationships are the foundation of business success.

TRUE.

The better your relationships, the better off you will be. Nurture all of your relationships and treat everyone you meet with respect.

4. You don't have to talk a lot to be a good conversationalist.

TRUE.

The best conversationalists say very little; they have skill in getting others to talk, and they know how to ask specific and open-ended questions. If you are sincerely interested in what others have to say and listen carefully to what is being said, you will be able to focus on other people and learn from them.

5. Most people are poor listeners.

TRUE.

Most of us hear only a fraction of what is being said. The best way to improve your listening is by focusing on what is being said. Listen more and talk less.

6. When you have a problem with someone you work with, tell your supervisor before doing anything else.

FALSE.

People problems are inevitable. Learn to deal with a variety of personalities. If you have a problem with someone, speak with that person. If you cannot resolve the problem or the situation is threatening, speak with your supervisor.

Chapter 13

The Attitude Advantage

YOUR ATTITUDE; YOUR CHOICE

This book identifies many areas in which your professionalism is displayed. The kind of impression you make, the way you carry yourself, your tone of voice, your actions, and the clothes you wear all reflect your feelings about yourself and your job.

In Chapter 4, you were introduced to the five components of your professional image:

Impression

Movement

Attitude

Grooming

Etiquette

It is essential to focus on each one of the five components equally because they all work together to help convey a positive and professional image. It's not enough to simply dress well and look great. You also need to carry yourself with confidence, put a smile on your face, and make sure your attitude is congruent with your actions. In other words, you'd better walk your talk, or your efforts will be in vain.

When I decided to leave college before graduating to go into sales, many skeptics told me it was a bad idea. After all, I didn't have a college degree or any relevant job experience. Cautious and concerned people told me I'd never get a job with so few qualifications, but I knew better. I knew I could relate well with people, and I was confident I would be good in sales.

I targeted companies, sent out résumés, and responded to ads, and I received calls for interviews. Upon meeting and interviewing with various people, I began to hear some of the same things over and over. "You don't have the qualifications we want, but you do seem to have what it takes to be a successful salesperson." "I like your enthusiasm and confidence." The qualities I had that were most attractive to the people I interviewed with were the qualities many of the more qualified job candidates were without. After several months, I was finally given an opportunity with a company, and I began my career in sales.

To this day, I believe that the reason I was hired and the reason I was successful was because of my attitude. What else could it be? I didn't have the qualifications my employer sought, but I did have drive and enthusiasm. I offered nothing more than my resolve to do well; it was my greatest asset. While other job seekers relied on experience, I relied solely on myself. There are many people who have impressive résumés, yet they have self doubt, lack ambition and initiative, and don't relate well to people. *The attitude you convey makes the difference.*

Some people complain about *everything* while others remain optimistic and cheerful. Either mind-set can be taken to an extreme, but given the choice, would you rather be around someone who is upbeat or someone who is downtrodden?

Your attitude is your choice; *you* are the one who determines your thoughts and reactions. You cannot control everything that happens to you, so don't bother trying. You *can,* however, control your *response* to what happens. The more conscious you are of your actions and thoughts, the more control you will have over them.

DESCRIBE YOURSELF

To help you evaluate your own attitude and image and become more aware of yourself, read through the following list of descriptive words and circle or make a note of any that you believe describe *you.* Look for the words that describe you as you are *now,* not how you'd like to be. Make your decisions quickly, without overanalyzing or thinking too much about each word. Your initial response will be most accurate.

creative	shy	fun	independent
diplomatic	extroverted	sophisticated	witty
dignified	satisfied	self-reliant	polished
calm	arrogant	confident	influential

distinctive	professional	controlled	successful
meek	cautious	respectful	impatient
wholesome	efficient	determined	reserved
self-centered	casual	masculine	enthusiastic
approachable	intellectual	original	delicate
innocent	flexible	classic	savvy
dramatic	controlling	flirtatious	active
authoritative	restrained	severe	unique
feminine	disciplined	cold	naive
gentle	friendly	gracious	fashionable
sarcastic	aggressive	elegant	persuasive
humble	attractive	stubborn	bold
loyal	negative	charming	open-minded
cheerful	precise	competitive	considerate
harmonious	inspiring	obedient	sociable
receptive	cordial	daring	soft-spoken
convincing	tolerant	persistent	optimistic
positive	accurate	restless	polite
peaceful	tough	distant	kind
outspoken	assertive	introverted	authentic

Now look over the words you selected and put a star next to the words you consider to be assets.

Next, look through the list of words you chose and place a check mark next to any words you picked that you believe are a detriment or might hold you back from achieving your goals.

Finally, read through the following list of the same words, this time circling or noting all of the words you feel are essential for success or that describe someone who is successful.

creative	shy	fun	independent
diplomatic	extroverted	sophisticated	witty
dignified	satisfied	self-reliant	polished
calm	arrogant	confident	influential

distinctive	professional	controlled	successful
meek	cautious	respectful	impatient
wholesome	efficient	determined	reserved
self-centered	casual	masculine	enthusiastic
approachable	intellectual	original	delicate
innocent	flexible	classic	savvy
dramatic	controlling	flirtatious	active
authoritative	restrained	severe	unique
feminine	disciplined	cold	naive
gentle	friendly	gracious	fashionable
sarcastic	aggressive	elegant	persuasive
humble	attractive	stubborn	bold
loyal	negative	charming	open-minded
cheerful	precise	competitive	considerate
harmonious	inspiring	obedient	sociable
receptive	cordial	daring	soft-spoken
convincing	tolerant	persistent	optimistic
positive	accurate	restless	polite
peaceful	tough	distant	kind
outspoken	assertive	introverted	authentic

Take some time to review the words you chose in the first part of the exercise—the words that describe *you*. Then examine those that you picked in the second part—traits of successful people.

- What words did you select in the second list (the characteristics of successful people) that you *didn't* select in the first list (your characteristics)?

- Which characteristics do you believe are necessary to be successful (the ones you picked in the second list) that you don't see in yourself?

- What do you need to do to make the characteristics you see yourself possessing (the first list) coincide with the traits you believe successful people have (the second list)?

- Read through the words you chose on the second list again, and put a star by three traits you will begin to work on.

Take your time with this exercise. The answers to what you need to do in order to be more professional are right before your eyes. Identifying and focusing on the traits you need to have and must work on developing are essential to gaining the edge.

BENEFITS OF A POSITIVE ATTITUDE

Your attitude is evident in everything you do. When you have a positive attitude, you increase your chances of success. You open yourself up to unforeseen possibilities, experience less stress, and feel a greater sense of personal contentment. When you maintain a positive outlook, you improve your chances of living a long and healthy life. Study after study has found a link between mental health and physical health. Your emotions affect you in many ways. The more positive you are and the better your attitude, the stronger your immune system will be. When your immune system is strong, your ability to fight off illness and disease is enhanced.

Opting to look on the bright side isn't always easy, nor is life always bright and cheery. You've seen bad things happen to good people. You know dreams don't always come true. You admit that not everyone can be trusted. As a result, you are cautious; you want to be *realistic*. Maybe you cling to your pessimistic, futile attitude to avoid creating false hope. Perhaps you're trying to protect yourself from being hurt or disappointed. Choosing to have a positive attitude is *not* the same as burying your head in the sand. You can be optimistic and at the same time, remain realistic. For example, if you want a job and find one you'd like to have, you apply for it. If you are looking to buy a house and find one you'd like to buy, you make an offer. You know there's a chance you might not get either, but you assume you've got a chance, and you hope you'll get what you want. When you hope it will work out, you are being both realistic and optimistic.

If someone else gets the job or house you wanted, you can get mad, feel sorry for yourself, or conclude that you are an unlucky person. But you don't *have to* feel that way. You can allow yourself to be momentarily disappointed, evaluate what went wrong and why, then move on and assume something better will come along. Over time, there's a good chance you'll theorize (and eventually realize) that there were aspects of the job you wouldn't have enjoyed or that the house you almost bought needed more work than you wanted to do. Eventually you will find a job you enjoy and a home that is better than the one you lost. When you do, you will be grateful the others fell through and understand the reason they did.

You have a choice; you can either let your losses get the best of you or *bring out the best in you*. Why not look for and learn valuable life lessons from your disappointments? Why not look for the *reason* something happened or how you contributed to it? What will it hurt to assume something better will come along?

ATTITUDES ABOUT AGE AND AGING

No matter what age you are, it can be an advantage or a disadvantage. The concepts in this book are for *anyone* who wants to improve his or her image at any phase. If you allow yourself to get stuck in a rut or refuse to change your ways, you will limit your opportunities. If you embrace technology and keep up with the times, you will remain competitive and your experience and maturity will be an added advantage.

If you are older and have been around while, it can be difficult to work for a younger person. You may think you know more than the young manager you work with, but be careful about offering free advice, telling others what to do, or talking about the way things used to be. Rank comes before age in business, and it is important to show respect for others.

Renee Ward, principal of the Forward Group, which publishes Seniors4Hire.org, has found increasing numbers of businesses recognizing the value of hiring and retaining older workers. Companies will always need people that can help them stay in business and grow and the experience and maturity that comes with age can be an asset. If you are looking to make a change or seeking employment, pay attention to some of the recommendations Seniors4Hire offers:

- Stay current or get current in your field or industry. Be knowledgeable of the latest buzz, new technologies, and best practices.

- Make sure your resumes don't go back any more than 10 years. Make sure your resume is tailored for a specific position, written for electronic scanners, and emphasizes the credentials needed by the company.

- Walk in to an interview assuming you will be given fair consideration. Show your eagerness, excitement, passion, and vitality.

- Demonstrate how your skills and accomplishments can contribute to the company's bottom line today and in the future. Don't rest on your past laurels.

Your state of mind affects *everything* you do no matter what stage of life you are in. You can be happy and successful at *any* age.

Your state of mind affects *everything* you do. Your attitude rubs off on *everyone* you're with. When you improve your attitude, you will improve the way you feel about yourself and others. As a result, others will change the way they feel about you. Following are some of the most important aspects of a successful, professional attitude and manner in business.

RESPECT OTHERS

Showing respect for others has been the underlying theme throughout this book. How you treat others is a reflection of how you value them. Many of the problems surrounding gender issues, diversity, and harassment would be eliminated if everyone lived with respect for others and their differences. It is the differences that make the workplace a place of learning. Your respect for others is visible in many ways.

- Do you treat everyone equally regardless of gender, ethnicity, or rank?

- Do you get to know people before judging them or their value?

- Do you honor others' cultural customs and personal preferences?

- Do you keep a comfortable distance when speaking with someone rather than invading his or her personal space?

- Do you respect an individual's title or rank by addressing him or her in a formal way?

- Do you respect time when meeting with someone or speaking on the telephone?

- Do you listen to what others have to say without correcting or interrupting?

- Do you respect differing opinions and views?

- Are you tolerant of others?

If you want others to respect you, start by respecting others. Don't be afraid of differences or try to intimidate other people; you cannot force respect, you have to earn it. Start by showing respect for *everyone*. Never overlook people or assume someone doesn't matter. For example, some people overlook the assistant they must deal with in order to get to the person they are trying to reach, which is a big mistake. An assistant is the closest person to your contact and can help you get through or make it difficult. But don't butter up the assistant only because you want something; putting on the charm when you want something from someone won't impress anyone. You either are a respectful, kind person, or you are not. A respectful attitude will not only make others feel good, but it will also make *you* look good. *By respecting others, you will earn respect in return.*

USE "PLEASE" AND "THANK YOU"

Little things make a big difference. A simple "please" attached to a request or a "thank you" when someone has done something for you can make all the difference in the world. Being courteous toward others makes people feel valued. It is the simplest way to motivate people and gain cooperation. In most cases, you can gain more cooperation by asking rather than telling. And people will be happy to help you when they can feel good about doing so. We all crave appreciation and need to feel that what we do matters. Whenever someone does something for you, show your appreciation; don't assume the person knows how appreciative you are. No matter how small the deed, say thank you when someone does something for you.

In addition, look for other ways to show your gratitude. If someone goes out of their way for you, go out of your way to express your thanks. If you know of a special food that person enjoys, pick it up and bring it to him or her. Offer to take that person's place when it's his or her turn to clean up the employee kitchen or pick up rolls for the morning meeting. Invite him or her to lunch, buy a blooming plant or flowers, write a personal note of thanks; find your special way of honoring the person who did something for you. And when you do express your thanks, always *be specific*; tell the person *what* you are thankful for and *why*. Showing your appreciation shows an attitude of gratitude. *Everyone craves appreciation; fill the craving.*

BE ON TIME

Due to circumstances beyond your control, you may find yourself, on occasion, falling behind schedule. Unfortunately, being late for one meeting in the morning can have a domino effect that ripples through the rest of your day. Consistent lateness can be interpreted as being negligent, careless, or disrespectful. It can make you appear disorganized, unprofessional, or out of control.

Too often we have a distorted view of what we can accomplish in any given day. Unexpected phone calls, problems, and delays you encounter can eat up huge amounts of time. But these unexpected happenings aren't really unexpected at all. You may not know the precise moment the phone will ring, but you can count on it ringing during the day. You can't predict every problem you'll face, but you can count on having problems. The things that take us by surprise and set us behind schedule are quite predictable and should be anticipated.

Learning to manage your time more effectively requires planning, personal commitment, and self-discipline. When you set your schedule or make appointments, allow extra time for delays you might encounter. Assume you will be interrupted, run into traffic delays, and have to deal with last-minute problems. You won't know what problem will surface or when, but you can be assured that something, or someone, is bound to interfere with your plans and ruin your good intentions. *Expect the unexpected and you will be better prepared to deal with whatever comes your way.*

The more control you have over your time, the more you will be able to accomplish. When you say you will do something and you do it, you become trustworthy and accountable. When you show up on time for appointments, you demonstrate your self-control and respect for others. The amount of time you keep someone waiting is proportionate to the value you place on that person. Never keep someone waiting longer than a few minutes. Time is precious and cannot be retrieved once it gets away from you. Use your time wisely, and make sure your attitude shows you value time. *Manage your time; don't let your time manage you.*

SPEAK POSITIVELY

Listen to the conversations you hear. What is the tone of most of them? Is it positive or negative? Although many conversations take on a negative spin, make sure you speak positively about your job, your organization, and your coworkers. It sounds simple, but is not. It is easy to find fault with others, talk bad about others, or complain about policies. It is easier to see the things that are not working than it is to identify the things that are. It's easier to find fault in others than it is to acknowledge their strengths.

Perhaps it's because negativity surrounds you. The television news plays one negative story after another. Join a group of coworkers in any office and you will hear plenty of complaints and lots of gossip about others. We know we shouldn't talk about others, but we do it anyway. It may make you feel more important in the moment, but even if you do succeed in making others look bad, chances are even better that you'll succeed in making *yourself* look bad.

It takes only one person to stop the cycle of negative chatter—you can be that person. Change the subject; offer a positive viewpoint, and take a stand against bad-mouthing others. There is plenty of despair out there; why don't you be the one who brings hope and happiness to others? Your attitude will be refreshing and you will be highly regarded. *Speak positively about others and they are more likely to speak positively about you.*

BE ENTHUSIASTIC

Although some equate enthusiasm with nothing more than cheering at a football game, being an enthusiastic professional is far more than that. Enthusiasm is an important business tool, yet it's one that many people misunderstand and avoid. Think of some of the encounters you've had when you were the customer. Think of the salespeople you've met who've lacked enthusiasm; they seemed to be saying to themselves, "Hmmm . . . maybe if I ignore them they'll go away." How did that make you feel?

Compare those people with others you've met who were happy, positive, and enthusiastic about seeing you walk through the door. Think about who would be most likely to get your business.

Enthusiasm is a quiet yet contagious energy that lets others know you are excited and passionate about what you do. Enthusiasm is often the difference between good and great service, and it differentiates an average experience from one that is superb.

When you are passionate, when you are interested, when you are excited, you are enthused. You can spot enthusiastic people because of the smiles on their faces. They have an extra beat in their steps. They seem genuinely happy to be with you and help you.

Enthusiasm comes naturally to some people, but others have to work at being enthusiastic. You can help yourself become more enthused. Start with a smile. Then *act* interested, *act* passionate, *act* like you care, and you will see and feel the difference. Enthusiasm is a great equalizer; it has nothing to do with talent, skill, or position. An enthusiastic attitude makes you welcome most anywhere. *Enthusiasm is contagious; start spreading it around.*

TAKE PRIDE IN EVERYTHING YOU DO

As Mark Twain once said, "Always do right. This will surprise some people and astonish the rest." No matter what position you hold, your job is important. Each person and every position is essential to an organization's overall success. Remember, no organization would accomplish much without all of the hard-working employees who support it. Your job is important. Work each day with energy and purpose.

Real progress takes time. You may not be working in your ideal job right now, but be patient. Everyone has to pay his or her dues, and you do too. Be willing to work your way up, but don't waste your time working at a job you despise. If you hate what you do, either find a new job or find a way to improve the job you have.

- If you don't feel important, do something important.

- If you don't feel valued, do something of value.

- If you aren't getting noticed, do something noticeable.

- If you don't get respect, do something respectable.

- If you aren't being acknowledged, start acknowledging others.

Look beyond the work you do and notice the people you see. Connect with someone new and make someone's day; you can find value in what you do. Your job may be temporary, but your reputation is long-lasting. Whatever you do and wherever you go, bring your pride with you. Do your best, because there is value in *everything* you do. *A job worth doing is a job worth doing well enough to be proud of it.*

SMILE

As discussed in Chapter 5, a smile can make you appear friendly, helpful, and positive. Smiling is important; your facial expression speaks for you before you have a chance to speak for yourself. A sincere smile is like an open door; it lets others know you welcome them and that you are open to being approached by them.

Most people would rather be around someone who is smiling than someone who is scowling. A smile is the fastest way there is to build rapport and acknowledge people and their ideas. Not only will you look better when you smile, you will look younger too!

If you are feeling down, smile and see how fast your spirits go up. If you feel unsure or insecure, smile and increase your confidence. If you are lonely, smile and attract other people. A smile can change your attitude and the attitude of others within seconds. Smile often and smile big; *like a picture, a smile really is worth a thousand words.*

BELIEVE IN YOURSELF

If you want others to believe in you, start by believing in yourself. If you don't, why should anyone else? You are your best salesperson, advocate, and promoter, so sell and promote your strengths, not your limitations. Don't tear yourself down or belittle yourself in front of other people; why draw attention to your imperfections? If you want people to believe in you, start by believing in yourself. Build yourself up and draw attention to your strengths.

Always be honest about your shortcomings, but never stop believing in your unlimited potential. Identify the things you want to improve or change and work on changing those things, but don't allow yourself to dwell on them. Listen to the manner in which you talk about yourself and become aware of the vision you create for others. If you put yourself down, you can't expect others to build you up. Always present yourself and talk about yourself with positive conviction.

Strength comes from within. Spend time with yourself. Journal, think, plan, dream, exercise, learn a new skill, do something for someone else, listen to music, read inspirational books, or do anything else you can do to nurture yourself. If you give away all of your time, thoughts, and self to others, you won't have anything left for yourself. People will take from you what you give away, as long as you allow them to.

If you have a dream of achieving something, hold onto that dream. Anything is possible; little is impossible. Be determined enough to overcome the obstacles you encounter and fight for what you believe. Share your dream with others and you will quickly find out who supports and believes in you and who questions you. You will never win the approval of everyone, so don't bother trying. Don't allow every naysayer you encounter get to you. Trust yourself, trust what you are doing, and believe in yourself. *You can achieve almost anything you want if you want it badly enough.*

BRING OUT THE BEST IN OTHERS

When you make others feel and look good, you will feel and look good too. Offering a sincere compliment is one way to make others feel good, and accepting a compliment graciously is important too. Some people purposely withhold kind remarks for others because they believe it will give the other person too much power. While you may assume someone has enough confidence or even an oversize ego, the truth is that most everyone can use a boost every now and then.

When you give of yourself and do or say something for the benefit of someone else, you benefit too. Even if you do succeed in making someone think more highly of himself or herself, that person can't help but think more highly of you too.

If you look for problems, you will find more than you can resolve. If you look for flaws in others, you will find them. But don't waste your time. No one needs or wants these things brought out. Most people are acutely aware of their limitations and imperfections and probably focus too heavily on them. However, few of us focus enough on our positive attributes. Most of us are more critical of ourselves than we need to be. It's always nice to receive some positive feedback.

If you want people to enjoy being around you, you've got to be enjoyable to be around. Do you prefer to be around people who make you feel good or bad? How do *you* make people feel? Do you bring out the *best* in others?

When you are with someone, affirm that person's positive attributes. Look for and focus on what makes someone unique, effective, or interesting, and then share what you discover with that person. Always aim to lift people up; don't bring anyone down. *Bring out the best in others and you'll bring out the best in yourself.*

ENJOY THE WORK YOU DO

Over the years, you will probably spend more time at work than at home. You will socialize more with your coworkers than with your friends, and you'll spend more time commuting than pursuing some of your personal interests.

The time commitment you make and give to a job is immense; don't waste your time doing something you despise. Spend your time doing something you enjoy. If you aren't happy at work, it is bound to carry over into other areas of your life. Your unhappiness at work can have an adverse affect on your relationships, your health, and your overall well-being. If you dread the thought of going to work each day, consider making a change. Life is too short.

If you are unhappy, determine why. If you are bored and need a change, consider requesting a move to another department or applying for different position. If that isn't enough, perhaps a move to another location or a different company is what you need. If that doesn't satisfy you, maybe you need an even bigger change, perhaps to a new field or an entirely new career. From the first job you accept to the last, chances are you will experience many changes. Whether you become part of a corporate downsizing or seek a better opportunity, you are likely to change jobs a number of times throughout your career. And although career changes are typically less frequent than job changes, they are not uncommon. Most people will change careers at some point, and sometimes they'll make several changes over the span of their lifetime.

If you are in a slump, a job or career change may be the solution. However, if you find yourself jumping from job to job in search of the elusive perfect job, you may never find it. Every job has advantages and disadvantages; every employee will like and dislike aspects of his or her job's duties. If you find problems with every job you have, the real problem may lie within *you.*

Many people grow both professionally *and* personally as a result of the changes and challenges they encounter in their work. No matter what your chosen profession, you can find meaning in what you do. You don't need to have a powerful position to have influence, and you don't need to do something unusual to leave a lasting legacy.

Befriend someone, offer your help, or simply smile and say hello to someone who's all alone. Make a difference in someone's life, and you will never be forgotten. Make it a habit, and you will find fulfillment wherever you go.

I have grown both mentally and emotionally as a result of my work. No matter what I've done, people have always told me that what I do looks like so much fun. I can't even count the number of times I've been told that I am lucky to have the job I have. When I hear this, I question what these people mean. Do they honestly think what I do is easy, something I just fell into, something given to me as a present?

When I started my business, it was anything but fun, and it was *not* easy. It was lonely at times; I worked alone, didn't have any clients, had no steady income, and was trying to sell a product few people wanted. Believe me, I've had many moments when I lost faith in myself and wondered what I was doing, but deep inside I believed I had a message people needed to hear. Even though some days I struggled to pull myself to the office, I did go. And when I did, I always ended up feeling better and enjoying myself. People think I'm lucky because they can see that I like what I do. What I do would not be considered fun to most people, and I don't always look forward to the work I have to do. But when I do it, I do everything I can to make it fun for myself and others. If I couldn't find a way to *like* what I do, I would have given up long ago.

If you are unhappy in your chosen field, figure out why. Identify something you'd enjoy doing more and consider making a change. It is never easy, and there's always a trade-off. Make your own fun and create your own luck, because no one else is going to do it for you.

I was making great money as a sales representative, but after seven years doing the same thing I was losing my zest; the challenge was gone. One of the hardest decisions I made was leaving and giving up a territory I built from scratch, but I knew I had reached my potential in that business and that it was time to move on. Once I did, I had to travel long distances, take chances and risks, work without making money, and create demand for something I believed in. Hard work, passion for what I do, and sheer determination has been responsible for my success. I *am* having fun and I *do* feel lucky, but these are things I've created myself. You, too, can create your own luck. You are the only one who can make yourself happy. Make sure you do something you enjoy and that you have fun doing it!

Become the kind of person who creates positive, rather than negative, energy. Remember, your overall success comes primarily from the way you handle yourself and others. *It all begins with the right attitude. Take control of yours.*

POINTS TO REMEMBER

1. **Respect others.**

2. **Be on time.**

3. **Speak positively about others.**

4. **Be enthusiastic.**

5. Take pride in everything you do.

6. Smile.

7. Believe in yourself.

8. Bring out the best in others.

9. Enjoy the work you do.

Chapter 14

Go for the Edge!

IT'S UP TO *YOU!*

*H*ow to Gain the Professional Edge was written to provide you with insight and information that will give you every advantage you need to succeed. This book covers many important issues, starting with who you are and where you want to go. *It's up to you* to set new goals, and *it's up to you* to accomplish them. *You* are responsible for what happens next.

By reading this book, you've been given the tools to create and convey a professional IMAGE in every one of five key areas:

Impression

Movement

Attitude

Grooming

Etiquette

You have the power to achieve your own professional edge. You have the information you need; *it's up to you* to make the principles in this book work. If you are open to others, open to their feedback, and open to change, I guarantee you'll have every opportunity to excel—and enjoy the process! Your attitude and openness will determine the way others respond to you. In order to bring out the best in others, you first need to bring out the best in *yourself*. Everything you *do* or *don't do* is determined by *you!*

FOUR SIMPLE RULES THAT GUARANTEE YOUR SUCCESS

We live in an era of constant change, and at times it may seem as though anything goes, but don't be fooled. You can do it *your* way, and you might defy the odds, but there are, and always have been, rules in business; they're no less real for being unwritten or unspoken.

The moment you accept a position, you accept all of the responsibilities that go with it. As you step into a new role, your performance will determine how successful you will be. You must play the part of a true professional, and you must play it exceptionally well.

Actors know what it takes to play a part well; an actor will make changes in appearance, mannerisms, and speech in order to *become* the character he or she plays. And you can learn from them. Pay attention to these four rules:

1. *Look* the part.

To be successful, you have to project an image with which your clients, your employer, and your colleagues are comfortable. Don't think that making changes to your image is giving up your individuality or compromising who you really are; you're being sensitive, savvy, and smart. To be successful, you need to project an image that your clients, your employer, and your colleagues are comfortable with.

The next time you enter a store or a party, pay attention to the clerk or the companion you seek out. It is likely you will gravitate toward those who look as if they can help you in a store or will be interesting to talk to at a party. What makes someone *look* approachable? Are they people close to your own age, educational level, and background—people who *look* like you? It's simple human nature, however predictable it might seem, to feel most comfortable with people who look, more or less, *like you.*

We also tend to favor the *expected* over the unexpected in others' appearance. Would you be more likely to trust a doctor in a lab coat carrying a stethoscope or one (perhaps equally competent) dressed in shorts and sunglasses? Would you be more apt to hire a carpenter wearing overalls and a tool belt or one wearing a sport coat and tie?

You actually have *more* latitude to be yourself and to contribute your particular skills and ideas when you *look the part* you want to play. By looking the part, you eliminate superficial barriers, enabling others to listen to and accept what you have to say. When it comes to clothing and grooming, *anyone* can enhance his or her look with attention to detail and up-to-date grooming and wardrobe tips—especially you.

2. *Act* the part.

You don't have to be a professional actor to *act* the part of a professional. You do, however, need to understand the role nonverbal communication plays in the way you come across to others. Acquiring new mannerisms and behaviors requires focus and determination. Controlling your gestures when you are under duress is something you can do to help you appear more confident. You need to walk the walk and talk the talk so that you appear the same as any successful person in your position.

Most business people will, at some point, find themselves in the position of introducing colleagues to one another, hosting or attending a business function, or socializing with clients and colleagues. These are just a few of the most common situations in which knowledge of business etiquette will see you through.

Knowing how to make yourself and others feel comfortable is an art, and can make all the difference in the way you are perceived. Etiquette is a skill worth perfecting if you are really serious about being successful in any field. When you *act* the part, you *become* the part.

3. *Be* the part.

Although a particular suit, hairstyle, or handshake can contribute to (or detract from) your professional image, your ability to demonstrate that you are capable, congenial, and constant will cinch the impression. Apply the "Three C's Test" as a quick way to monitor and modulate your encounters with the various "audiences" and "theaters" of your working life:

> **Capable**: Do you look and act like somebody who can do the job—not only the job you have, but the one you're striving toward?

> **Congenial**: Do you look and act like someone your clients, customers, boss, and coworkers can talk to and work with? Are you sincere, approachable, friendly, and helpful?

> **Consistent**: Do you look and act trustworthy? Are you dependable, the kind of person people can count on, because you do what you say?

The creative director of an ad agency, the attorney, and the manager of a high-fashion retail store all need to come across as capable, congenial, and consistent *in their particular setting*. They are unlikely to dress or behave alike. But the ones who are successful will look, act and be within the norm of what is expected in their particular industry and workplace. You'll be more successful if you are attentive to what that norm is in the job you have or the job you want, and you operate within it. It's that simple.

4. *Think* the part.

With so much focus on your *outer* image, be careful not to neglect your *inner* image. Your thoughts influence your actions; improve your performance by improving your thinking. Think your way to success, and think positively.

Your thoughts about and response to the changes that take place play a key role in how successful you will be. Your willingness to step outside of your comfort zone and take chances will benefit you.

Change is something many people resist, but change is an important part of life, both at work and at home. Over time, we change our tastes, our friends, our interests, our goals, and our jobs. We change because we *choose* to and at times because we *have* to. Either way, change can be good.

Even a downsizing situation, which no employee can control, can turn into a positive experience. Although initially the news can be devastating, many people eventually uncover new interests, find new opportunities, go into business for themselves, or end up reevaluating and fine-tuning their goals. Embrace change. Think of it as a chance to change the way you're doing things, to grow and improve.

Risk presents opportunities to experience great success by stretching yourself beyond the ordinary. The only way to go from *wanting* something to *having* something is by *doing* something. For years, I had the dream of becoming a business-advice columnist. My public relations person gave me the number of the business editor of our local newspaper after I told her about my idea for the column. After vacillating about whether I should try to contact the editor, I got up enough courage to make the call. I could tell he wasn't enthused, and just as he was about to hang up the phone, I convinced him to meet me for lunch.

I had to work with this editor for a full year writing sample columns, pitching other articles, and calling him regularly to check in. When a previous columnist stopped writing his column, my window of opportunity opened and I received the call I had been waiting and hoping for.

One phone call, and taking a big risk, forced me to stretch, step out of what I ordinarily did, and create something new. The results were well worth it. Take risks. Don't *wait* for things to happen to you, *make them happen!*

TAKE CARE OF YOURSELF

When I answered the phone, my friend Kathie, who was on the other end, was surprised. "I didn't think I'd ever talk to you again!" she said. Although we used to meet for lunch on a regular basis, we had been struggling to find the time to get together. When she asked me to meet her for lunch that day, I hesitated. It wasn't that I had plans; I just had so many other things I needed to do. I was feeling guilty about taking time away from work and also guilty for not being a good friend. As I wavered in my decision, citing the reasons another day would be better for us to meet, she interrupted me. "Sue, *stop*. We haven't seen each other in three months, and if we don't do it today, it will be another three months before we do. You need to eat, you need to take a break, and you need to get out and have some fun. I won't take no for an answer." I was still resistant, but I couldn't argue with her. She was insistent, and she was right; I wasn't taking good care of myself or my relationships. I needed to make time for myself *and* my friends.

Life gets busy. We've got work to do, families to raise, friends to see, committees to serve, and goals to accomplish. Too often we forget to take proper care of ourselves. When we finally remember, the things we decided to do are rarely a top priority. No one can do for you what you must do for yourself.

Work smarter not harder. You don't have to work seven days a week or put in extra hours each day to be successful. While the willingness to work hard is an asset, your *productivity* is even more important. If you are always bringing work home with you, working holidays and weekends, are the first to arrive and the last to leave each day, something is amiss. Identify the reasons why you feel the need to do so much more than others—and why you choose to work harder than you need to. It's good to be dedicated to your work, but not when work is all you think or care about. Working longer hours does not ensure you will be more effective or more productive than someone else. If you spend too much time at work, not only will your personal life suffer, but you are likely to burn out and then your work will suffer.

Make good use of the time you spend at work and learn to let go of whatever it is you are holding on to. You don't have to be perfect nor must you do everything yourself. Everyone needs down time; time away from work is essential for your well being. If you aren't sure what you should be doing differently or how to work smarter, seek guidance from someone else. The first step toward working smarter is acknowledging when you need help. The second step is being willing to ask for help when you need it.

Be a friend—to *yourself*. If you always end up last on your list, it's time to move yourself up to the top. If you don't think enough of yourself to make *you* a priority, no one else will either. Be the *best* kind of friend: supportive, encouraging, caring, understanding, nurturing. If you wouldn't belittle a friend, don't belittle yourself. If you'd do something nice for a friend, do something nice for yourself. You really can be your own best friend, and you will be better for it.

Track your accomplishments. Keep track of your accomplishments. Create a success file—save the notes that made you smile and keep records of your achievements. Write down the compliments you receive so you can read them when you need a boost. You may not think it matters now, but you'll be glad you kept track of your accomplishments when you're interviewing for a new position, asking for a raise, or are in need of a boost on a dreary day.

Learn the *easy* way. You don't have to learn all of life's lessons the hard way or go through the school of hard knocks. Learn and benefit from others. Don't hesitate to ask for help or seek advice. When you do, pay attention to what you hear.

When I started my business, I met with a retired bank president who offered his perspective and advice. I've never forgotten his words of wisdom that day. "Go out and buy a business journal. Write in it every day; keep a record of the experiences you have and the stories people share. Eventually you'll forget the details of your journey. Your journal will give you the material you need to write a book someday."

His advice was some of the best I've ever received. I became lax over the years and have some gaps in my writing, but what I do have, I treasure. *You* can follow his advice; you can start your journal today. I highly recommend you do.

Be your own advocate. Don't be modest, don't be shy, and don't expect someone else to do what *you* need to do. If you want something, ask for it. If you need something, announce it. Boast a little; pat yourself on the back. Pick yourself up when you're feeling down. No one is going to ask what *you* want or need; you'll have to ask yourself. If you don't ask, the answer is always no!

Minimize stress. Stress is inevitable, but you can learn to control and minimize the amount of stress you incur. The more control you have over the things you do, the less stress you are likely to feel. While it isn't always possible to control your environment or the things that happen, do what you can to have as much control over your life as possible.

If you are increasingly impatient and irritable, always feel you have more to do than you can get done, suffer with frequent headaches, indigestion, feel sluggish no matter how much sleep you get, don't enjoy the things that used to bring you pleasure, and are sleeping more but never feel rested, it may be due to stress. These are common reactions to stress, but everyone reacts differently. It is important to recognize your reactions and triggers to stress.

Managing stress is easier when you take good care of yourself. The healthier and more vibrant you are, the stronger you will be physically and emotionally and the better able you will be to deal with stress when it occurs.

Be healthy. You don't have to be sick to get well; adapt a healthier lifestyle and you will feel better, look better, and increase your stamina.

- **Eat *real* food.** If you get it from a machine, a package, or a box, it isn't *real* food. Eat more fruits and vegetables, and drink more water instead of filling up on sodas, sugar-laden juices, and other high-calorie drinks. If you don't believe that eating real food makes a difference, try it and see— the more real food you eat, the better you will feel.

- **Exercise.** If you don't have time, then take the stairs or walk for five, 10, or 15 minutes. Any amount of exercise is better than no exercise. It doesn't have to be regimented or routine. Move, stretch, breathe, do whatever you can. Every little bit makes a difference and makes you healthier.

- **Laugh.** Let go and laugh out loud! Studies have found a number of benefits gained from laughing: The sick heal faster, the burdened feel lighter, and the anxious feel calmer. Don't laugh at someone else—learn to laugh at *yourself;* it's what makes comedians so endearing. Don't be hard on yourself when you make a mistake—look for the *humorous* side of the lesson you learned. Laughing feels good, and it's good for you. Laugh often. Laugh out loud. Laugh until your stomach hurts from laughing. Let yourself go; laugh a healthy, hearty laugh. Watch a funny movie, laugh at someone's joke, do something silly. Laugh for no reason at all. Laugh your way to health, happiness, and cheer.

- **Express yourself.** If you have something to say, say it. Don't avoid your feelings. If you stuff them, they'll find some way to come out, and probably at the wrong time. Be honest with yourself and others. Cry or even yell if you must, but those emotions are best kept *out* of the office. Keeping your emotions intact doesn't mean you have to be emotionless. Whether your feelings are positive, negative, or somewhere in between, you're better off getting *rid* of them than stuffing them.

- **Take a time-out.** Close your eyes and relax. Breathe deeply. Sigh. Get a massage. Do yoga. Glance through a magazine. Read a chapter of a book. Write down your thoughts. Watch a sunset. Meditate. Listen to music. Daydream. Slow down. Walk around the block. Count your blessings. Take a nap. Take a bubble bath. Make time for yourself. Take time for yourself. You deserve it. *Enjoy* your day, every day.

Strive for balance in your life. It's a fact of life: there will always be more for you to do than time for you to do it. The older you get and the more responsibility you have, the more difficult it becomes to strike a healthy balance, but it is essential that you do. The most important thing you can do is to prioritize your commitments and let go of those things that are not important. Your time and energy should go to the people and projects you are most committed to. You'll never please everyone, so don't even try, but do try to please yourself and those you care most about.

If you neglect your family and friends because of work or neglect work because of family and friends, either way you will suffer. There will be times when work has to come before family and occasions when family has to come before work, but you shouldn't have to sacrifice one for the other in the long term.

Give yourself permission to have some down time, even if it is time doing nothing at all. Limit the number of commitments you make when you can in order to have free time to do what you choose. Spontaneity is important and so is the freedom that comes with choosing what you want to do on a day off.

Don't be afraid to ask for help when you need it—you needn't do everything yourself. When you are well-balanced, you aren't plagued by guilt or worried about all the things you have to do. You have to work at achieving balance, but it is work that pays off in huge benefits. You will be happier, healthier, and ultimately more effective when your life is in balance.

ONE STEP AT A TIME

Several years ago, I was asked to present the closing session of an all-day conference. My task was to tie together the day's activities and motivate those in attendance to put the information they had gathered that day to use in their own lives. I knew they'd be asked to evaluate the speakers they'd heard that day, and realizing I'd be evaluated motivated me to create something new. I thought about how easy it is to judge others yet how difficult it can be to judge ourselves. I decided to create an evaluation for them to fill out, not just on me, the speaker, but on *themselves* as well.

"How did *you* come across today?" I asked. "Open-minded? Attentive? Friendly?" Some of the attendees began to sit up and listen.

"Did you give your undivided attention to the speakers? Were you participating 100 percent?" I saw others shift in their chairs.

I continued with my questions, pointing out how easy it is to evaluate others, to be full of opinions and advice for them, and even to judge them harshly. But how honest are most of us when evaluating *ourselves?* How often do we stop and think about how effectively we come across? Are your actions part of a *plan* or simply random reactions to whatever happens? Following are a few of the points I made in my speech for you to think about as you work on gaining your professional edge.

- We all have good days and bad days. The people with whom we resonate are those who are positive, upbeat, and make us feel good. You can be the kind of person others like to have around, even when you are having a bad day. You might have to put on an act at first, *pretending* to feel terrific until you really *do* feel terrific. Try it—it works! Some days you'll need to push yourself harder than others. There will be times you'll have to act upbeat even if you don't feel it, but in no time at all, you may be surprised how real the feeling can be. You have more control over your days and your feelings than you think.

- We all influence and impact others. How do you want to be remembered? What do you want people to think of when your name comes up? *The people who leave a lasting impression on us are often those who exceed our expectations.*

I've had conversations with people long after they participated in my program, and I am always interested to hear the things they tell me.

- "I changed my hairstyle."
- "I shaved my mustache."
- "I always remember to pass the salt and pepper *together.*"
- "I always wear a jacket."
- "I've remembered to give a two-pump handshake."
- "I'm more optimistic and positive."

What interests me most is how every person picks up something different, even when they were in the same workshop. And although initially my reaction has sometimes been, "Is that *all* you remember?" I really am thrilled to hear there are one or two things people pick up, because I know I've reached them in some way. I've realized that walking away with just one or two ideas is a huge step in the self-improvement process. People can't change who they are overnight, but they can change in small steps.

- Gaining the professional edge is not a one-shot, overnight accomplishment. It's the result of a long-term commitment to looking at yourself honestly and objectively, being open to constructive comments, and creating and refining your professional image *every day*. Are you willing to make that commitment?

- Gaining the professional edge is within your grasp—and your future. As you continue to apply the strategies you've learned by reading this book, your confidence will increase and you will become a person with that extra something: *the professional edge.*

- Gaining the professional edge elicits change. As you continue to change, you will notice changes in others too. People will respond differently to you and you to them. Lead the way and become a positive role model for others. It only takes 21 days to make or break a habit. Why not start making changes today?

Think about how much more effective our workplaces would be and the better service we would receive if everyone we came into contact with used the principles in this book. As you continue to put your knowledge into practice, measure your progress every day. Give yourself credit for and acknowledge the subtle and minor changes you make, as well as the more monumental ones.

I always enjoy hearing the ways people are able to use this book or about a point that made a difference for them. If you have a success story or are struggling with something, please let me hear from you. Although I cannot promise to respond to each letter personally, I may be able to use my column to address a problem you're having.

Remember:

- You can create and project the professional image you want to.

- You can manage the message you send.

- You can achieve the success you desire.

- *You can gain the professional edge!*

Recommended Reading

Baldrige, Letitia. *New Manners for New Times: A Complete Guide to Etiquette.* New York: Scribner, 2003.

Berman Fortgang, Laura. *Take Yourself to the Top.* New York: Warner Books, 1998.

Bolles, Richard Nelson and Mark Emery Bolles. *What Color is your Parachute? 2005: A Practical Manual for Job Hunters and Career Changers.* California: Ten Speed Press, 2004.

Cameron, Julia. *The Artist's Way: A Spiritual Path to Higher Creativity.* New York: Putnam, 2002.

Carnegie, Dale. *Dale Carnegie's Lifetime Plan for Success: How to Win Friends & Influence People and How to Stop Worrying & Start Living.* New York: BBS Publishing, 1998.

Chopra, Deepak. *The Seven Spiritual Laws of Success: A Practical Guide to the Fulfillment of Your Dreams.* Novato, CA: New World Library, 1995.

Covey, Stephen. *Seven Habits of Highly Effective People.* New York: Simon & Schuster, 1990.

Goleman, Daniel. *Emotional Intelligence: Why It Can Matter More Than I.Q. for Character Health and Lifelong Achievement.* New York: Bantam, 1995.

Hill, Napoleon. *Think and Grow Rich.* New York: Ballantine, 1976.

Hoff, Ron. *"I Can See You Naked" A New Revised Edition of the National Bestseller on Making Fearless Presentations.* Missouri: Andrews and McMeel, 1992.

Johnson, Spencer. *Who Moved My Cheese? An Amazing Way to Deal with Change in Your Work and in Your Life.* New York: Penguin Putnam, 1998.

Jolley, Willie. *It Only Takes a Minute to Change Your Life!* New York: St. Martin's Press, 1997.

Jones, Laurie Beth. *The Path; Creating Your Mission Statement for Work and for Life.* New York: Hyperion, 1969.

Keller, Jeff. *Attitude Is Everything: Change Your Attitude . . . and You Change Your Life.* Tampa, FL: INTI Publishing, 1999.

Klauser, Henriette and Anne Klauser. *Write It Down Make It Happen: Knowing What You Want and Getting It.* New York: Simon & Schuster, 2001.

Krannich, Ronald. *Change Your Job, Change Your Life: High Impact Strategies for Finding Great Jobs in the Decade Ahead.* Virginia: Impact Publications, 2000.

Leider, Richard J. *The Power of Purpose: Creating Meaning in Your Life and Work.* San Francisco: Barrett Kohler Publishers, Inc, 1997.

Lundin, Stephen C., John Christianson, and Harry Paul. *Fish! A Remarkable Way to Boost Morale and Improve Results.* New York: Hyperion Press, 2000.

Mackenzie, Alex. *The Time Trap: The Classic Book on Time Management.* New York: Amacom, 1990, 1997.

McGraw, Phillip C. *Self Matters: Creating Your Life from the Inside Out.* New York: Hyperion, 1999.

Morem, Susan. *101 Tips for Graduates: A Code of Conduct for Success and Happiness in Life.* New York: Ferguson, 2005.

Morem, Susan. *How to Get a Job and Keep It.* New York: Ferguson, 2002.

Post, Peggy and Peter Post. *The Etiquette Advantage in Business: Personal Skills for Professional Success.* New York: Harper Collins, 1999.

Rath, Tom and Donald Clifton. *How Full is Your Bucket? Positive Strategies for Work and Life.* New York: Gallup Press, 2004.

Richardson, Cheryl. *Take Time for Your Life: A Personal Coach's Seven-Step Program for Creating the Life You Want.* New York: Broadway Books, 1998.

Robbins, Anthony. *Awaken the Giant Within: How to Take Immediate Control of Your Mental, Emotional, Physical, and Financial Destiny.* New York: Simon and Schuster, 2001.

Schlenger, Sunny. *How to be Organized in Spite of Yourself: Time and Space Management That Works With Your Personal Style.* New York: Penguin, 1999.

Schwartz, David J. *The Magic of Thinking Big.* New York: Simon & Schuster, 1987.

Sinetar, Marsha. *Do What You Love, The Money Will Follow: Discovering Your Right Livelihood.* New York: Dell, 1989.

Tracy, Brian. *Maximum Achievement: Strategies and Skills That Will Unlock Your Hidden Powers to Succeed.* New York: Simon & Schuster, 1995.

Tullier, L. Michelle. *Networking for Everyone! Connecting With People for Career and Job Success.* Indiana: Jist Works, Inc., 1998.

Yate, Martin. *Knock 'Em Dead 2005; The Ultimate Job Seeker Guide.* Massachusetts: Adams Media 2004.